Visual Language Guide
Spanish

Barron's

Grammar Overview 6

Quick Overview 9

General Information 15

Conversation 25

On the Move 47

Overnight Accommodations 85

Eating and Drinking 105

Shopping 137

Beach, Sports, and Nature 179

Culture and Entertainment 195

Offices and Institutions 201

Health 207

Business Travel 217

Glossary 221

Sentence Structure

Sentence structure follows the general pattern for all Romance languages:

Article	Subject	Adjective	Verb	Adverb	Object
The	policeman	tall	spoke	slowly	with my husband.
El	policía	alto	hablaba	despacio	con mi marido.

Articles

In Spanish nouns are either masculine (usually ending in -**o**) or feminine (usually ending in -**a**):

> the dog - el perro / the dogs - los perros
> the school - la escuela / the schools - las escuelas

The neuter **lo** is often used before adjectives and sometimes before adverbs:

> lo bueno - the good thing

The indefinite articles are **un** and **una**

Nouns

The plural is usually formed by adding -**s**:

> muchacho - muchachos (boys)
> muchacha - muchachas (girls)

There are some exceptions to this basic rule. Nouns that end with a consonant, in -**í**, or -**ú** add -**es** to the end in the plural.

> nación - naciones
> reloj - relojes

Nouns that end in -**s** after an unstressed vowel remain the same: **el paraguas** - **los paraguas**

Possessive / Indirect Object

The possessive uses the preposition **de**; indirect objects are expressed using **a**. In certain cases these prepositions combine with the articles:

> la casa del Sr. González (Mr. Gonzales' house)
> la risa de las chicas (the girls' laughter)

Pronouns

Subject		Object stressed	unstressed	Possessive 1	Possessive 2
I	yo	a mí de mí	me	mi / mis	el mío / los míos la mía / las mías
you	tú (fam.)	a ti / de ti	te	tu / tus	el tuyo / los tuyos la tuya / las tuyas
	usted	a usted de usted	le / lo	su / sus	el suyo / los suyos la suya / las suyas
he	él	a él de él	le / lo	su / sus	el suyo / los suyos la suya / las suyas
she	ella	a ella de ella	le / la	su / sus	el suyo / la suya la suya / las suyas

we	nosotros	a nosotros	nos	nuestro, -os	el nuestro, los nuestros
	nosotras	a nosotras		nuestra, -as	la nuestra, las nuestras
		de nosotros			
		de nosotras			
you	vosotros	a vosotros	os	vuestro, -os	el vuestro, los vuestros
(fam.)	vosotras	a vosotras		vuestra, -as	la vuestra, las vuestras
		de vosotros			
		de vosotras			
you	ustedes	a ustedes	les / los	su / sus	el suyo / los suyos
		de ustedes	les / las		la suya / las suyas
they	ellos	a ellos	les / los	su / sus	el suyo / la suya
	ellas	a ellas	les / las		la suya / las suyas
		de ellos			
		de ellas			

Possessive 1 is used as a possessive adjective before nouns (mi coche); Possessive 2 is used alone as a possessive pronoun (el mío).

Adjectives

Adjectives normally are placed after the nouns they modify and change in number and gender:

> **un perro grande** – a large dog
> **unos perros grandes** – large dogs

Comparatives generally are formed using **más: grande – más grande**

Adverbs

Adverbs are generally (but not always) formed with the ending **–mente**, which is added to the feminine form of the adjective:

> **rápido – rápidamente**
> **amable – amablemente**

Of course there are exceptions to this rule: **bueno – bien**

Helping Verbs and Modal Verbs

ser / estar	tener / haber	hacer
to be	to have	to make, to do
soy/estoy	tengo/he	hago
eres/estás	tienes/has	haces
es/está	tiene/ha	hace
somos/estamos	tenemos/hemos	hacemos
sois/estáis	tenéis/habéis	hacéis
son/están	tienen/had	hacen

Ser expresses a permanent condition; **estar** expresses temporary conditions and is used to indicate all locations.
Tener expresses possession or feeling; **haber** is used in conjugating verbs.

Verbs

There are three regular verb conjugations. In addition there are a lot of irregular verbs – too many to include in the framework of this book.

	comprar to buy	vender to sell	partir to leave
yo	compro	vendo	parto
tú	compras	vendes	partes
él, ella	compra	vende	parte
nosotros, -as	compramos	vendemos	partimos
vosotros, -as	compráis	vendéis	partís
ellos, ellas	compran	venden	parten

Negation

Negation is formed using the word **no**, e.g. **No fumo.**

Pronunciation

We have made a conscious decision to avoid phonetic spelling. Experience shows that tiresome stammering through phonetic spelling leads to painful results. In addition, you'll be able to handle practically everything in this book without it anyway. Here are the most important rules for pronunciation. Note that stress is underlined.

	Rule	Example	Pronunciation
c	before **e** or **i**, like the lisped English **th** (in Spain); like **s** in **see** (Latin America); otherwise, like the hard **c** in **can**	ciego casa	thee-<u>eh</u>-goh see-<u>eh</u>-goh kah-sah
ch	like the **ch** in **chocolate**	muchacho	moo-<u>chah</u>-choh
g	before **e** or **i**, like the **ch** in the name **Bach**; otherwise like the hard **g** in **golf**	gitano gala	chee-<u>tah</u>-noh gah-lah
gu	**u** is not pronounced when followed by **e** or **i**	guitarra	gee-<u>tahr</u>-rah
h	always silent	helados	eh-<u>lah</u>-dohs
j	like the **ch** in the name **Bach**	mojo	<u>moh</u>-choh
ñ	like the **ny** in **canyon**	niño	<u>neen</u>-yoh
q	always used with **u** and pronounced like **k** in **kilo**	queso	<u>keh</u>-soh
r	trilled when surrounded by vowels; at the beginning of a word, rolled forcefully	pero rojo	<u>peh</u>-roh <u>rroh</u>-hoh
rr	rolled forcefully	perro	<u>peh</u>-rroh
s	as in the English word **sun** (not a **z**-sound)	casa esbelto sed	<u>kah</u>-sah ehs-<u>behl</u>-toh sehd
v	pronounced partway between **v** and **b**	severo enviar	seh-<u>veh</u>-roh (seh-<u>beh</u>-roh) ehn-vee-<u>ahr</u> (ehn-bee-<u>ahr</u>)
z	like the lisped English **th** (in Spain); or like **s** (Latin America)	zapato eficaz	thah-<u>pah</u>-toh (sah-<u>pah</u>-toh) eh-fee-<u>kath</u> (eh-fee-<u>kahs</u>)

Quick Overview

The 11 Most Important Words

yes **Sí**

no **No**

please **Por favor**

Thank you! / Thanks! **Gracias**

I'm sorry! / Sorry! / Excuse Me!
¡Perdón!

Don't mention it! **No hay de qué.**

Good-bye! **¡Adiós!**

How are you? **¿Cómo estás?**

Fine, thanks. **Bien, gracias.**

Help! **¡Socorro!**

Hello!
¡Buenos días!

The 22 Most Important Expressions

My name is ...
Me llamo ...

I'm from the United States.
Soy de los Estados Unidos.

Can you please help me?
¿Puede ayudarme, por favor?

Pardon me?
¿Cómo dice usted?

What is this?
¿Qué es esto?

How much does this cost?
¿Cuánto cuesta esto?

Do you speak English?
¿Habla usted inglés?

I don't understand you.
No le entiendo.

I only speak a little bit of Spanish.
Yo hablo sólo un poco de español.

Please speak slowly.
Por favor, hable usted despacio.

Can you please repeat that?
¿Puede repetir, por favor?

Can you write that down?
¿Puede escribirlo, por favor?

How do you say that in Spanish?
¿Cómo se dice eso en español?

Please show it to me in this book.
Por favor, enséñemelo en este libro.

Just a minute.
Un momento.

I'm hungry.
Tengo hambre.

I'm thirsty.
Tengo sed.

Leave me alone!
¡Déjeme en paz!

Get away!
¡Lárgate!

What would you recommend?
¿Qué me recomienda?

Where is the bathroom?
¿Dónde están los lavabos?

I am lost.
Me he perdido.

If there is something you don't understand, you can of course say *no comprendo*, which is shorter and a little more polite.

What You Often Hear

Can I help you?
¿En qué puedo ayudarle?

With pleasure.
Con mucho gusto.

Don't mention it.
De nada.

I'm sorry.
Lo siento.

We are completely full.
Está todo completo.

Doesn't matter. / That's all right.
No importa.

Where are you from?
¿De dónde es usted?

Too bad!
¡Qué lástima! ¡Qué pena!

Please is generally expressed as *por favor*. But in the case of *please shut the door,* you say *se ruega cerrar lu puerta.*

The 33 Most Important Verbs

ask (-ed) **preguntar (pregunté, preguntado)**

believe (-ed) **creer (creí, creído)**

buy (bought, bought) **comprar (compré, comprado)**

can (could, could) **poder (pude, podido)**

come (came, come) **venir (vine, venido)**

do (did, done) **hacer (hice, hecho)**

eat (ate, eaten) **comer (comí, comido)**

feel (felt, felt) **sentir (sentí, sentido)**

find (found, found) **encontrar (encontré, encontrado)**

get (got, got) **obtener (obtuve, obtenido)**

give (gave, given) **dar (di, dado)**

go (went, gone) **ir (fui, ido)**

have (had, had) **tener (tuve, tenido)**

hear (heard, heard) **oír (oí, oído)**

know (knew, known) **saber (supe, sabido)**

let (let, let) **dejar (dejé, dejado)**

like (-ed) **gustar (gusté, gustado)**

listen (-ed) **escuchar (escuché, escuchado)**

look for ... (looked for ...) **buscar (busqué, buscado)**

must (must, must) / have to... (had to ...) **deber (debí, debido)**

read (read, read) **leer (leí, leído)**

recommend (-ed) **recomendar (recomendé, recomendado)**

say (said, said) **decir (dije, dicho)**

see (saw, seen) **ver (vi, visto)**

sell (sold, sold) **vender (vendí, vendido)**

smell (-ed) **oler (olí, olido)**

speak (spoke, spoken) **hablar (hablé, hablado)**

take (took, taken) **tomar (tomé, tomado)**

taste (-ed) **degustar (degusté, degustado)**

tell (told, told) **contar (conté, contado)**

think (thought, thought) **pensar (pensé, pensado)**

work (-ed) **trabajar (trabajé, trabajado)**

write (wrote, written) **escribir (escribí, escrito)**

Constructing Sentences

Even if you don't know much about languages you can easily construct the easiest sentences. These formulas will help you. Plug in the words you need to replace the underlined words. It's courteous to begin questions and requests by saying, "Pardon me..."

Excuse me, do you have ...
Perdone, tiene ...

I'm hungry.
Tengo hambre.

I would like a double room.
Quisiera una habitación doble.

Do you have track shoes?
¿Tiene zapatos de gimnasia?

Are there any oranges?
¿Hay naranjas?

I would rather have bananas.
Prefiero plátanos.

I would like some mineral water.
Quisiera agua mineral, por favor.

I need a band-aid.
Necesito una tirita.

I'm looking for a hotel.
Busco un hotel.

Can you tell me what time it is?
¿Podría decirme qué hora es?

Would you please bring me a fork?
¿Me puede traer un tenedor, por favor?

If you want to reserve a single room, you say *una habitación individual* or *sencilla.*

Everyday Conversation

Achoo!
¡achís! (estornudo)
Bless you!
¡Jesús! ¡Salud!

Have a nice day!
¡Que pase un buen día!
Thanks, same to you!
Gracias, igualmente.

I'll have the special of the day.
Para mí el menú del día.
So will I.
Para mí también.

I don't feel well today.
Hoy, no me siento bien.
Get well soon!
¡Que se mejore!

Have fun!
¡Que se divierta!
You, too!
Gracias, igualmente.

You can also ask *How are you?* by saying *¿Qué tal?* and avoiding the need to choose a salutation.

Comparatives

old, older, oldest
viejo, más viejo que, el más viejo

good, better, best
bueno, mejor, óptimo

hot, hotter, hottest
caliente, más caliente que, el más caliente

high, higher, highest
alto, más alto que, el más alto

young, younger, youngest
joven, más joven que, el más joven,

cold, colder, coldest
frío, más frío que, el más frío

short, shorter, shortest
corto, más corto que, el más corto

long, longer, longest
largo, más largo que, el más largo

slow, slower, slowest
lento, más lento que, el más lento

bad, worse, worst
malo, peor, pésimo

fast, faster, fastest
rápido, más rápido que, el más rápido

beautiful, more beautiful, most beautiful
bonito, más bonito que, el más bonito

deep, deeper, deepest
profundo, más profundo que, el más profundo

broad, broader, broadest
ancho, más ancho que, el más ancho

Opposites

all – nothing
todo – nada

old – young
viejo – joven

old – new
viejo – nuevo

outside – inside
fuera – dentro

early – late
temprano – tarde

big – small
grande – pequeño

good – bad
bueno – malo

right – wrong
correcto – falso

fast – slow
rápido – lento

beautiful – ugly
bonito – feo

strong – weak
fuerte – débil

expensive – cheap
caro – barato

much – little
mucho – poco

full – empty
lleno – vacío

hot – cold
caliente – frío

If you mean to say *old shoes*, you say *zapatos viejos*; *an old lady*, however, is *una señora anciana*.

Important Vocabulary

all **todos**

when **cuando**

other **otros / otras**

on **en**

from **de**

at **a**

then **entonces**

that **eso**

therefore **por eso**

these **estos / estas**

through **por**

a, an **un, uno**

some / a few **algunos / algunas**

for **para**

same **mismo, igual**

their **su**

in **en**

each **cada uno**

now **ahora**

with **con**

still **todavía**

only **sólo**

although **aunque**

or **o**

without **sin**

very **muy**

such **tal**

and **y**

of / from **de**

before **antes de**

because **porque**

little **poco**

if **si**

like **como**

again **de nuevo**

Questions About Questions

when? **¿cuándo?**

what? **¿qué?**

why? **¿por qué?**

who? **¿quién?**

where? **¿dónde?**

how? **¿cómo?**

how much? **¿cuánto?**

how many? **¿cuántos?**

how far is ...? **¿A qué distancia está ...?**

how long? **¿cuánto tiempo?**

This and That

there **allá**

this one **éste / ésta**

that one **ése / ésa**

here **aquí**

The expression *Pardon me?* may be expressed more compactly using *¿Cómo?* (What?).

General Information

Cardinal Numbers

zero **cero**

one **uno**

two **dos**

three **tres**

four **cuatro**

five **cinco**

six **seis**

seven **siete**

eight **ocho**

nine **nueve**

ten **diez**

twenty **veinte**

thirty **treinta**

forty **cuarenta**

fifty **cincuenta**

sixty **sesenta**

seventy **setenta**

eighty **ochenta**

ninety **noventa**

one hundred **ciento**

one thousand **mil**

ten thousand **diez mil**

one hundred thousand **cien mil**

one million **un millón**

one billion **mil millones**

Ordinal Numbers

first (1st) **primero**

second (2nd) **segundo**

third (3rd) **tercero**

fourth (4th) **cuarto**

fifth (5th) **quinto**

sixth (6th) **sexto**

seventh (7th) **séptimo**

eighth (8th) **octavo**

ninth (9th) **noveno**

tenth (10th) **décimo**

twentieth (20th) **vigésimo**

thirtieth (30th) **trigésimo**

Fractions and Quantities

one eighth **un octavo**

one quarter **un cuarto**

one half **medio**

three quarters **tres cuartos**

once **una vez**

twice **dos veces**

thrice **tres veces**

half **medio**

half **mitad**

double **el doble**

a little **un poco**

a pair **un par**

a dozen **una docena**

enough **bastante / suficiente**

too much **demasiado**

many **muchos / muchas**

more **más**

The page numbers in this book are written out. That way you can easily find any number you need.

Weights

gram **el gramo**
pound **la libra**
kilo **el kilo**
ton **la tonelada**
ounce **la onza**

Fluids

liter **el litro**
one quarter liter **un cuarto de litro**
one half liter **medio litro**

Length

millimeter **el milímetro**
centimeter **el centímetro**
meter **el metro**
kilometer **el kilómetro**
inch **la pulgada**
foot **el pie**
yard **la yarda**
mile **la milla**

Area

square meter **el metro cuadrado**
square kilometer **el kilómetro cuadrado**

Conversions

1 ounce (oz)		= 28,35 g
1 pound (lb)	= 16 ounces	= 453,59 g
1 ton	= 2000 pounds	= 907 kg
1/4 pound		= 113 g
1/2 pound		= 227 g
100 g	= 3.527 oz	
1 kg	= 2.205 lb	
1 inch (in)		= 2,54 cm
1 foot (ft)	= 12 inches	= 0,35 m
1 yard (yd)	= 3 feet	= 0,9 m
1 mile (mi)	= 1760 yards	= 1,6 km
1 cm	= 0.39 in	
1 km	= 0.62 mi	
1 square foot (ft^2)		= 930 cm^2
1 acre (A)		= 4047 m^2
1 m^2	= 0.386 mi^2	
1 ha	= 2.471 acres	
1 pint (pt)		= 0,47 l
1 quart (qt)	= 2 pints	= 0,95 l
1 gallone (gal)	= 4 quarts	= 3,79 l
1/4 l	= 0.26 qt	
1/2 l	= 0.53 qt	
1 l	= 1.057 qt	
	= 0.264 gal	

In Spain and South America, *medio kilo* (a *half-kilo*) roughly equals a pound.

Date and Time

When do you arrive?
¿Cuándo llega usted?

We arrive on the 15th of July.
Nosotros llegamos el 15 de julio.

That is, in two weeks.
Entonces, dentro de 15 días.

What is the date today?
¿A qué día estamos? ¿Qué día es hoy?

Today is the 1st of July.
Estamos al primero de julio / Hoy es el primero de julio.

At what time must we be there?
¿A qué hora tenemos que estar?

At 3 o'clock in the afternoon.
A las quince horas.

How long will you stay?
¿Cuánto tiempo se queda usted?

We will stay until the 12th of August.
Nos quedamos hasta el 12 de agosto.

When Spaniards and people from South America speak of *fifteen days*, they mean two weeks—in other words, fourteen days.

Days of the Week

Monday **lunes**
Tuesday **martes**
Wednesday **miércoles**
Thursday **jueves**
Friday **viernes**
Saturday **sábado**
Sunday **domingo**

Months

January **enero**
February **febrero**
March **marzo**
April **abril**
May **mayo**
June **junio**
July **julio**
August **agosto**
September **septiembre**
October **octubre**
November **noviembre**
December **diciembre**

Holidays

New Year's Day **Año Nuevo**
Good Friday **Viernes Santo**
Easter **Pascua**
Whitsun, Pentecost **Pentecostés**
Christmas **Navidad**
Happy Easter! **¡Felices Pascuas!**
New Year's Eve **Noche Vieja**
Merry Christmas! **¡Feliz Navidad!**
Happy New Year! **¡Feliz Año Nuevo! / ¡Próspero Año Nuevo!**

Times

in the evening **por la tarde**
That is too early. **Es demasiado temprano.**
That is too late. **Es demasiado tarde.**
earlier **más temprano**
yesterday **ayer**
today **hoy**
in two weeks **dentro de quince días**
year **año**
now **ahora**
at noon **mediodía**
midnight **medianoche**
month **mes**
tomorrow **mañana**
in the afternoon **por la tarde**
at night **por la noche**
sunrise **la salida del sol**
sunset **la puesta del sol**
later **más tarde**
hourly **cada hora**
day **día**
daily **diariamente**
the day after tomorrow **pasado mañana**
the day before yesterday **anteayer**
previously **antes**
in the morning **por la mañana**
weekend **el fin de semana**

Seasons

spring **la primavera**
summer **el verano**
autumn / fall **el otoño**
winter **el invierno**
high season **la temporada alta**
off season / low season **la temporada baja**

In Spain neither Easter Monday nor Whit Monday is a holiday.

Telling Time

Can you tell me what time it is?
¿Me puede decir qué hora es?

Ten minutes past three.
Las tres y diez minutos.

Does your watch
have the right time?
**¿Funciona bien su
reloj?**

Of course.
Claro.

My watch is slow.
Mi reloj está atrasado.
I am sorry, I'm late.
Lo siento, me he retrasado.

If you want to say *My watch is fast*, in Spanish it's *Mi reloj está adelantado.*

two o'clock
las dos

five past two
las dos y cinco

ten past two / two ten
las dos y diez

quarter past two
las dos y cuarto

two thirty
las dos y media

two thirty-five
las tres menos veinticinco

Once the long hand passes the half-hour mark, the minutes are subtracted from the next hour; therefore, twenty to three is *three minus twenty*.

twenty to four
las cuatro menos veinte

quarter to four
las cuatro menos cuarto

five to three
las tres menos cinco

exactly 12 noon
las doce en punto

Can you please tell me the time?
¿Me puede decir qué hora es?

hour
la hora

minute
el minuto

second
el segundo

in ten minutes
dentro de diez minutos

in an hour
dentro de una hora

in half an hour
dentro de media hora

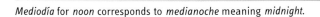

Mediodía for *noon* corresponds to *medianoche* meaning *midnight*.

The Weather

Storms in the northeast. Skies are almost clear south of the Canary and Balearic Islands, Andalusia, Murcia, south of Valencia, La Mancha, and Estremadura. Partly cloudy in the central regions, north of the Balearic and Canary Islands, north of Valencia and in the mid-south mountain areas, especially Gredos and the Aracena-Nevada mountain ranges. Cloudy south of Castile and Leon, north of La Mancha and north of Valencia and Aragon, Rioja, Navarre and the interior of Catalonia, with occasional downpours in the Cantabrian Mountains. Cloudy skies with rain in the Cantabrian-Pyrenean range and in Galicia, with worsening weather in the Atlantic coast.

Tormentas en el noroeste. Cielo casi despejado en el sur de Canarias, Baleares, Andalucía, Murcia, al sur de Valencia, al sur de La Mancha y en Extremadura. Parcialmente nuboso en el centro, norte de Baleares, de Canarias, al norte de Valencia y en las zonas montañosas de la parte central del sur, especialmente en Gredos, sierra de Aracena y Nevada. Intervalos nubosos en el sur de Castilla y de León, norte de La Mancha, al norte de Valencia y de Aragón, Rioja, Navarra e interior de Cataluña, y con chubascos ocasionales en el Cantábrico. Cielo nuboso con precipitaciones en la cordillera cántabro-pirenaica y en Galicia, más abundantes en la costa atlántica.

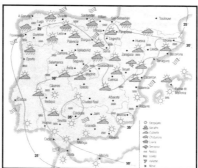

How will the weather be today?	**¿Qué tiempo hará hoy?**
It will stay nice.	**Seguirá haciendo buen tiempo.**
It will become nice.	**Habrá buen tiempo.**
It's supposed to rain.	**Puede que llueva.**
How long has it been raining?	**¿Cuánto tiempo lleva lloviendo?**
How much longer will it rain?	**¿Cuánto tiempo seguirá lloviendo?**
What is the temperature today?	**¿A cuántos grados estamos hoy?**
It is 15 degrees Celsius	**Estamos a 15 grados.**
Is it always so hot?	**¿Siempre hace tanto calor?**
It froze at night.	**Esta noche ha helado.**
The streets are ...	**Las calles están ...**
wet.	**mojadas.**
slippery.	**heladas.**
snow-covered.	**cubiertas de nieve.**
dry.	**secas.**

In case of ice, you may see a sign saying *Peligro de heladas* (ice danger).

clearing **el despejo**

lightning **el relámpago**

thunder **el trueno**

ice **el hielo**

frost **la helada**

storm **la tormenta**

sheet ice **el hielo resbaladizo**

sleet **la nieve granizada**

hail **el granizo**

heat **el calor**

high pressure **alta presión**

maximum values **los valores máximos**

high tide **la marea alta**

air **el aire**

humidity **la humedad**

moderately warm **calor moderado**

fog **la niebla**

drizzle **la llovizna**

ozone **el ozono**

puddle **el charco**

powder (snow) **la nieve polvo**

rain **la lluvia**

showers **el chaparrón**

snow **la nieve**

snow chains **las cadenas antideslizantes**

sun **el sol**

storm **la tormenta**

typhoon **el tifón**

thaw **el deshielo**

low pressure **baja presión**

minimum values **los valores mínimos**

flood **la inundación**

little change **pocos cambios**

wind **el viento**

tornado **el ciclón**

clouds **las nubes**

Fahrenheit and Celsius

Temperatures in the United States are measured in degrees Fahrenheit, but in Spain and Latin America they measure in degrees Celsius. To convert Fahrenheit to Celsius, deduct 32 and multiply by 5/9. To convert Celsius to Fahrenheit, multiply by 9/5 and add 32.

°F	°C	°F	°C
0	−17.8	78	25.6
10	−12.2	79	26.1
15	−9.4	80	26.7
20	−6.7	81	27.2
25	−3.9	82	27.8
30	−1.1	83	28.3
32	0.0	84	28.9
35	1.7	85	29.4
40	4.4	86	30.0
45	7.2	87	30.6
50	10.0	88	31.1
60	15.6	89	31.7
61	16.1	90	32.2
62	16.7	91	32.8
63	17.2	92	33.3
64	17.8	93	33.9
65	18.3	94	34.4
66	18.9	95	35.0
67	19.4	96	35.6
68	20.0	97	36.1
69	20.6	98	36.7
70	21.1	99	37.2
71	21.7	100	37.8
72	22.2	101	38.3
73	22.8	102	38.9
74	23.3	103	39.4
75	23.9	104	40.0
76	24.4	105	40.6
77	25.0	106	41.1

A high is *una zona de alta presión*; logically, then, a low is *una zona de baja presión*.

Don't Forget!

rubber boots
las botas de goma

umbrella
el paraguas

It is ... **Está / hace / hay ...**
cloudy. **Está nublado.**
hazy. **Está brumoso.**
very hot. **Hace mucho calor.**
cold. **Hace frío.**
foggy. **Hay niebla.**
muggy. **Hace calor sofocante.**
sunny. **Hace sol.**
stormy. **Está tempestuoso.**
dry. **Está seco.**
warm. **Hace calor.**
variable / changeable. **Está inestable.**
windy / breezy. **Hace viento.**

It is ... **Está ...**
raining. **lloviendo.**
snowing. **Nevando.**

sunglasses
las gafas para el sol

parasol / sun umbrella
la sombrilla

Pronunciation

A, like **Argentina**	J, like **Jaén**	S, like **Sevilla**
B, like **Bolivia**	K, like **Kuwait**	T, like **Teruel**
C, like **Colombia**	L, like **Lugo**	U, like **Uruguay**
D, like **Dinamarca**	M, like **México**	V, like **Valencia**
E, like **España**	N, like **Nicaragua**	W, like **Washington**
F, like **Francia**	O, like **Oviedo**	X, like **xilófono**
G, like **Guatemala**	P, like **Panamá**	Y, like **Yemen**
H, like **Honduras**	Q, like **Quito**	Z, like **Zaragoza**
I, like **Italia**	R, like **Roma**	

In weather expressions such as *The weather is nice*, the Spanish often use the verb *to make/to do*, so in this case it would be *Hace buen tiempo*.

Conversation

First Contact

Latin Americans are open and friendly toward tourists. Typically, they will appreciate and celebrate your attempts to communicate in Spanish, and most upper-middle-class Latinos will know enough English for at least basic communication.

Attitudes toward their own countries and to those of English speakers usually vary with the size of the country and the political inclinations of the people, but more courtesy usually prevails. Blessed be the tourist who is modest and not overly critical.

In Spain you will meet many people who have a basic knowledge of English, especially in the Canary Islands and on Mallorca. The Spanish value courtesy, which they perceive as mutual respect. They have an evident self-confidence and generally have a high opinion of their country.

At first contact, a Spaniard may appear a little reserved, not to mention arrogant. That's just an old defense mechanism against all strangers, and it's quickly put aside as soon as you get to know each other a little better.

Greetings in Spanish, in Spain as well as in Latin America, basically follow the sun. From morning to noon, you say *Buenos días*; in the afternoon, to around five or six o'clock, the greeting is *Buenas tardes*; and in the evening, *Buenas noches*. When people say good-bye, they commonly say *Hasta luego*, which corresponds to our *See you later*, or *Adiós*.

After the general greeting, it's usual to add *¿Cómo está?* or *¿Cómo estás?* in formal or familiar terms, respectively. If you want to steer clear of the formal/informal issue, you can also say *¿Qué tal?* (How's it going?), although this is slightly more informal. In a formal introduction, such as when a Spanish acquaintance introduces some friends or his wife to you, you respond with *Mucho gusto*, which corresponds to our *Pleased to meet you*.

Hello!
¡Hola!

Good morning.
Buenos días.

Good day.
Buenos días.

Good evening.
Buenas tardes.

Good night.
Buenas noches.

How are you?
¿Cómo está?

Fine, thank you.
Bien, gracias.

What is your name?
¿Cómo se llama?

Good-bye.
Adiós.

Pardon me?
¿Cómo dice usted?

Do you speak English?
¿Habla usted inglés?

I have not understood you.
No le he entendido.

Unfortunately, I speak only a little bit of Spanish.
Desgraciadamente hablo muy poco español.

Can you please repeat that?
¿Puede repetirlo, por favor?

Can you please write that down?
¿Me lo puede anotar, por favor?

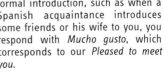

Of course has lots of nuances in Spanish; you can say *claro*, *por supuesto*, or *seguro* (sure).

Hello!
¡Hola!

Good day!
¡Buenos días!

How are you?
¿Cómo está usted?

Fine, thanks.
Bien, gracias.

Nice meeting you.
Encantado de verlo.

Same here!
El gusto es mío.

Good-bye!
¡Adiós! ¡Hasta luego!

It was nice to have met you.
Ha sido un placer saludarle.

In Spanish *hola* is a very common but slightly familiar greeting word. On the telephone people say *Diga* (Spain) or *Aló?* (America).

What You Hear

¿De dónde es usted?
Where are you from?

¿Cuánto tiempo lleva usted aquí?
How long have you been here?

¿Le gusta?
Do you like it?

¿Es la primera vez que viene?
Is it your first time here?

¿Cuánto tiempo se queda?
How long are you staying?

Permítame que le presente.
May I introduce you?

Familiar Greetings

How is it going?
¿Cómo va?

What's happening? / What's going on?
¿Qué pasa?

Hi, there!
¡Oiga!

Hi folks!
¡Hola amigos!

Hi pal!
¡Hola compañero!

Good to see you!
¡Me alegro de verte!

What's new?
¿Qué tal?

Doing great!
¡Estoy muy bien!

Doing okay.
Regular.

Have a nice day.
¡Que tenga un buen día!

See you later!
¡Hasta pronto!

Take care!
¡Cúidate!

So long!
Hasta luego.

Set Phrases

Oh, really?
¿De veras?

That is right.
Eso es cierto.

That is interesting.
Eso es interesante.

That is news to me.
No lo sabía.

I agree.
Estoy de acuerdo.

I don't agree.
No estoy de acuerdo.

I like that.
Eso me gusta.

That would be nice.
Sería magnífico.

Great!
¡Fantástico!

Could be.
Podría ser.

Maybe.
Quizás.

Probably.
Probablemente.

I don't know.
No sé.

Just a minute, please.
Un momento, por favor.

May I? / Excuse me!
¿Me permite ...?

Good luck!
¡Buena suerte!

Have fun!
¡Que te diviertas!

All the best!
¡Que te vaya bien!

Welcome!
¡Bienvenido!

Unfortunately, I have no time.
Desgraciadamente no tengo tiempo.

I'll be right back.
En seguida vuelvo.

The word *luck* is translated by *la suerte*; when it means *good fortune*, the word is *la felicidad* (the adjective is *feliz*).

Excuse Me!

Excuse me, how much do
these shoes cost?
**Perdone, ¿cuánto cuestan
estos zapatos?**

I'm sorry, I don't work here.
Lo siento, yo no trabajo aquí.

Excuse me please!
¡Perdone!

No problem!
¡No importa!

Instead of *perdón* you can also say *disculpe*, for example, when you want to create a little space for yourself in the bus.

Introductions

My name is ...
Yo me llamo ...

What is your name?
¿Cómo se llama usted?

How old are you?
¿Cuántos años tiene usted?

I am 25 years old.
Tengo 25 años.

Are you married?
¿Está usted casado?

I am single.
Soy soltero.

Do you have any children?
¿Tiene usted hijos?

What do you do for a living?
¿A qué se dedica usted?

Where are you travelling to?
¿Adónde viaja usted?

How long will you stay?
¿Cuánto tiempo se queda?

I am on ...
Estoy ...
a business trip.
en viaje de negocios.
vacation.
de vacaciones.
I am traveling on to ...
Continuaré mi viaje a ...

I would like to visit the following cities.
Me gustaría visitar las siguientes ciudades.

I am spending the night ...
Paso la noche ...
in a hotel.
en un hotel.
with friends.
en casa de amigos.

It was very nice to meet you.
Encantado de haberlo conocido.

May I introduce?
Permítame que le presente.

Forms of Address

	Singular	Abbreviation	Plural	Abbreviation
Mr.	Señor	Sr.	Señores	Sres.
Mrs.	Señora	Sra.	Señoras	Sras.
Miss	Señorita	Srta.	Señoritas	Srtas.
Ladies and Gentlemen			Señoras y señores	

If you want to say *My name is*, you can leave off the subject of the sentence and simply say *Me llamo*.

Where Are You From?

Where are you from?
¿De dónde es usted?

I'm from the United States.
Soy de los Estados Unidos.

I'm from England.
Soy de Inglaterra.

I'm from Australia.
Soy de Australia.

Be diplomatic: Spaniards and Latin Americans are *very* patriotic.

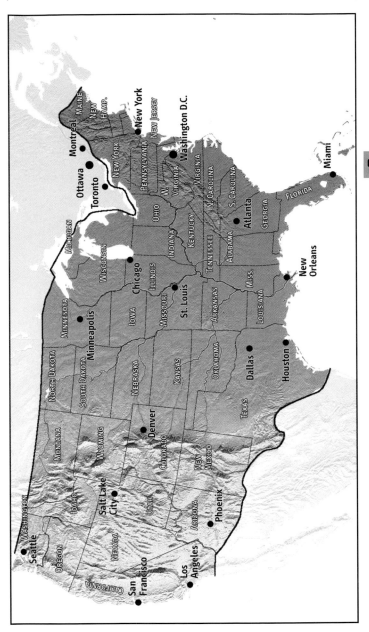

Show your friends where you are from and have them show you where they live.

Relatives

husband	**el marido**	aunt	**la tía**
wife	**la mujer**	grandson	**el nieto**
friend	**el amigo**	cousin	**la prima**
friend / acquaintance	**el conocido**	cousin	**el primo**
fiancée	**la novia**	nephew	**el sobrino**
fiancé	**el novio**	niece	**la sobrina**
daughter	**la hija**		
son	**el hijo**		
brother	**el hermano**		
sister	**la hermana**		
father	**el padre**		
mother	**la madre**		
grandfather	**el abuelo**		
grandmother	**la abuela**		
son-in-law	**el yerno**		
daughter-in-law	**la nuera**		
father-in-law	**el suegro**		
mother-in-law	**la suegra**		
uncle	**el tío**		

Occupations

What do you do for a living?
¿A qué se dedica?

I work in a factory.
Trabajo en una fábrica.

I work for the XYZ company.
Trabajo en la empresa XYZ.

I work in retail sales.
Trabajo en el comercio al pormenor.

I'm still at school.
Todavía voy al colegio.

What are you studying?
¿Qué estudia?

I'm studying architecture.
Estudio arquitectura.

I am an official / a civil servant
Soy funcionario.

In order to designate one's parents you should use the word for *father (el padre)* in the plural: *los padres.*

Professions

doctor
el médico

construction worker
el albañil

cook
el cocinero

painter
el pintor

mason
el albañil

chimney sweep
el deshollinador

department head **el jefe de departamento**

geriatric nurse **el enfermero geriátrico**

employee **el empleado**

lawyer **el abogado**

worker **el obrero**

unemployed **el desempleado**

architect **el arquitecto**

architecture **la arquitectura**

army **el ejército**

doctor's assistant **la auxiliar de médico**

trainee **el aprendiz**

mechanic **el mecánico**

author **el autor**

baker **el panadero**

official / civil servant **el funcionario**

economist **el economista**

biologist **el biólogo**

bookkeeper **el contable**

bookseller **el librero**

chemistry **la química**

chemist **el químico**

roofer **el tejador**

decorator **el decorador**

pharmacist **el farmacéutico**

computer expert **el experto de informática**

For *unemployed* you can also say *parado* (Spain) or *desempleado* (America).

Professions

retail **el comercio al por menor**

electrician **el electricista**

teacher **el educador / la educadora**

skilled worker / specialist **el obrero especializado**

photographer **el fotógrafo**

freelancer **el profesional independiente**

hairdresser **el peluquero**

management level **el nivel administrativo**

gardener **el jardinero**

hotelier **el propietario de un hotel, restaurante, etc.**

English language and literature **la filología inglesa**

glazier **el vidriero**

craftsperson **el artesano**

housewife **la ama de casa**

lawyer **el abogado**

jeweler **el joyero**

businessman / merchant **el comerciante**

waiter **el camarero**

car mechanic **el mecánico de automóviles**

nurse **la enfermera**

artist **el artista**

farmer **el agricultor**

teacher **el profesor**

broker / agent **el corredor (de bolsa, de comercio)**

manager **el gerente**

mechanic **el mecánico**

medicine **la medicina**

master **el maestro**

butcher **el carnicero**

musician **el músico**

notary **el notario**

government service / public service **el servicio público**

optician **el óptico**

homemaker **la ama de casa**

midwife **la partera**

paramedic **el paramédico**

college **la universidad**

industry **la industria**

engineer **el ingeniero**

plumber **el plomero, el fontanero**

journalist **el periodista**

law **el derecho**

A general term for teacher is *el profesor*; an elementary school teacher is *un maestro.*

Professions

locksmith **el cerrajero**
tailor **el sastre**
carpenter **el carpintero**
writer **el escritor**
shoemaker **el zapatero**
student **el alumno**
tax advisor **el asesor fiscal**
student **el estudiante**
taxi driver / cab driver **el taxista**
veterinarian **el veterinario**
watchmaker **el relojero**
retraining **la readaptación profesional**
entrepreneur / businessman **el empresario**
salesperson **el vendedor**
administration **la administración**
scientist **el científico**
dentist **el dentista**
dental technician **el técnico dental**
carpenter **el carpintero**

priest **el sacerdote**
pharmacy **la farmacia**
philosophy **la filosofía**
physics **la física**
police officer **el policía**
president **el presidente**
production **la producción**
professor **el profesor**
programmer **el programador**

psychologist **el psicólogo**
psychology **la psicología**
lawyer **el abogado**
retired person **el jubilado**
judge **el juez**
actor **el actor**

Another term for a university professor is *un catedrático*.

How Are You?

How are you?
¿Cómo está usted?

So-so.
Regular.

Great!
Muy bien.

I feel terrific!
Me siento de maravilla.

I have a wonderful feeling!
Tengo una sensación maravillosa.

I am in love.
Estoy enamorado.

I'm not feeling very well.
No me siento muy bien.

I am ...
Estoy ...
    depressed.
    deprimido.
    frustrated.
    frustrado.

tired.
cansado.
sick.
enfermo.
angry.
enojado.
annoyed.
molesto.

I am feeling cold.
Tengo frío.

I am feeling warm.
Tengo calor.

I am worried.
Estoy preocupado.

Terms of Endearment

Sweetheart.
Tesoro.

Darling.
Cariño.

The Spanish language uses many terms of endearment.

Congratulations

All the best!
¡Que te vaya bien!

Lots of success!
¡Mucho éxito!

Good luck!
¡Buena suerte!

Get well soon!
¡Que te mejores!

Congratulations ...
Felicidades ...
  on your birthday.
  por tu cumpleaños.
  on your promotion.
  por el ascenso.
  on the birth of your son /
  daughter.
  por el nacimiento de tu hija / hijo.
  on your engagement.
  por el compromiso.
  on your wedding.
  por la boda.
  on your silver wedding
  anniversary.
  por las bodas de plata.
  on your golden wedding
  anniversary.
  por las bodas de oro.

Opinion

What is your opinion?
¿Cuál es su opinión?

I totally agree with you.
Soy de su opinión.

I have a different opinion.
No soy de la misma opinión.

In my opinion ...
En mi opinión ...
  we should go back.
  deberíamos regresar.
  we should turn back.
  deberíamos volver.
  we should go home.
  deberíamos volver a casa.
  that is wrong.
  eso es incorrecto.
  that is right.
  eso es correcto.

Enthusiasm

amazing
asombroso

fantastic
fantástico

gorgeous
magnífico

great
estupendo

awesome
excelente

wonderful
maravilloso

Indignation

What a mess!
¡Qué porquería!

That is shameless!
¡Es un descaro!

Nonsense!
¡Tonterías!

Stop that!
¡Déjelo!

Leave me alone!
¡Déjeme en paz!

Don't you dare!
¡No se atreva!

What nerve!
¡Qué desvergüenza!

When you congratulate someone in Spain, instead of *felicidades* you can say *enhorabuena.*

Problems

Can you please help me!
¡Ayúdeme, por favor!

I don't see well.
No veo bien.

I don't hear well.
No oigo bien.

I feel sick.
Me siento mal.

I am dizzy.
Estoy mareado.

Please call a doctor.
Por favor, llame a un doctor.

Insults

Fool!
¡Imbécil!

Shit!
¡Mierda!

Idiot!
¡Idiota!

Imbecile!
¡Estúpido!

Moron!
¡Cretino!

Dumb bitch!
¡Bruta!

First Approach

May I join you?
¿Puedo sentarme aquí?

Are you travelling alone?
¿Viaja usted sola?

Are you married?
¿Está usted casada?

Do you have a boyfriend?
¿Tiene novio?

I think you're very nice.
Usted es muy simpática.

You are really sweet.
Eres muy agradable.

Do you have anything planned for this evening?
¿Qué planes tiene para esta noche?

Shall we do something together?
¿Salimos juntos?

Shall we go out together this evening?
¿Salimos juntos esta noche?

May I invite you to lunch / dinner?
¿Me permite invitarla a comer?

When should we meet?
¿Cuándo nos vemos?

At 8 o'clock in front of the movie theater.
A las ocho enfrente del cine.

I can pick you up.
¿Puedo pasar a recogerla?

I am looking forward to it.
Lo espero con mucho gusto.

Thank you for a wonderful evening.
Gracias por la maravillosa velada.

I would be very happy if I could see you again.
Me encantaría volver a verla.

Can I bring you home?
¿Me permite que la lleve a su casa?

Spaniards love to curse: *vete a la mierda* (go to hell, although the location is somewhat stronger), *métetelo por el culo* (stick it up your ass) and *carajo* (damn).

Agreement

May I join you?
¿Puedo sentarme aquí?

Sure, why not?
¿Por qué no?

Would you like something to drink?
¿Desea tomar algo?

Yes, that's a good idea.
Sí, gracias, me parece muy buena idea.

I think you're very nice.
Usted es muy simpática.

Do you have anything planned for this evening?
¿Qué planes tiene para esta noche?

I am meeting my husband.
Tengo que encontrarme con mi marido.

Tomar can mean both *to drink* and *to take.*

Polite but Firm

I am waiting for ...
Estoy esperando a ...
  my husband.
  mi marido.
  my wife.
  mi mujer.
  my boyfriend.
  mi novio.
  my girlfriend.
  mi novia.

It was nice meeting you, but unfortunately I have to go now.
Encantado de conocerlo, pero desgraciadamente ahora tengo que marcharme.

Unfortunately, I have no time.
Desgraciadamente no tengo tiempo.

I already have something else planned.
Tengo ya otros planes.

Leave me alone, please!
¡Por favor déjeme en paz!

Please go now!
¡Por favor, vete!

You are bothering me.
Me estás molestando.

Impolite and Very Firm

Stop that!
¡Deje éso!

Stop that immediately!
¡Basta ya!

Go away!
¡Lárgate!

Get the hell out!
¡Vete al carajo!

Take your hands off me!
¡Manos quietas!

I'll call the police!
¡Llamo a la policía!

This person is becoming offensive.
Esta persona me está importunando.

This person is threatening me.
Esta persona me está amenazando.

Things Are Getting Serious!

I have fallen in love with you.
Me he enamorado de ti.

I would like to make love to you.
Quisiera hacer el amor contigo.

Your place or mine?
¿Vamos a tu casa o a la mía?

But only with a condom!
¡Pero sólo con condón!

Friendship is delineated quite clearly in Spanish. *Un amigo* is a friend to the death; anybody else is just *a conocido*, an acquaintance.

On the Phone

Good day. This is the Barron's publishing house. May I help you?
Editorial Barron's, buenos días. ¿En qué puedo servirle?

I would like to speak to Mr. García.
Quisiera hablar con el Sr. García.

Who is calling?
¿Con quién hablo?

My name is Juan Bueno.
Me llamo Juan Bueno.

Just a minute, I'll connect you.
Un momento, ahora lo comunico.

Unfortunately, the line is busy. Would you like to hold?
Desgraciadamente la línea está ocupada. ¿Le importaría esperar?

I'll call again later.
Llamaré más tarde.

During decades the telephone systems of Latin America were expensive and unreliable. Fiberoptics and satellite communication has changed the picture.

Using the Telephone

Is Pablo there?
¿Está Pablo?

Pablo speaking.
Con él habla.

To whom am I speaking?
¿Con quién hablo?

Could you connect me with Mr. García?
¿Podría ponerme con el Sr. García?

Please stay on the line / Please hold.
Espere un momento, por favor.

There is no reply.
No responde nadie.

He is on another line.
Está en otra línea.

Can I leave a message?
¿Puedo dejar un recado?

Can you please repeat the phone number slowly?
¿Puede repetir despacio el número de teléfono, por favor?

I'm sorry, I have dialled the wrong number.
Perdone, me he equivocado de número.

Excuse me, I didn't understand your name.
Lo siento, no he entendido su nombre.

Can I call you back?
¿Puedo volver a llamarle?

Thanks for your phone call.
Muchas gracias por su llamada.

There is no such number.
Número inexistente.

cell phone, cellular
el móvil / el celular

receiver
el auricular

dial tone **la señal de línea libre**

phone call **la llamada telefónica**

answering machine **el contestador automático, la contestadora**

information **el servicio de información**

busy signal **la señal de línea ocupada**

classified directory / yellow pages
las páginas amarillas

direct dialling **la marcación / selección directa**

connection **la conexión**

long distance call **la llamada de larga distancia**

charge **la tarifa telefónica**

card telephone **el teléfono de tarjeta**

telephone connection / telephone line **la línea**

pay phone / coin-operated telephone **el teléfono público de monedas**

emergency **la llamada de socorro**

local call **la llamada local**

collect call **la llamada de cobro revertido**

telephone book **la guía telefónica**

phone card **la tarjeta telefónica**

telephone booth / phone booth **la cabina telefónica**

switchboard **la central telefónica**

area code **el prefijo**

For *speaking* you can also say *al habla.*

A Personal Letter

Pedro Ramírez
c / Mar Menor, 15
74423 Almería
Spain

June 6, 2001

Dear Pedro,

Thanks for your letter and your kind invitation.
As we discussed, we will arrive at your place next Thursday at about
6:00 p.m. We're really looking forward to it!

Yours truly,
María

Pedro Ramírez
C / Mar Menor, 15
74423 Almería
España

6 de junio 2001

Querido Pedro:

Muchas gracias por tu carta y por tu gentil invitación.
Según hemos convenido, llegaremos el jueves próximo a eso de las
seis de la tarde. ¡Esperamos con impaciencia llegar!

Recibe un cordial saludo
María

In Spanish after the salutation you use a colon, and the text begins with a capital letter.

A Business Letter

....

June 6, 2001
Re: your letter of June 4, 2001

Dear Mr. López:

Thank you for your aforementioned letter.
We confirm our appointment for this Thursday at
about 6 p.m. Please find attached a few documents
which will be useful in preparing for our
discussions.
If you have any further questions, please feel
free to call on me at any time.

Sincerely,

Juan Pérez
Manager

---

6 de junio de 2001
Asunto: Su carta fechada 4 de junio de 2001

Estimado Sr. López:

Agradecemos su carta arriba mencionada y le
confirmamos la cita concertada para el jueves
próximo a las 18:00 horas.
Anexo a la presente sírvase encontrar algunos
documentos que le podrán ser de utilidad a la
hora de preparar nuestra conversación.

Si desea aclarar cualquier tipo de cuestión, no
dude en llamarme.

Atentamente
Juan Pérez
Director

The greeting *Ladies and Gentlemen* has not become common in Spain; instead
they say *Gentlemen*. However, in South America, *Damas y caballeros* is fine.

Salutations

Dear Ms. Rodríguez ...
Estimada Sra. Rodríguez ...

Dear Mr. Rodríguez ...
Estimado Sr. Rodríguez ...

Dear Ms. Rodríguez ...
Querida Sra. Rodríguez ...

Dear Sirs ...
Distinguidos Señores ...

Greetings

Good day, how are you?
Buenos días, ¿cómo está usted?

Hello, how are things?
Buenos días, ¿qué tal?

Hi, how are you doing?
Hola, ¿cómo estás?

Hi, what's up?
Hola, ¿qué pasa?

Important Vocabulary

sender
el remitente

address
la dirección

enclosure
el anexo

salutation
la salutación

reference
la referencia

letterhead
el membrete

date
la fecha

registered mail
el correo certificado

recipient
el destinatario

closing
la despedida

post office box (P.O. Box)
el apartado postal

zip code
el código postal

stamp
el sello / la estampilla

envelope
el sobre

In Spain, stamps are *sellos*; in South America, they are *estampillas*.

Subjects

ballet **el ballet**	opera **la ópera**
television **la televisión**	politics **la política**
film **la película**	press **la prensa**
jazz **el jazz**	radio **la radio**
cinema **el cine**	religion **la religión**
concert **el concierto**	sports **el deporte**
culture **la cultura**	theater **el teatro**
literature **la literatura**	economy / finance **la economía**
music **la música**	magazine **la revista**
news **las noticias**	newspaper **el periódico**

Politics

Although some Latin American countries were plagued by political instability in the 1970s and 1980s, constitutional republics are currently the norm. The appeal of a strong executive and the presence of personality cults in some Latin countries add color to political life – where else will you see presidents dancing cha cha at political rallies and representatives *(diputados)* having their love lives discussed in such detail on TV talk shows.

In Spain, after the end of the authoritarian Franco regime, the country returned to constitutional monarchy; in other words, the head of the national government is the King, who nevertheless governs with greatly restricted authority within a democratic framework.

The Spanish Parliament, *Las Cortes*, is a bicameral parliament that consists of a senate and a house of representatives. This has obvious parallels to the structure of the government in the United States. The Prime Minister is the head of the government; he is appointed by the King at the recommendation of the parties.

President **el presidente**

senator **el senador**

Senate **el senado**

House of Representatives **la cámara de diputados**

representative **el diputado**

vote **el voto**

political refugee **el solicitante de asilo**

citizens' action / citizens' initiative **la iniciativa cívica**

democracy **la democracia**

immigration **la inmigración**

coalition **la coalición**

kingdom **el reino**

parliament **el parlamento**

government **el gobierno**

taxes **los impuestos**

constitution **la constitución**

elections **las elecciones**

Spaniards like to discuss politics. As a guest you should be polite and refrain from criticizing.

At the Border

Your passport!
¡Su pasaporte!

Your passport has expired.
Su pasaporte está caducado.

How long are you staying?
¿Cuánto tiempo se queda usted?

How much money do you have with you?
¿Cuánto dinero lleva encima?

Do you have anything to declare?
¿Tiene algo que declarar?

Please open your suitcase.
Por favor, abra su maleta.

Can you show me a receipt?
¿Puede presentar la factura?

You have to declare that.
Ésto tiene que declararlo.

If you are an American citizen, you will need only a valid passport to enter Spain or any Latin American country (Cuba excepted). Some countries will accept your American driver's license, some may not. Better safe than sorry: find out in advance or get an international driver's permit.

The same rule applies to your belongings, for nobody will object to your suits and shoes, but problems may arise if you bring large amounts of expensive gifts and audio/video equipment. Check with the consulates of the countries you plan to visit.

You can go through.
Puede pasar.

There are no more border checks within the European Union, but if you arrive to Spain from the United States you should expect the usual treatment given to all foreigners. Even if you arrive from a European Union country, spot checks do occur. Always keep your passport and your driver's license with you.

Instead of checking for terrorists, Latin Americans are far more interested in finding *narcotraficantes*.

Customs Regulations

If you are a tourist carrying a reasonable amount of clothes, photographic and video equipment, and modest gifts for friends and relatives, you should have no problems anywhere in Latin America or Spain. However, when in doubt, call the consulate of the country you plan to visit.

Within the European Union you may transport goods for your personal use in practically unlimited quantities. The following quantities are allowed:

Alcoholic drinks

    20 liters of liquor under 22% vol.
    10 liters of liquor over 22% vol.
    90 liters wine (including a maximum of 60 liters of sparkling wine)
    110 liters of beer

Tobacco

    800 cigarettes
    400 cigarillos
    200 cigars
    1 kg tobacco

No limit on coffee, tea, and perfume.

Customs

I have nothing to declare.
No tengo nada que declarar.

These are gifts.
Son regalos.

These are personal belongings.
Son objetos personales.

I want to declare merchandise in the value of ...
Quiero declarar mercancía por un valor de ....

departure
la salida

arrival
la entrada

export
la exportación

import
la importación

declarable goods
mercancía sujeta a declaración

customs
la aduana

customs declaration
la declaración de aduana

customs regulations
las disposiciones aduaneras

customs check
la inspección aduanera

duty-free
exento de derechos de aduana

dutiable
sujeto a derechos de aduana

The institution of customs is *la aduana*; the customs duty that you have to pay is *los derechos de aduana*.

Booking a Flight

I would like to make a reservation to New York.
Quiero reservar un vuelo a Nueva York.

For when?
¿Para cuándo?

Next Tuesday.
Para el martes que viene.

One way?
¿Sólo de ida?

Round trip.
De ida y vuelta.

The flight leaves at 3:40 p.m.
El vuelo sale a las 15.40 horas.

Is there an earlier flight?
¿Hay algún vuelo que salga antes?

I'm sorry, that flight is full.
Lo siento, ese vuelo está completo.

For *next Tuesday* you can say either *el martes que viene* or *el martes próximo.*

Booking a Flight

Where is the American counter?
¿Dónde está la ventanilla de American?

When is the next flight to New York?
¿Cuándo sale el siguiente vuelo a Nueva York?

Are seats still available?
¿Quedan asientos libres?

What does the flight cost?
¿Cuánto cuesta el vuelo?

I would like to confirm my flight to New York.
Quiero confirmar el vuelo a Nueva York.

Is there a stopover?
¿Es un vuelo con escala?

Is there a connecting flight?
¿Hay un vuelo de enlace?

My flight number is ...
El número de mi vuelo es el ...

How much baggage can I take?
¿Qué cantidad de equipaje puedo llevar?

Can I take this as hand luggage?
¿Puedo llevar ésto como equipaje de mano?

Is there an extra charge for excess weight?

I would like to change my flight to New York.
Quiero cambiar mi vuelo a Nueva York.

At what time must I be at the airport?
¿Cuándo tengo que estar en el aeropuerto?

How long is the flight?
¿Cuánto tiempo dura el vuelo?

¿Tengo que pagar recargo por exceso de peso?

Are there any reduced rates?
¿Tiene billetes más económicos?

Are there special fares for children?
¿Hay tarifas especiales para niños?

If the flight is overbooked, I would be prepared to take the next flight.
Si el vuelo estuviera completo, estaría yo dispuesto a tomar el siguiente.

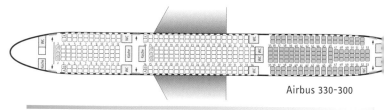

Airbus 330-300

Quiero simply means *I want*. If you want to be more polite, say *quisiera (I would like)*.

Security Check

Last call for flight LH465 to New York.
Última llamada para el vuelo LH465 a Nueva York.

Excuse me, my flight leaves in a few minutes. Would you please let me through?
Perdone, mi vuelo sale dentro de pocos minutos. ¿Me deja usted pasar, por favor?

I am in a hurry myself.
Yo también tengo prisa.

 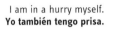

Put all objects into this receptacle.
Ponga todos los objetos en este recipiente.

Open your bag.
Abra su bolsa.

Switch on your laptop.
Encienda su computadora portátil.

Passenger Jones, booked to New York, is requested to proceed immediately to gate 12.
Se ruega al pasajero Jones, con destino a Nueva York, se presente urgentemente en la puerta 12.

To be in a hurry is *tener prisa*; the opposite is *no hay prisa*.

On the Plane

We are sorry, but smoking is forbidden inside the aircraft.
Lo sentimos, pero se prohíbe fumar dentro de la aeronave.

Please fasten your seatbelts!
¡Abróchense los cinturones!

Where can I put this?
¿Dónde puedo poner ésto?

Could I please have something to drink?
Perdone, ¿podría traerme algo de beber, por favor?

Could you please pour me another coffee?
¿Podría darme un poco más de café, por favor?

Could you please bring me a blanket?
¿Podría traerme una manta, por favor?

Do you have any toys for my children?
¿Tiene usted algún juguete para mis hijos?

Can you heat up the baby food?
¿Podría calentarme la comida del bebé?

Do you also have vegetarian meals?
¿También tienen comida vegetariana?

Can you give me something for nausea?
¿Tiene algo para la náusea?

What is our cruising altitude?
¿A qué altura estamos volando?

Will we arrive on time?
¿Llegaremos puntuales?

When can I use my laptop?
¿Cuándo puedo utilizar mi computadora portátil?

Arrival

When does my connecting flight leave?
¿Cuándo sale mi vuelo de enlace?

I have missed my flight.
He perdido el vuelo.

I can't find my luggage.
No encuentro mi equipaje.

My luggage has been lost.
Se ha perdido mi equipaje.

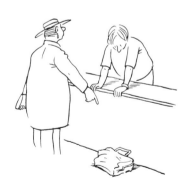

My suitcase has been damaged.
Mi maleta ha sido dañada.

For *cigarettes* you can use either *los cigarrillos* or the word *cigarros*; these are different from *los puros*, which means *cigars*.

Important Vocabulary

suitcase
la maleta

traveling bag
la bolsa de viaje

flight number **el número del vuelo**
flight schedule **el horario de vuelo**
plane ticket **el pasaje de avión**
gate **la puerta de embarque**
aisle seat **el asiento junto al pasillo**
luggage / baggage **el equipaje**
luggage claim **la devolución del equipaje**
luggage carts **el carro de las maletas**
belt **el cinturón**

backpack / knapsack
la mochila

takeoff **la salida**
departure time **la hora de salida**
arrival time **la hora de llegada**
connecting flight **el vuelo de enlace**
crew **la tripulación**
boarding pass **la tarjeta de embarque**
landing / disembarkation form **el formulario de entrada**

window seat **el asiento junto a la ventana**

hand luggage **el equipaje de mano**
landing **el aterrizaje**
forbidden items **artículos prohibidos**
passenger **el pasajero**
luggage inspection **inspección de equipaje**
return flight **el vuelo de vuelta**
counter **la ventanilla**
life jacket **el chaleco salvavidas**
security check **el control de seguridad**
meeting place **el punto de encuentro**
excess luggage **el exceso de equipaje**
delay **el retraso**
stopover **la escala**

La escala is the ladder, the scale, the ruler, and less frequently, the stopover.

Taxi

Where is the nearest taxi stand?
¿Dónde está la parada de taxis más cercana?

Taxi, please!
¡Taxi, por favor!

I would like to order a taxi for 10 o'clock.
Quiero pedir un taxi para las 10 horas.

Can you please send a taxi immediately?
¿Puede mandarme inmediatamente un taxi?

Please take me...
Por favor, lléveme ...
   to the hotel ...
   al hotel ...
   to this street...
   a esta calle...
   downtown.
   al centro de la ciudad.
   to the airport.
   al aeropuerto.
   to the railway station.
   a la estación de ferrocarriles.

What will the fare cost, approximately?
¿Cuánto cuesta la carrera más o menos?

Take the shortest / fastest route, please.
Tome el camino más corto / rápido, por favor.

Straight ahead here, please.
Siga aquí derecho, por favor.

Turn right / left here.
Gire a la derecha / izquierda.

Please stop here.
Pare aquí, por favor.

Stop at the next crossroad.
Pare en el cruce siguiente.

Please wait for me here.
Espéreme aquí, por favor.

How much do I owe you?
¿Cuánto le debo?

We agreed on another amount.
Habíamos convenido otra cantidad.

That seems too much!
¡Me parece demasiado caro!

I would like a receipt.
Quisiera un recibo, por favor

Keep the change!
¡Está bien así!

That is for you.
Es para usted.

You can keep the change.
Quédese con el cambio.

Could you please put our luggage into the trunk?
¿Podría meter nuestro equipaje en el maletero, por favor?

Could you please help me to get in?
¿Puede ayudarme a subir, por favor?

Do you know an inexpensive hotel in the neighborhood?
¿Conoce usted un hotel barato por aquí cerca?

Another word for *train station* is *la estación de trenes.*

Renting a Car

I would like to rent a car for a week.
Quiero alquilar un coche por una semana.

Which kind of car would you like?
¿Qué tipo de coche quiere usted?

A medium-size car.
Un coche mediano.

Let's see what we have. That will cost 250 euros per week.
Véamos cuáles hay. Éste cuesta 250 euros a la semana.

Can I see your driver's license?
¿Me permite ver su carnet de conducir?
Please sign here.
Firme aquí, por favor.

When the car has been filled up with gas, it has *el tanque lleno* and *está con el tanque lleno.*

Renting a Car

Do you have weekend rates?
¿Hay tarifas especiales para el fin de semana?

Do you have any special offers?
¿Hay ofertas especiales?

Do you have any better offers?
¿Hay otras ofertas más económicas?

Can I return the car elsewhere?
¿Puedo entregar el coche en otro sitio?

At what time do I have to return the vehicle?
¿A qué hora tengo que entregar el coche?

Is this with unlimited mileage?
¿El número de kilómetros es ilimitado?

Do I have to leave a deposit?
¿Tengo que depositar una fianza?

Is the gas tank full?
¿Está lleno el tanque?

Do I have to return the car with a full tank?
¿Tengo que entregar el coche con el tanque lleno?

Could you explain to me what the different types of insurance are?
¿Podría usted explicarme los diferentes tipos de seguro?

I would like comprehensive insurance.
Quisiera un seguro a todo riesgo.

How much is the deductible?
¿Cuánto se deduce de la compensación?

Can my partner drive the car too?
¿Está permitido que mi compañero conduzca?

Does the car have ...
¿Tiene el vehículo ...
   air conditioning?
   aire acondicionado?
   power steering?
   dirección asistida?
   ABS?
   ABS?

anti-theft device?
inmovilizador electrónico antirrobo?

Do you have a road map?
¿Tiene usted un mapa de carreteras?

What's the fastest way through the city?
¿Cuál es el camino más rápido para atravesar la ciudad?

How can I bypass the city center?
¿Cómo puedo evitar pasar por el centro de la ciudad?

What's the best way to go downtown?
¿Cuál es el mejor camino para llegar al centro de la ciudad?

If you say the letters ABS in Spanish, you have to say *AH BEH EHSSEH*.

The Car

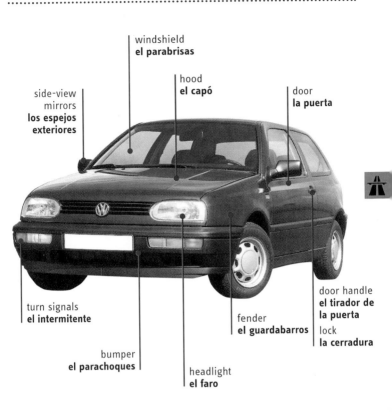

windshield
el parabrisas

hood
el capó

door
la puerta

side-view
mirrors
**los espejos
exteriores**

turn signals
el intermitente

door handle
**el tirador de
la puerta**

fender
el guardabarros

lock
la cerradura

bumper
el parachoques

headlight
el faro

wheel
la rueda

tires
los neumáticos

rim
la llanta

For hood, you can also say *la capota* instead of *el capó*.

The Car

steering wheel
el volante

gear lever
la palanca del cambio

exhaust
el tubo de escape

brake
el freno

tachometer
el tacómetro

gas pedal
el acelerador

hand brake / emergency brake
el freno de mano

glove compartment
la guantera

rear
la parte trasera

rear windshield
la luneta trasera

trunk
el maletero

clutch
el embrague

motor
el motor

rear view mirrors
el retrovisor

windshield wipers
los limpiaparabrisas

seat belt
el cinturón de seguridad

speedometer
el velocímetro

fuel gauge
el indicador de la gasolina

emergency flashers
las intermitentes de emergencia

For *coupling* there is also the general term *el acoplamiento*; the *clutch* is *el embrague*.

The Motorcycle

seat **el asiento**
flasher / blinker **la luz intermitente**
brake light **la luz de parada**
brake cable **el cable de freno**
motor **el motor**
tail light **la luz trasera**
headlights **los faros**
tank **el tanque**
drum brake **el freno de tambor**
carburetor **el carburador**

For *exhaust pipe* you can use the shortened form *escape* instead of *tubo de escape.*

On the Move

Excuse me, how do I get to ...
Perdone, ¿cómo se llega a ...?

Can you show me that on the map?
¿Puede enseñármelo en el mapa?

Can you show me where I am on the map?
¿Puede indicarme en el mapa dónde estoy?

Where is the nearest gas station?
¿Dónde está la próxima gasolinera?

Where is the nearest repair shop?
¿Dónde está el taller más cercano?

traffic light
el semáforo

turnpike
la autopista

interstate highway
la carretera nacional

crossroad
el cruce

country road
la carretera regional

Is that the street that goes to ...?
¿Es éste el camino a ...?

How far is it to ...?
¿Qué distancia hay de aquí a ...?

Directions

You are in the wrong place.
Se ha equivocado de camino.

You must drive back.
Tiene que regresar.

Straight ahead.
Todo recto.

Go to the first crossroad.
Siga hasta el primer cruce.

Turn right at the next corner.
Al llegar a la esquina siguiente, gire a la derecha.

Follow the signs.
Siga las señales.

Turn left at the traffic lights.
Al llegar al semáforo gire a la izquierda.

You sometimes will encounter signs marked *estación de servicio* for gas station.

Notices and Traffic Signs

Caution! **¡Atención!**

exit **salida**

keep driveway clear **dejar libre la salida**

construction **obras**

one-way street **calle de dirección única**

junction **desembocadura**

form lanes **enfilarse**

single-lane traffic **carretera de una sola vía**

end of no parking zone **fin de prohibido estacionar**

road narrows **paso estrecho**

crosswalk **cruce de peatones**

pedestrian zone **zona peatonal**

danger **peligro**

dangerous curve **curva peligrosa**

gradient **desnivel**

speed limit **limitación de velocidad**

hairpin bend **curva en herradura**

no stopping **prohibido parar**

no entry **prohibido el acceso**

rotary traffic **circulación giratoria**

crossing **el cruce**

slow lane **vía para vehículos lentos**

drive slowly **conducir despacio**

slow down **modere la velocidad**

truck **el camión**

no parking **prohibido estacionar**

parking garage **el garaje**

parking lot **el estacionamiento**

parking lot ticket machine **la boletera de estacionamiento**

radar control **control por radar**

bicycle path **pista para bicicletas**

keep right **circular por la derecha**

right lane has right of way **dar la preferencia a la derecha**

no right turn **prohibido girar a la derecha**

loose gravel **gravilla suelta**

slippery when wet **peligro de deslizamiento**

dead end **callejón sin salida**

turn on headlights **encender las luces del automóvil**

danger of skidding **resbaladizo**

expressway **la autovía**

school-bus stop **la parada del autobús escolar**

traffic jam **el embotellamiento**

road construction **obras**

toll **el peaje**

underground parking garage **el garaje subterráneo**

no passing **prohibido adelantar**

bypass **la circunvalación**

detour **la desviación**

traffic lights **el semáforo**

heed right of way **ceda el paso**

yield right of way **ceda el paso**

Caution! **¡Atención!**

no u-turn **prohibido virar en U**

toll booth **la estación de peaje**

Obras simply means *work*, and in the figurative sense *Men Working* (on a road or construction site).

Parking

Can I park here?
¿Puedo estacionar aquí?

How long can I park here?
¿Cuánto tiempo puedo estar estacionado?

Where is there ...
¿Dónde hay ...
   a parking lot?
   un estacionamiento?
   an underground parking garage?
   un garaje subterráneo?
   a parking building?
   una torre de estacionamiento?

What are the parking charges ...
¿Cuánto cuesta el estacionamiento ...

   per hour?
   por hora?
   per day?
   al día?

Is the parking lot attended?
¿Es un estacionamiento vigilado?

During what hours is the parking building open?
¿Cuál es el horario de apertura de la torre de estacionamiento?

Is the parking building open the whole night?
¿Está abierta durante toda la noche la torre de estacionamiento?

Where is the cashier?
¿Dónde está la caja?

Where is the parking ticket machine?
¿Dónde está la boletera de estacionamiento?

Can you give me change?
¿Puede usted cambiarme el dinero?

I have lost my parking ticket.
He perdido el boleto.

parking meter
el parquímetro

At the Gas Station

gas pump
el surtidor de gasolina

gas can
la lata de gasolina

gas
la gasolina

oil
el aceite

super
la gasolina súper

regular
la gasolina corriente

unleaded
sin plomo

diesel
el dieseloil

brake fluid
el líquido del freno

A ticket dispenser can also be translated as *un distribuidor de billetes*.

Filling Up

Octane Ratings

In the US, gasolines have the following octane ratings:

Regular: 89

Mid-grade: 91

Super: 94

Compare these ratings with those of Spain or whatever Latin American country you happen to visit.

Where is the nearest gas station?
¿Dónde está la próxima gasolinera?

Please fill it up.
Lleno, por favor

Give me 30 euros' worth please.
Echeme 30 euros, por favor.

I need one quart of oil.
Necesito un litro de aceite.

   Can you check ...
   Por favor mire ...
   the oil.
   el nivel del aceite.
   the tire pressure.
   la presión de los neumáticos.
   the antifreeze.
   el anticongelante.

Please fill the windshield washer fluid.
Por favor, relléneme el depósito del agua.

Can you do an oil change?
¿Me puede hacer un cambio de aceite?

Would you please clean the windshield?
¿Me limpia el parabrisas, por favor?

Could you wash the car?
¿Me puede lavar el coche?

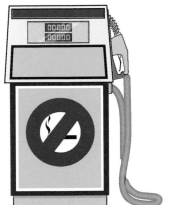

How much do I owe you?
¿Cuánto le debo?

Do you have a map?
¿Tiene usted un mapa de carreteras?

Where are the toilets?
¿Dónde están los lavabos?

The Spanish people commonly use the word *baño* (meaning bath) for toilet; or else they say *ir al servicio*.

Breakdowns

Can you help me? I've had a breakdown.
¿Puede ayudarme? Tengo una avería.

What is wrong?
¿Qué pasa?

The motor won't start.
El motor no arranca.

Let me have a look.
Déjeme echar un vistazo.

I think you have to take it to the repair shop.
Temo que tendrá que ir a un taller.

Can you tow my car?
¿Puede usted remolcarme?

¿Qué pasa? (What's happening?) is a Spanish expression that can be used in practically any situation.

I've had a breakdown.
Tengo una avería.

I have a problem ...
Tengo problemas ...
  with the battery.
  con la batería.
  with the steering.
  con la dirección.
  when starting.
  al arrancar.
  with the lights.
  con la luz.
  with the brakes.
  al frenar.
  with changing gears.
  con la caja de cambios.

I have a flat tire.
La rueda está pinchada.

It won't start.
No arranca.

The motor splutters / misses.
El motor funciona irregularmente.

I'm out of gas.
Quedé sin gasolina.

Do you know of a repair shop nearby?
¿Sabe usted si hay un taller por aquí cerca?

Can you take me to the nearest gas station?
¿Puede llevarme a la siguiente gasolinera?

Can you tow me?
¿Puede remolcarme?

Can you push me?
¿Puede empujarme?

Can you repair it?
¿Puede repararlo?

Can I drive any farther with the car?
¿Puedo seguir conduciendo?

When will it be ready?
¿Cuándo estará listo?

Can I phone from here?
¿Puedo hacer una llamada?

Please connect me with my car rental agency.
Póngame con la agencia que me ha alquilado el coche, por favor.

gas can
la lata de gasolina

warning triangle
el triángulo de emergencia

tools
las herramientas

breakdown / towing service **el servicio de grúa**

towing cable **el cable para remolcar**

breakdown assistance **el servicio de averías**

jumper cables **los cables de empalme para la puesta en marcha**

jack **el gato**

emergency flashers **las luces intermitentes**

Breakdown assistance can also be translated as *asistencia en carretera*.

In the Repair Shop

There's something wrong with the brakes.
Los frenos no funcionan bien.

My car is losing oil.
Mi coche pierde aceite.

The warning light is on.
El indicador luminoso está encendido.

Change the spark plugs please.
Por favor, cambie las bujías.

Can you recharge the battery?
¿Podría cargar la batería?

Can you fix the tire?
¿Puede reparar el neumático?

Can you take a look at it?
¿Puede echarle un vistazo?

Can you repair it?
¿Puede repararlo?

Something is wrong with the motor.
Hay algo que no funciona en el motor.

How long will it take?
¿Cuánto tiempo tomará?

What will it cost?
¿Cuánto costará?

starter **motor de arranque**	gears / transmission **la caja de cambios**
brake lining **el forro del freno**	light bulb **la bombilla**
brakes **los frenos**	heater **el calefactor**
brake fluid **el líquido del freno**	rear axle **el eje trasero**
brake light **la luz del freno**	horn **la bocina**
gasket **la junta**	cable **el cable**
fuel injector pump **el inyector**	v-belt **la correa en cuña**
spare wheel **la rueda de recambio**	air conditioning **el climatizador**
spare tire **el neumático de recambio**	radiator **el radiador**
spare parts **las piezas de recambio**	coolant / antifreeze **el anticongelante**
backfire **encendido defectuoso**	short circuit **el cortocircuito**

A V-belt is *una correa en V*, so remember to pronounce *veh*, not vee.

battery
la batería

distributor
el distribuidor

pistons
los pistones

water pump
la bomba del agua

shock absorber
el amortiguador

spark plug
la bujía

steering
la dirección

headlight flasher
el indicador luminoso

dynamo
la dínamo

motor
el motor

oil filter
el filtro del aceite

taillight
la luz trasera

fuse
el fusible

seat
el asiento

valve
la válvula

carburetor
el carburador

front axle
el eje delantero

ignition
el encendido

cylinder head
la culata

sunroof
el techo corredizo

Another word for the headlight flasher is *el avisador luminoso*.

Traffic Regulations, Violations

Driving in Latin America should be an unforgettable experience, either because you checked carefully the rates at the car rental agency (including insurance and free mileage), drove mainly in daylight, and stayed at hotels/motels approved by your tourist guide, or because you did none of these things.

The freedom that driving provides, the chance to stop at a breathtaking spot for as long as you like, should be judiciously balanced with the uneven quality of roads and services available in the Spanish continent.

Spain has an excellent highway and hotel system. Its traffic regulations have been "harmonized" with those of the European Union: towing with private vehicles is forbidden. Using a telephone while driving is permitted only with a hands-free headset. No passing 100 meters before a hilltop and on roads where you don't have at least a 200-meter view. Speed limits: in town, 50 km/h; out of town, 90; high-speed highways, 100; divided highways, 120. The seat belt law is in effect.

Drivers who commit infractions are required to pay promptly. The highway police are likely to deal summarily with tourists. Fines as of 2001: DWI, 300 euros and higher; 20 km/h over the speed limit: 90 euros and higher; red light infraction: 90 euros and higher; passing violation, 90 euros and higher; parking infraction: up to 90 euros.

Emergency
   Police: 112
   Accident assistance: 061

You were driving too fast.
Usted iba conduciendo a una velocidad demasiado alta.

You went through a red light.
Se saltó el semáforo en rojo.

You did not give the right of way.
Usted no cedió el paso.

You cannot park here.
Usted no puede estacionar aquí.

Passing is not allowed here.
Está prohibido adelantar.

You have had too much to drink.
Usted ha bebido demasiado.

Never forget that on the highway you are dealing with kilometers per hour, not miles per hour.

Accidents

There has been an accident.
Hubo un accidente.

I've had an accident.
Sufrí un accidente.

Some people have been injured.
Hay heridos.

Do you have any bandages?
¿Tiene usted vendajes?

Please call ...
Por favor, llame ...
   the police.
   a la policía.
   an ambulance.
   una ambulancia.
   a tow truck.
   el servicio de grúa.

My name is ...
Me llamo ...

I am a tourist.
Soy turista.

What is your name and address?
¿Cuál es su nombre y su dirección?

Please give me your insurance number.
Deme el número de su seguro, por favor.

I need witnesses.
Necesito testigos.

I have witnesses.
Tengo testigos.

It was my fault.
Fue culpa mía.

It was your fault.
Fue culpa suya.

I had the right of way.
Yo tenía la preferencia.

You did not keep enough distance.
Usted no respetó la distancia de seguridad.

You braked suddenly.
Usted frenó inesperadamente.

Please inform my family. The number is ...
Por favor, informe a mi familia. El número es el ...

Towing service is *el servicio de remolque* and *el servicio de grúa*.

The Bicycle

saddle
el sillín

handlebars
el manillar

saddlebags
las bolsas

chain
la cadena

pedal
el pedal

tires
los neumáticos

gearshift
el cambio de marchas

reflector
el reflector

antitheft cable **el cable antirrobos**
bicycle pump **la bomba para neumáticos**
rims **las llantas**
repair kit **el bote de parches**
hand brake **el freno de mano**
chain guard **el cubrecadenas**
cover **la cubierta**
mountain bike **la todocamino**
nut **la tuerca**
hub **el cubo**
wheel **la rueda**

racing bike **la bicicleta de carreras**
taillight **la luz trasera**
inner tube **la cámara de aire**
mudguard **el guardabarros**
spoke **el rayo**
valve **la válvula**
headlight **la luz delantera**
front fork **la horquilla de la rueda delantera**
tool **la herramienta**
gear **el engranaje**

Another common word for *bicycle* is *bici*.

Renting a Bicycle

I would like to rent a bicycle.
Quisiera alquilar una bicicleta.

Gladly. We have a big selection.
Con mucho gusto. Tenemos un amplio surtido.

I would like something more sporty.
Quisiera algo más deportivo.

How is this one?
¿Qué le parece ésta?

How many speeds
does the bicycle
have?
**¿Cuántas marchas
tiene la bicicleta?**

Twelve.
Doce.

The *gear* can also be *el cambio.*

Renting a Bicycle

How much does a bicycle cost per day?
¿Cuánto cuesta el alquiler de una bicicleta al día?

That is too expensive.
Es demasiado caro.

Do I have to leave you a deposit?
¿Tengo que depositar una fianza?

Are longer rentals cheaper?
¿Dan descuento si se alquila por más tiempo?

Do you also rent ...
¿También alquila ...

  saddlebags?
  bolsas?
  rain gear?
  impermeables?
  children's seats?
  sillines para niños?
  children's bicycles?
  bicicletas para niños?
  repair kits?
  estuches de reparación?
  helmets?
  cascos?

Can you show us a scenic route from ... to ...?
¿Puede indicarnos una ruta bonita de ... a ...?

Can you show me an easier route?
¿Puede indicarme un recorrido más sencillo?

Do you have information about bicycle routes in the area?
¿Tiene folletos con información sobre las rutas de esta zona?

Is there a lot of traffic on this route?
¿Hay mucho tráfico en ese camino?

We have children with us.
Vamos con niños.

Is this bicycle route suitable for children?
¿Es una ruta adecuada para los niños?

I have a flat tire.
El neumático está pinchado.

Can you lend me your repair kit?
¿Me puede prestar su bote de parches?

I fell off my bike.
Me he caído.

Do you have bandages?
¿Tiene vendajes?

Translations for *caution* are *fianza* and *caución* (Spain) or *cuidado* (America).

Buying Tickets

A ticket to Madrid, please.
Un billete para Madrid, por favor.

One-way or round-trip?
¿De ida y vuelta?

Only one way, please.
Sólo de ida, por favor.

When does the next train leave?
¿Cuándo sale el próximo tren?

At 10:28 on platform 3.
A las diez y veintiocho en el andén 3.

The Spanish word for *platform* (at the railroad station) is *el andén*.

At the Ticket Window

I would like a train timetable.
Quisiera un horario de los trenes.

I would like like to go by train
from ... to ...
Quisiera viajar en tren de ...a ....

When does the next train leave?
¿Cuándo sale el próximo tren?

What does the round trip cost?
¿Cuánto cuesta el billete de ida y vuelta?

Are there special offers for tourists?
¿Hay precios especiales para turistas?

There is discount for ...
¿Hay tarifas especiales para ...
children?
niños?
schoolchildren?
estudiantes?
college students?
universitarios?
senior citizens?
jubilados?
families?
familias?

I would like to have ...
Quisiera ...
a place in the sleeping car.
una plaza en el coche-cama.
a sleeping compartment for ...
persons.
un compartimiento para ... personas.
a reclining seat.
un asiento reclinable.
first-class ticket.
un billete de primera clase.

Do I have to reserve a seat?
¿Tengo que reservar el asiento?

I would like to reserve a window seat.
Quisiera reservar un asiento junto a la ventana.

Is that a nonstop train?
¿Es un tren directo?

Does the train stop at Madrid?
¿El tren para en Madrid?

Does the train have a dining car?
¿Hay un vagón-restaurante en el tren?

Do I have to change trains?
¿Tengo que hacer transbordo?

From which track does the train depart?
¿De qué andén sale el tren?

Where can I check in my luggage?
¿Dónde puedo dejar mi equipaje?

Can I take my bicycle?
¿Puedo llevar mi bicicleta?

What does that cost?
¿Cuánto cuesta?

Written Inquiry

Nonpotable water
Agua no potable

Occupied
Ocupado

Vacant
Libre

Emergency brake
Freno de emergencia

Exit
Salida

Toilets
Servicios higiénicos

Non-potable water is *agua no potable*; therefore, *drinking water* is *agua potable*.

On the Platform / On the Train

Does the train to Madrid leave from this platform?
¿El tren para Madrid sale de este andén?

Where does the train to Madrid leave?
¿De dónde sale el tren para Madrid?

Is this the train to Madrid?
¿Es éste el tren para Madrid?

Does the train go via Madrid?
¿Este tren pasa por Madrid?

Is the train from Madrid delayed?
¿Viene con retraso el tren de Madrid?

How long is the delay?
¿Cuánto tiempo lleva de retraso?

When will it arrive at Barcelona?
¿Cuándo llegará a Barcelona?

Is this seat occupied?
¿Está ocupado este asiento?

This is my seat. I have reserved it.
Este asiento es mío. Lo he reservado.

May I ...
¿Puedo ...
open the window?
abrir la ventana?
close the window?
cerrar la ventana?

Is there a smoking car?
¿Hay un vagón para fumadores?

Where are we?
¿Dónde estamos?

How long do we stop here?
¿Cuánto tiempo dura esta parada?

Will we arrive on time?
¿Llegaremos puntuales?

Will I make my connecting train?
¿Llego a tiempo para hacer el transbordo al otro tren?

From which track does my connecting train leave?
¿De qué andén sale el tren de enlace?

Where is the dining car?
¿Dónde está el vagón-restaurante?

Where can I buy something to drink?
¿Dónde puedo comprar algo de beber?

Where are the toilets?
¿Dónde están los servicios higiénicos?

What You Hear

El tren para Madrid está a punto de llegar al andén número tres.
The train to Madrid is arriving on track 3.

El tren para Madrid, que sale del andén tres, lleva diez minutos de retraso.
The train to Madrid on track 3 is delayed by ten minutes.

¡Suba, por favor!
All aboard!

¿Dónde has dejado los billetes?
Where did you leave the tickets?

Los billetes, por favor.
The tickets, please.

Si compra el billete en el tren, tiene que pagar un suplemento.
If you buy the ticket on the train, you have to pay a surcharge.

Dentro de pocos minutos llegaremos a Madrid.
In few minutes, we will arrive in Madrid.

With means of transportation, *to get in* is *subir*; *to get out* is *bajar*.

Important Vocabulary

departure **la salida**

compartment **el compartimiento**

stopover **la parada**

information **la información**

car-train **el autotren**

railway station **la estación de ferrocarril**

platform **el andén**

express train **el tren directo**

express train **el tren rápido**

railroad **el ferrocarril**

last stop **la estación final**

reduction / discount **la reducción de tarifa**

ticket **el billete**

ticket counter **la taquilla**

timetable **el horario del tren**

family ticket **el billete con tarifa familiar**

window seat **el asiento junto a la ventana**

lost-and-found office **la oficina de objetos perdidos**

aisle **el pasillo**

baggage **el equipaje**

baggage deposit **el maletero**

checkroom **la consigna**

track **el andén**

group card **el billete de tarifa de grupo**

sleeper **el coche-litera**

locomotive **la locomotora**

local traffic **el tráfico local**

emergency brake **el freno de emergencia**

reservation / reserved seat ticket **el billete de reserva de asiento**

reservation **la reservación**

round-trip ticket **el billete de ida y vuelta**

ticket checker **el revisor**

sleeping car **el coche-cama**

locker **la consigna automática**

dining car **el vagón-restaurante**

commuter train **el tren local**

car number **el número del vagón**

waiting room **la sala de espera**

washroom **el cuarto de aseo**

newsstand **el quiosco**

surcharge **el suplemento del billete**

porter **el mozo de estación**

A suitcase is *una maleta*; a large travel trunk is *un baúl*.

Taking the Bus

I would like to travel by bus for two weeks in this area.
Quisiera viajar durante dos semanas en autobús para recorrer esta región.

Do you any have special offers?
¿Hay alguna oferta especial?

Do you give a discount for ...
¿Hay descuentos para ...
    college students?
    universitarios?
    schoolchildren?
    estudiantes?
    senior citizens?
    jubilados?
    handicapped?
    minusválidos?
    groups?
    grupos?
    families?
    familias?

Is it cheaper to buy a round trip ticket?
¿Es más conveniente comprar un billete de ida y vuelta?

Is it possible to reserve seats?
¿Es posible reservar asientos?

From which platform does the bus leave?
¿De qué andén sale el autobús?

Will the passengers be called for departure?
¿Hay llamadas para los pasajeros?

Does the bus have ...
¿El autobús tiene ...
    air-conditioning?
    aire acondicionado?

    reclining seats?
    asientos reclinables?
    a toilet?
    servicios higiénicos?

When do I have to be at the bus station?
¿Cuándo tengo que estar en la estación de autobuses?

Do I have to transfer?
¿Tengo que hacer transbordo?

Where / when is the next stop?
¿Dónde / cuándo es la siguiente parada?

How long does the trip take?
¿Cuánto tiempo dura el viaje?

Where does this bus go to?
¿A dónde va este autobús?

Aire acondicionado is the most common expression for *air conditioning*. It's easy to remember because it's so similar to the English.

Traveling by Boat

I would like to have a timetable.
Quisiera un itinerario de los barcos.

When does the next ship leave for Key West?
¿Cuándo sale el próximo barco a Key West?

I would like to have a ticket to Key West.
Quisiera un billete para Key West.

How much does the trip cost?
¿Cuánto cuesta el viaje?

Are there any special offers for tourists?

¿Hay ofertas especiales para turistas?

Is the ticket also valid for the return trip?

¿El billete también vale para la vuelta?
¿El billete también vale para la vuelta?

I would like to take my car along.
Quisiera llevar el coche.

What does that cost?
¿Cuánto cuesta?

When do we have to board?
¿Cuándo tenemos que embarcarnos?

How long does the crossing take?
¿Cuánto tiempo dura la travesía?

What ports do we visit?
¿En qué puertos hacemos escala?

I would like a round-trip ticket for 11 o'clock.
Quisiera un billete para la gira de las once.

On Board

I am looking for cabin no. 12.
Estoy buscando el camarote número doce.

Can I have another cabin?
¿Puede darme otro camarote?

Can I have an outside cabin?
¿Puedo tener un camarote exterior?

How much more does that cost?
¿Cuánto tengo que pagar extra?

Where is my luggage?
¿Dónde está mi equipaje?

Where is the dining room?
¿Dónde está el comedor?

When is the meal served?
¿A qué hora se sirve la comida?

When do we leave?
¿Cuándo salimos?

How long is the stop?
¿Cuánto tiempo dura la escala?

Can I go ashore?
¿Puedo bajar del barco?

When do I have to be back?
¿Cuándo tengo que estar de regreso?

I am feeling sick.
Me siento mal.

Do you have anything for seasickness?
¿Tiene algo para el mareo?

Another word for *ferry* is *el transbordador*. The word *ferry* is also used.

deck chair
**la silla de
cubierta**

lighthouse
el faro

life preserver
el salvavidas

life jacket
**el chaleco
salvavidas**

anchor **el ancla**

mooring **el atracadero**

outside cabin **el camarote exterior**

car ferry **el transbordador de
automóviles**

port **babor**

bow **la proa**

steamer **el barco de vapor**

deck **la cubierta**

single cabin **el camarote individual**

ferry **el ferry**

ticket **el billete**

mainland **la tierra firme**

riverboat trip **el viaje fluvial**

freighter **el buque mercante**

harbor **el puerto**

harbor tour **el recorrido en barco
por el puerto**

stern **la popa**

inside cabin **el camarote interno**

yacht **el yate**

boat **el bote**

quay **el muelle**

berth / cabin **el camarote**

captain **el capitán**

cruise **el crucero**

coast **la costa**

shore excursion **la excursión al
interior**

jetty **el embarcadero**

reclining seat **el asiento reclinable**

rubber raft / rubber dinghy **el
aerodeslizador**

crew **la tripulación**

sailor **el marinero**

motorboat **la motolancha**

hurricane **el huracán**

lifeboat **el bote salvavidas**

rowboat **el bote de remos**

round-trip **la gira / el recorrido / la
excursión**

swell **la
marejada**

seasick
mareado

sail **la vela**

sailboat **el
barco de vela**

starboard
estribor

steward **el camarero del barco**

storm **la tormenta**

hydrofoil **el acuaplano**

wave **la ola**

double cabin **el camarote doble**

Crucero means the crossing as well as the vessel.

Asking for Directions

Excuse me, how do I get to El Prado?
¿Perdone, cómo se llega al Prado?

Straight ahead, take the second street on the left, then the third on the right.
Siempre recto, la segunda a la izquierda, luego la tercera a la derecha.

The third left?
¿La tercera a la izquierda?

No, the second left. There is a gas station, then a supermarket and after that some traffic lights.
No, la segunda a la izquierda, allí hay una gasolinera, luego un supermercado y después un semáforo.

You mean left at the gas station?
¿Entonces en la gasolinera giro a la izquierda?

No, that is too early. Left at the traffic lights.
No, la gasolinera está antes, debe girar en el semáforo.

Maybe ten minutes.
Unos diez minutos.

Is it far?
¿Está lejos?

Ah, thank you. I should be able to find it.
Muchas gracias, seguro que lo encuentro.

Behind is *detrás* in a geographical sense; for rank or order the word *después* is used.

What You Hear

Lo siento, no lo sé.
I'm sorry, I don't know.

No soy de aquí.
I am not from here.

Está lejos.
It is far.

No está lejos.
It is not far.

Cruce la calle.
Cross the street.

No puede perderse.
You cannot miss it.

Vuelva a preguntar.
Ask once again.

Traveling on Foot

Excuse me, can you help me?
Perdone, ¿me puede ayudar?

I am looking for Thomson Street.
Busco la calle Thomson.

Can you show it to me on the map?
¿Puede mostrármelo en el mapa?

How far is Lincoln Center?
¿A qué distancia está Lincoln Center?

traffic light
el semáforo

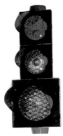

Can I take a bus?
¿Se puede ir en autobús?

Where are the nearest toilets?
¿Dónde están los servicios higiénicos más cercanos?

bridge
el puente

pedestrian zone
la zona peatonal

alley
el callejón

buildings
los edificios

street number
el número de la casa

downtown
el centro de la ciudad

crossing
el cruce

park
el parque

square / place
la plaza

street
la calle

Most Spanish people don't walk very much; they are more likely to take a taxi.

Directions

 left
a la izquierda

 right
a la derecha

straight ahead
siempre recto

the first left
la primera a la izquierda

the second right
la segunda a la derecha

in front of
delante de

behind
detrás de

after
después de

Todo recto and *todo derecho* both mean *straight ahead*.

Local Traffic

Where is the nearest ...
¿Dónde está el (la) próximo (-a) ...
  subway station?
  estación de metro?
  bus stop?
  parada de autobús?
  streetcar stop?
  parada de tranvía?

When does the next bus leave?
¿Cuándo sale el siguiente autobús?

When does the last subway train leave?
¿Cuándo sale el último metro?

Where can I buy a ticket?
¿Dónde puedo comprar el billete?

Can you help me? I don't know how to use the vending machine.
¿Me podría ayudar? Yo no sé cómo funciona la máquina vendedora.

What is this button for?
¿Para qué sirve este botón?

I would like to go to ... Which ticket must I buy?
Quiero ir a ... ¿Qué billete tengo que comprar?

Can you give me change for this?
¿Puede cambiarme el billete en monedas?

How much does a trip cost?
¿Cuánto cuesta el billete?

How much does the round trip cost?
¿Cuánto cuesta el billete de ida y vuelta?

Do you also have ...
¿Hay también ...
  multiple ride tickets?
  billetes múltiples?
  day tickets?
  billetes válidos por un sólo día?
  weekly tickets?
  billetes semanales?
  monthly tickets?
  billetes mensuales?
  tourist tickets?
  billetes para turistas?

How long is this ticket valid?
¿Cuánto tiempo es válido este billete?

Can I travel as often as I like with this ticket?
¿Puedo utilizar este billete más de una vez?

I can get off and then back on again with the same ticket?
¿Puedo bajar y subir con el mismo billete?

Is this ticket also valid for the return trip?
¿Este billete también vale para la vuelta?

Is this ticket also valid for the bus / the subway?
¿Este billete también vale para el autobús / el metro?

Which line goes to ...?
¿Qué línea va a ...?

In which direction do I have to go?
¿Qué dirección debo tomar?

Where do I have to transfer?
¿Dónde tengo que hacer transbordo?

In Mexico a bus is *un camion*, which really should mean *truck*. In Central America it is a *guagua*, which really should mean *baby*.

What is the name of the next station?
¿Cómo se llama la próxima estación?

How many stops are there?
¿Cuántas paradas son?

Can you please tell me when we reach the stop?
¿Puede avisarme en cuanto lleguemos a la parada?

What do I have to do when I want to get off?
¿Qué tengo que hacer para bajarme?

I did not know that the ticket was not valid here.
No sabía que el billete no era válido aquí.

I have lost the ticket.
He perdido el billete.

I have left something behind in the bus.
He olvidado algo en el autobús.

Can you tell me where the lost-and-found office is?
¿Puede decirme dónde guardan objetos perdidos?

subway
el metro

bus
el autobús

streetcar
el tranvía

last stop
la estación final

driver
el chofer

ticket
el billete

ticket vending machine
la vendedora de billetes

timetable
el horario / el itinerario

stop
la parada

ticket inspector
el inspector

ticket checker
el revisor

day ticket
el billete válido por un día

one-week ticket
el billete semanal

season ticket
el billete estacional

A ticket in Spain is *un billete*; in South America it's *un boleto*.

Overnight Accommodations

Where Can One Spend the Night?

Although all Latin American capitals will have at least a few dozens of first-class hotels and hundreds of more modest accommodations, diversity is the norm in smaller cities.

Research is everything; use the internet and good tourist guides, and you will be pleased. And never forget to appreciate the personal and friendly service you will get at most places.

Spain is a common tourist destination, so it has a well developed tourism infrastructure, and acceptable accommodations are the norm.

That may not necessarily be the case in the country, where you may have to place a higher value on atmosphere than on luxury.

In addition to all grades of hotels, there are the *paradores*, which are often high-quality overnight accommodations run by the state (often in old castles), plus the *mesones* and *hostales*, which are equivalent to a pension.

farm	**la granja**
bungalow	**la casita campestre**
campsite	**el camping**
YWCA	**Asociación de jóvenes cristianas**
YMCA	**Asociación de jóvenes cristianos**
vacation house	**la casa de vacaciones**
vacation apartment	**el apartamento de vacaciones**
hotel	**el hotel**
youth hostel	**el albergue juvenil**
motel	**el motel**
private guest house / bed and breakfast	**las habitaciones en casas particulares**
single room	**la habitación simple**
double room	**la habitación doble**
suite	**la suite**
breakfast	**el desayuno**
half board	**la media pensión**
full board / American plan	**la pensión completa**
room only / European plan	**la habitación sin desayuno**

Written Inquiry

Habitación libre
Rooms available / Vacancies

Todo lleno
No vacancy

La oferta especial
Special offer

A bungalow is also called *un chalé*.

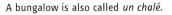

Finding a Room

Is there a good hotel here?
¿Hay por acá un buen hotel?

How is the hotel?
¿Cómo es el hotel?

I am looking for a room for ...
Busco una habitación para ...
 one night.
 una noche.
 three days.
 tres días.
 a week.
 una semana.

Do you still have rooms available?
¿Quedan habitaciones libres?

What does it cost?
¿Cuánto cuesta?

Is there a discount for children?
¿Hay descuento para niños?

That is too expensive.
Es demasiado caro.

Do you have something less expensive?
¿Hay algo más barato?

Do you have a list of private guest houses?
¿Tiene una lista de casas particulares que alquilen habitaciones?

Where else can I find a vacant room in this vicinity?
¿Dónde puedo encontrar una habitación libre aquí cerca?

What is the address?
¿Cuál es la dirección?

Can you please write down the address?
¿Podría anotarme la dirección, por favor?

How can I get there?
¿Dónde se encuentra?

Is it far?
¿Está lejos?

Written Inquiry

To Whom It May Concern:

We would like to rent a room for two people, with shower or bath, from August 7 through 15, preferably with a view of the ocean and a balcony.

Please tell us the price for a double room, with breakfast, half board, and full board.

Sincerely,

Estimadas señoras y señores,

Quisiéramos reservar una habitación del 7 al 15 de agosto, para dos personas con ducha o baño, de ser posible con balcón y vista al mar.

Por favor, indíquenos los precios de una habitación doble con desayuno, media pensión y pensión completa.

Atentamente

The word *dormitorio* (bedroom) is also used for *dormitory*. Mexicans call it *la recámara*.

Reserving by Phone

Please give me room reservations.
Póngame con la encargada de reservaciones, por favor.

Just a minute, I will connect you.
Un momento, le comunico.

Grand Hotel, room reservations. May I help you?
Gran hotel, reservaciones. ¿En qué puedo servirle?

I would like to have a room for tonight.
Quisiera reservar un habitación para esta noche.

About 5 p.m.
Alrededor de las 17 horas.

When will you arrive?
¿A qué hora llega?

We will reserve your room until 6 p.m. If you will be arriving later, please let us know.
Le reservaremos la habitación hasta las 18 horas. Si llega más tarde, por favor llámenos.

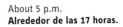

When you reserve a hotel room you should report to *la recepción*.

At the Reception Desk

Good day, I would
like a room for one
night.
**Buenos días, quisiera
una habitación para
una noche.**

We have a double room
for 120 euros.
**Tenemos una habitación
doble por 120 euros.**

That's fine. Can I pay by
credit card?
**De acuerdo. ¿Puedo pagar
con la tarjeta de crédito?**

Of course.
Sí, claro.

Can I look at the
room?
**¿Puedo ver la
habitación?**

Yes, of course.
Sí, cómo no.

Good, I will take
it.
**De acuerdo, me
quedo con la
habitación.**

The keys are here. The room
number is 212, on the second
floor.
**Aquí tiene las llaves. El número
de su habitación es el 212 y está
en el segundo piso.**

Cómo no meaning *certainly* or *of course* is very common and (fortunately) easy
to remember.

I have reserved a room.
He reservado una habitación.

Can I look at the room?
¿Puedo ver la habitación?

I will take the room.
Me quedo con la habitación.

I don't like the room.
La habitación no me gusta.

The room is ...
La habitación es ...
    too small.
    demasiado pequeña.
    too noisy.
    demasiado ruidosa.
    too dark.
    demasiado oscura.

Can I have another room?
¿Podría darme otra habitación?

Do you have something ...
¿Hay alguna habitación ...
    quieter?
    más tranquila?
    bigger?
    más grande?
    cheaper?
    más barata?
    with a balcony?
    con balcón?

Do you have non-smoking rooms?
¿Tienen habitaciones para no fumadores?

Do you have rooms with three beds?
¿Tienen habitaciones con tres camas?

Could you put in a third bed?
¿Podría poner otra cama más?

Is there an elevator?
¿Hay ascensor?

Is breakfast included?
¿El desayuno está incluido?

Where can I park my car?
¿Dónde puedo dejar el coche?

Do you have a garage?
¿Hay garaje?

I will stay for two nights.
Me quedo dos noches.

I don't yet know how long we will stay.
No sé todavía cuánto tiempo nos quedaremos.

Can we still get something to eat in the neighborhood?
¿Hay algún sitio aquí cerca donde podamos comer a esta hora?

Please bring the luggage to the room.
Lleve el equipaje a la habitación, por favor.

What You Hear
• •

Está todo lleno.
We are full.

¿A qué nombre?
In whose name?

¿Cuánto tiempo desea quedarse?
How long would you like to stay?

Llene el formulario, por favor.
Fill in the registration form, please.

¿Me enseña su pasaporte, por favor?
May I see your passport?

Firme aquí, por favor.
Please sign here.

To distinguish a single bed from a double with no chance of confusion, you should add *individual* or *sencilla* to *cama*.

Requests and Desires

I would like to extend my stay by one night.
Me gustaría quedarme una noche más.

The key for room 212, please.
La llave de la habitación 212, por favor.

I have locked myself out of my room.
La puerta se ha cerrado con las llaves dentro.

I have lost my key.
He perdido la llave.

Can you put that into your safe?
¿Podría poner esto en su caja fuerte?

Is there any mail for me?
¿Me ha llegado alguna carta?

I am expecting a phone call.
Estoy esperando una llamada telefónica.

Please inform them that I ...
Por favor, deje dicho que ...
   will call them back.
   volveré a llamar.
   will be back in the evening.
   vuelvo esta tarde.

I would like to leave a message for Mr. García.
Quisiera dejar un mensaje para el Sr. García.

When is breakfast served?
¿A qué hora sirven el desayuno?

Where can one have breakfast?
¿Dónde puedo desayunar?

Is the hotel open the whole night?
¿Está abierto el hotel durante toda la noche?

When must I check out of the room?
¿Cuándo debo dejar libre la habitación?

Can you wake me at 8 o'clock?
¿Podría despertarme a las 8?

Can you please bring me a towel?
¿Podría traerme una toalla, por favor?

Can I have an extra blanket?
¿Podría darme otra manta?

Can you get a typewriter for me?
¿Podría conseguirme una máquina de escribir?

Can I send a fax from here?
¿Puedo mandar un fax desde aquí?

DO NOT DISTURB!

If you are expecting mail, you can also ask, *¿Me ha llegado algún correo?*

The Hotel Staff

manager
el director

receptionist
el recepcionista

bell boy
el mozo

porter
el portero

chambermaid
la camarera

room service
el servicio de habitaciones

Complaints

The key doesn't fit.
La llave no entra.

The door won't open.
La puerta no se abre.

The room has not been made.
No han arreglado la habitación.

The bathroom is dirty.
El baño está sucio.

There are no towels.
No tengo toallas.

The window can't be opened / closed.
La ventana no se puede abrir / cerrar.

Departure

We are leaving tomorrow morning.
Nos marchamos mañana por la mañana.

We are leaving now.
Nos marchamos ahora.

I would like the bill.
Me da la cuenta, por favor.

Can I pay by credit card?
¿Puedo pagar con tarjeta del crédito?

I am paying cash.
Pago en efectivo.

I think that you made a mistake.
Creo que se ha equivocado.

Can I leave my luggage with you for the day?
¿Podría dejar aquí mi equipaje todo el día?

Could you call me a taxi?
¿Podría llamar un taxi?

We were very pleased.
Nos ha gustado.

Please get my luggage.
Me podría traer mi equipaje, por favor.

When you leave, you simply say *Nos marchamos*.

Accessories

adapter
el adaptador

child's bed
la cama para el niño

ashtray
el cenicero

suitcase
la maleta

iron
la plancha

pillows
las almohadas

TV
el televisor

refrigerator
el frigorífico

light bulb
la bombilla

sewing kit
los avíos de costura

towel
la toalla

lock
la cerradura

comb
el peine

key
la llave

In South America a light bulb is also called *un foco*.

telephone
el teléfono

bathroom
el excusado

alarm clock
el despertador

toothbrush
el cepillo de dientes

bed **la cama**
blanket **la manta**
bedsheet **la sábana**
stationery **el papel de cartas**
double bed **la cama doble**
shower **la ducha**
single bed **la cama individual**
ice cube **el cubito de hielo**
electricity **la electricidad**
floor **el piso**
window **la ventana**
hair dryer **el secador**
breakfast **el desayuno**
luggage **el equipaje**
half board **media pensión**
high season **temporada alta**
electric blanket **la manta eléctrica**
heating **la calefacción**
cold water **el agua fría**
babysitting / child care **el cuidado del niño**

reception desk **el registro**
elevator **el ascensor**
bath **el baño**
bathrobe **el albornoz**
bath towel **la toalla de baño**

hangers **las perchas**
wardrobe / closet **el armario**
air-conditioning **el climatizador**
lamp **la lámpara**
mattress **el colchón**
ocean view **la vista al mar**
mini-bar **el minibar**
low season **la temporada baja**

bathtub **la bañera**
balcony **el balcón**

In Spain an elevator is *un ascensor*; in South America, it is often called *un elevador*.

Accessories

night table **la mesita de noche**
off season **fuera de temporada**
wastepaper basket **la papelera**
radio **la radio**
bill **la factura**
reservation **la reservación**
restaurant **el restaurante**
reception **la recepción**
shutters **la persiana**
quiet **tranquilo**
safe **la caja fuerte**
wardrobe / closet **el armario**
desk / writing table **el escritorio**

toilet paper **el papel higiénico**
door **la puerta**
fan / ventilator **el ventilador**
extension cord **el prolongador**
full board **la pensión completa**
curtain **la cortina**
pre-season **la pretemporada**
warm water **el agua caliente**
wash basin **el lavabo**
water **el agua**
valuables **los objetos de valor**
toothpaste **la pasta dentífrica**
room **la habitación**
room number **el número de la habitación**
to the street **a la calle**

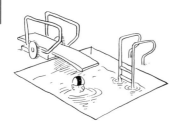

swimming pool **la piscina**
soap **el jabón**
armchair **el sillón**
mirror **el espejo**
socket **la toma de corriente**
plug **el enchufe**
floor **el piso**
plug / stopper **el tapón**
beach **la playa**
chair **la silla**
terrace **la terraza**

A bill in a store is *una factura*; in a restaurant, it's *una cuenta*.

Reserving a Vacation Home

Vacation apartment
El apartamento de vacaciones

Vacation house
La casa de vacaciones

We are looking for a vacation apartment for three weeks.
Buscamos un apartamento de vacaciones para tres semanas.

We have rented a vacation apartment for three weeks.
Hemos alquilado un apartamento de vacaciones por tres semanas.

There are four of us.
Somos cuatro.

We need two bedrooms.
Necesitamos dos habitaciones.

We need four beds.
Necesitamos cuatro camas.

How many beds are there in the house?
¿Cuántas camas hay en la casa?

Where do I pick up the keys?
¿Dónde tengo que recoger las llaves?

Is the vacation apartment completely furnished?
¿El apartamento de vacaciones está completamente amueblado?

Do we have to bring bed linen?
¿Tenemos que traer ropa de cama?

What does it cost to rent bed linen?
¿Cuánto cuesta el alquiler de la ropa de cama?

Does the house have central heating?
¿Hay calefacción central en la casa?

Does the apartment have a phone?
¿El apartamento tiene teléfono?

Can I make outgoing telephone calls, or only receive incoming calls?
¿Puedo hacer llamadas telefónicas o sólo recibirlas?

Is the final cleaning included?
¿Está incluida la limpieza final?

What does the final cleaning cost?
¿Cuánto cuesta la limpieza final?

ocean view
la vista al mar

A *vacation spot* is *un centro de recreo*.

Vacation Home: Practical Matters

Where are the garbage cans / trash cans?
¿Dónde están los cubos de basura?

Do I have to separate the garbage?
¿Tengo que clasificar la basura?

When is the trash / garbage picked up?
¿Cuándo recogen la basura?

Whom should I contact if there are problems?
¿A quién puedo dirigirme si hubiera algún problema?

Can you give me the phone number?
¿Puede dejarme el número de teléfono?

During our stay, a glass broke.
Durante nuestra estancia se ha roto un vaso.

How much do I owe you for it?
¿Cuánto le debo?

The windowpane broke.
Se ha roto el cristal de la ventana.

Where can I have it repaired?
¿Dónde puedo llevarlo a reparar?

Where can one ...
¿Dónde puedo ...
  shop?
  ir de compras?
  make a phone call?

llamar por teléfono?
do the laundry?
lavar la ropa?
hang up the laundry?
tender la ropa?

The toilet is clogged.
El excusado está obturado.

The heating isn't working.
La calefacción no funciona.

There is no water.
No hay agua.

There is no hot water.
No hay agua caliente.

The faucet is dripping.
El grifo gotea.

→ Also see HOUSEWARES, p. 159; TOOLS, p. 164; CAMPING EQUIPMENT, p. 165.

There is or *there are* is translated in Spanish by *hay*.

Equipment

cutlery /
silverware
los cubiertos

refrigerator
el frigorífico

TV
el televisor

light switch
el interruptor de la luz

gas range
la hornilla de gas

frying pan
la sartén

dishes
la vajilla

lock
la cerradura

glass
el vaso / la copa

key
la llave

grill
la parrilla

vacuum cleaner
la aspiradora

saucepan /
pot
la olla

socket
la toma de corriente

Common terms for *refrigerator* are *el refrigerador* and *la nevera*.

chair
la silla

telephone
el teléfono

plate / dish
el plato

VCR / video
recorder
**la grabadora
de vídeo**

faucet
el grifo

bath **el baño**
balcony **el balcón**
bed **la cama**
hot water heater **el calentador**
shower **la ducha**
electric range **la cocina / el hornillo
eléctrico**
window **la ventana**
window pane **el cristal de la
ventana**
dishwasher **el lavaplatos**
heating **la calefacción**
coffee machine **la cafetera**
chimney **la chimenea**
coal heating **la calefacción de
carbón**
kitchen **la cocina**
microwave **el microondas**
radio **la radio**
bedroom **el dormitorio**
terrace **la terraza**
table **la mesa**
toaster **el tostador**
door **la puerta**
hot water **el agua caliente**
clothes dryer **la secadora**
washing machine **la lavadora**
living room **la sala**

Important Vocabulary

date of departure **la fecha de salida**
date of arrival **la fecha de llegada**
apartment **el apartamento**
bungalow **la casita de campo**
vacation spot **el lugar turístico**
vacation house **la casa de
vacaciones**
vacation apartment **el apartamento
de vacaciones**
garage **el garaje**

ocean view **la vista al mar**
rent **el alquiler**
garbage **la basura**
garbage can **el cubo de la basura**
extra costs **los gastos adicionales**
power **la corriente**
voltage **el voltaje / la tensión
eléctrica**
landlord **el alquilador**

Added expenses are sometimes referred to as *los gastos imprevistos.*

Youth Hostels

Do you still have rooms available?
¿Quedan habitaciones libres?

Do you also have rooms only for women?
¿Tiene también habitaciones sólo para mujeres?

What is the cost of...
¿Cuánto cuesta ...
  an overnight stay?
  por una noche?
  bed linen?
  la ropa de cama?
  a lockable cupboard?
  un armario con llave?

Is there any other reasonably priced accommodation?
¿Hay habitaciones más baratas?

Can I use my own sleeping bag?
¿Puedo utilizar mi saco de dormir?

Do you have bed linen?
¿Tiene la ropa de cama?

Where is ...
¿Dónde está ...
  the washroom?
  el cuarto de aseo?
  the shower?
  la ducha?
  the toilet?
  el excusado?

Do you have lockers?
¿Hay cajas de seguridad?

When do you close in the evening?
¿Cuándo cierra de noche?

Do you close during the day?
¿Cierra durante el día?

Is breakfast served?
¿Hay servicio de desayuno?

What does the breakfast cost?
¿Cuánto cuesta el desayuno?

When is breakfast served?
¿A qué hora sirven el desayuno?

Is it possible to work in exchange for the room and breakfast?
¿Es posible trabajar a cambio de pernoctación y desayuno?

Are there reduced rates for longer stays?
¿Me cuesta menos si me quedo más tiempo?

Where can I leave a message?
¿Dónde puedo dejar un recado?

Can I leave a message with you?
¿Puedo dejarle un mensaje?

Can I have mail sent here?
¿Puedo pedir que me envíen aquí mi correspondencia?

Has any mail come for me?
¿Ha llegado correo para mí?

Is the area safe at night?
¿Esta zona es segura de noche?

Which bus lines go from here ...
¿Qué líneas de autobuses salen de aquí ...
  to the railway station?
  a la estación de ferrocarril?
  to the harbor?
  al puerto?
  to the beach?
  a la playa?
  to the airport?
  al aeropuerto?
  downtown?
  al centro de la ciudad?

Can I have another room tonight?
¿Puedo dormir en otra habitación esta noche?

Can I leave my luggage here until 12 o'clock?
¿Puedo dejar mi equipaje aquí hasta las 12?

¿Cuánto cuesta? (How much is it?) is one of the expressions you will use most frequently in Spanish.

At the Campground

Do you still have vacant camping spots?
¿Quedan sitios libres?

Do I have to register in advance?
¿Tengo que hacer una reservación?

How far in advance?
¿Con cuánto tiempo de antelación?

What does it cost per night for ...
¿Cuánto se paga por noche por ...

a tent?
una tienda?
a trailer?
una caravana?
a camper?
una autocaravana?
one person?
una persona?
a car?
un coche?
a cottage?
una cabaña?

We will stay for three days / weeks.
Nos quedaremos tres días / semanas.

Can you tell me how to get to my camping spot?
¿Puede decribirme cómo llegar al lugar de camping?

Where are the ...
¿Dónde están ...
toilets?
los servicios higiénicos?

washrooms?
servicios de aseo?
showers?
las duchas?
garbage cans?
los contenedores de basura?

What voltage is used here ?
¿Qué voltaje hay aquí?

Is there a grocery store?
¿Hay tienda de comestibles?

Are we allowed to light fires?
¿Está permitido encender fuego?

Is there someone on duty at night?
¿Está el camping vigilado por la noche?

Where can I speak to the ranger?
¿Dónde encuentro al guardabosque?

Which is the windy side?
¿Cuál es el lado expuesto al viento?

Can you please lend me a tent peg?
¿Me puede prestar una estaca, por favor?

Where can I rent / exchange gas cylinders?
¿Dónde puedo comprar / cambiar la bombona de gas?

Another word for *tent* is *una tienda de campaña.*

kerosene lamp /
hurricane lamp
**la lámpara de
petróleo**

plug
el enchufe

electrical connection
la toma de corriente

gas cylinder
la bombona de gas

gas stove
el hornillo de gas

tent peg
la estaca

children's playground
el parque infantil

grocery store
la tienda de comestibles

rental fee
el costo del arriendo

coins
las monedas

propane
el gas propano

drinking water
el agua potable

washing machine
la lavadora

washroom
el cuarto de aseo

water connection
el suministro de agua

camper
la autocaravana

trailer
la caravana

tent
la tienda

tent pole
el palo de la tienda

→ Also see Housewares, p. 159;
Tools, p. 164; Camping Equipment,
p. 165

A *hotplate* is *un hornillo eléctrico* in Spanish.

On the Farm

tractor
el tractor

harvester
la segadora-trilladora

field
el campo

grain
el cereal

ear of grain
la espiga

A *farm* is translated by either *una granja* or *una finca*.

straw
la paja

hay
el heno

horse
el caballo

donkey
el asno

pig
el cerdo

Instead of *un cerdo* for pig, you can also say *un cochino*.

goat
la cabra

chick
el polluelo

sheep
la oveja

goose
el ganso

cow
la vaca

duck
el pato

calf
el becerro

turkey
el pavo

rooster / cock
el gallo

cat
el gato

chicken
la gallina

dog
el perro

If he calls you a *perro*, he is saying that you are a miser. If she calls you a *pe-rrito*, she is saying that you are her little doggie.

Eating and Drinking

Cuisine

Latin American cuisine often depends on geography. Be wise and look for fish dishes in coastal cities and hearty stews in the mountains and valleys.

Every country has its own typical dishes, and you should ask for them. This is your chance to be adventurous and to taste dishes you have never seen before (ask for the recipes and write them down!).

The same applies to drinks: why ask for the usual whiskey or vodka, when Chile has wines that often surpass those of France, and Peru's *pisco* (grape-derived firewater with an exquisite bouquet) is known throughout the continent.

Note: dinner in America starts usually around eight, but in Spain it is around ten.

The cuisine of Spain is fairly substantial. It uses a lot of salt and fat. At the coast you absolutely must sample the fish and shellfish.

The two best known dishes of this country are *paella* (rice with vegetables, mussels, fish, and chicken), and the cold soup *gazpacho* (tomato juice, cucumber, and pepperoni, prepared with vinegar and garlic), which is an excellent choice on a hot day.

The main meal of the day is the evening meal *(la cena)*. The mid-day meal *(el almuerzo)* is a step down from that and is taken mainly in the form of *tapas*: small, often very delicate appetizers such as *calamares* (squid), *almejas* (mussels), or simply potatoes with mayonnaise. People also have a glass of wine.

Breakfast doesn't amount to much. A coffee and croissant are about all there is. The Spanish much prefer their *aperitivo*, which they have in the late morning or in the middle of the day in the form of a snack, accompanied by a glass of wine.

Where to Turn

Tasca
A typical restaurant where people normally eat tapas and drink wine (tavern).

Freiduría
A simple restaurant where you can get fried fish (normally *pescaítos*, in a free and easy atmosphere).

Marisquería
Exclusively fish and seafood restaurant.

Mesón
Restaurant with plain cooking.

Venta
A simple restaurant outside the city in the mountains, etc.

Chiringuito
A type of beach pub where service is outdoors.

Cafetería
The place to get breakfast and between-meal snacks.

Churrería
This is where you get the *churros* (a sweet pastry eaten with breakfast), accompanied by a cup of hot chocolate.

Tetería
Especially in Granada, a tea parlor with a somewhat oriental atmosphere.

Heladería
An ice cream parlor.

Bar de copas
A nightclub or a bar.

Spanish people like to eat out a lot. With good restaurants it's a good idea to make a reservation.

Meals

breakfast
el desayuno

lunch
el almuerzo

dinner
la cena

What You Hear

¿Ha reservado mesa?
Do you have a reservation?

¿Fumador o no fumador?
Smoking or non-smoking?

¿Quiere tomar primero un aperitivo?
Would you like a drink before your meal?

¿Quiere pedir?
Would you like to order?

Los platos del día son ...
Today's specials are ...

Le recomiendo ...
I recommend ...

Lo siento, ya no nos queda.
I'm sorry, we're out of that.

¿Qué quiere de tomar?
What would you like to drink?

¿Me permite servirle un poco más?
Can I give you another?

¿Está todo bien?
Is everything okay?

¿Desea algo más?
Would you like anything else?

¿Ha sido de su agrado?
Did you enjoy your meal?

Meal Times

Breakfast, 7 – 10 a.m.
Desayuno, 7 – 10 a.m.

Lunch, 1 – 3 p.m.
Almuerzo, 13 – 15 p.m.

Dinner, 9 – 11:30 p.m.
Cena, 21 – 23:30 p.m.

What You Often Need

Where are the restrooms?
¿Dónde están los servicios?

Can you please pour me another one?
¿Me sirve un poco más, por favor?

Can I please have the menu again?
¿Podría traerme otra vez el menú?

I would like to order.
Quisiera pedir.

Can you bring the wine list?
¿Podría traerme la carta de vinos?

No thank you, I'm full / that's all.
No gracias, estoy satisfecho.

Can I pay by credit card?
¿Puedo pagar con tarjeta de crédito?

Signs and Posters

Carry-out
Comida para llevar

You may order until nine o'clock.
Aceptamos pedidos hasta las 21 horas.

Please wait to be seated.
Por favor espere hasta que le indiquemos una mesa.

Please pay the cashier.
Por favor pague en la caja.

Today's / Daily Special
Menú del día

The verb *comer* is used for eating in general; it can also be used with particular reference to the midday meal.

In a Restaurant

In mid-summer in Madrid the temperature can reach 104 degrees (40 degrees C), so it's not too surprising that the Spanish put off the evening meal as long as possible, to the dismay of people who are accustomed to having dinner early.

In Barcelona, for example, you will find no restaurants open before nine o'clock in the evening, and in Madrid if you go into a restaurant shortly after nine o'clock, you are likely to be the first customer.

If you are hungry after going to a late movie, you can still get something to eat in most restaurants even after midnight.

Only in tourist areas have the guests' wishes been acceded to by opening the restaurants earlier. Things are different in Latin America, where dinner hours start around eight.

Spanish people, in Europe and in America, see a connection between the duration and the quality of a meal. A good meal always takes time. Eating is also a social experience; in addition to satisfying the palate, it serves the purpose of a social gathering that can occupy several hours.

Service generally is included in the bill, but the server still expects a tip, and there are no hard and fast rules concerning the amount; five to ten percent should be adequate.

In certain circles and in the business world Spaniards still place significant value on appropriate dress. If you want to dine in a five-star restaurant, for example, you won't get in without a jacket and tie no matter how persuasive you are.

I am hungry.
Tengo hambre.

Can you recommend a good restaurant?
¿Puede recomendarme un buen restaurante?

I would like something to eat.
Quisiera comer algo.

I would just like a bite of something.
Sólo quiero comerme un bocadillo.

I would just like something to drink.
Sólo quiero beber algo.

I would like to have breakfast.
Quisiera desayunar.

I would like to have dinner.
Quisiera cenar.

I would like to have lunch.
Quisiera almorzar.

Tomar means both *to take* and *to drink*. The server will usually ask you *Qué quisiera tomar?*

Ordering

I'm sorry!
¡Perdone!

Yes, sir?
¿Sí, señor?

Can I please have
the menu?
**¿Podría traerme el
menú, por favor?**

Of course. Just a
minute.
**Claro. Un
momento.**

Would you like to you order?
¿Desea pedir?

Thanks!
¡Gracias!

Don't mention it.
De nada.

What do you recommend?
¿Qué me recomienda?

I recommend the day's special.
Le recomiendo el plato del día.

Thanks! I would like ...
¡Gracias! Quisiera ...

When you want to pay, you say *Lu cuenta por favor.*

Making a Reservation

I would like to reserve a table ...
Quisiera reservar una mesa ...
   for six people.
   para seis personas.
   for tonight.
   para esta noche.
   for eight p.m.
   para las 20.

I have reserved a table in the name of Hayes.
He reservado una mesa a nombre del Sr. Hayes.

I would like a table ...
Quisiera una mesa ...
   at the window.
   junto a la ventana.

   in a quiet corner.
   en un rincón tranquilo.

Do you have a smoking / non-smoking area?
¿Hay un área de fumadores / no fumadores?

Where can we wait?
¿Dónde podemos esperar?

How long will we have to wait?
¿Cuánto tiempo tenemos que esperar?

Ordering

The menu and wine list, please.
El menú y la lista de vinos, por favor.

What do you particularly recommend?
¿Me puede sugerir algo especial?

Can we order the beverages right now?
¿Podemos pedir las bebidas de inmediato?

Do you also have children's / senior citizens' portions?
¿Hay raciones para niños / personas de edad?

Are there also vegetarian dishes?
¿Hay también comida vegetariana?

Is there any alcohol in this dish?
¿Este plato contiene alcohol?

I am a diabetic.
Soy diabético.

I am not very hungry. Can I have a small portion?
No tengo mucha hambre. ¿Puede traerme una ración pequeña?

I will have ...
Quiero ...

Can you prepare the dish without garlic?
¿Puede preparar este plato sin ajo?

One bottle of wine, please.
Una botella de vino, por favor.

The term *senior citizens* can't be translated literally into Spanish; the term is *personas de edad*.

Paying

I would like to pay the bill, please.
Quisiera pagar la cuenta, por favor.

I am in a hurry.
Tengo prisa.

Is the tip included in the bill?
¿Está incluida la propina en la cuenta?

Everything on one bill, please.
Todo junto, por favor.

Separate bills, please.
Cuentas separadas, por favor.

Do you take ...
¿Aceptan ...

credit cards?
tarjetas de crédito?
travellers checks?
cheques de viajero?
checks?
cheques?

I'm afraid you haven't totaled that up right.
Creo que usted se ha equivocado en la cuenta.

I did not have that.
No he pedido eso.

The change is yours.
El cambio es para usted.

Praise

The meal was excellent.
La comida estuvo deliciosa.

I liked it.
Me ha gustado mucho.

Thank you very much, the service was excellent.
Muchas gracias, el servicio ha sido excelente.

We will recommend this place.
Recomendaremos este sitio a los demás.

Complaints

I didn't order that.
No he pedido eso.

The meat is too hard.
La carne está dura.

Have you forgotten us?
¿Se ha olvidado de nosotros?

I am sorry, but I was not pleased.
Lo siento, pero no he quedado complacido.

The service was ...
El servicio ha sido ...
sloppy.
desatento.
unfriendly.
poco amable.

The meal was ...
La comida estuvo ...
too salty.
demasiado salada.
cold.
fría.

In Spanish you don't say that the bread is old, but that it's *hard*.

On the Table

ashtray
el cenicero

cup
la taza

silverware
los cubiertos

plate
el plato

fork
el tenedor

beverage **la bebida**
pepper **la pimienta**
salt **la sal**
bowl **el plato hondo**
mustard **la mostaza**
teaspoon **la cucharilla**
tablecloth **el mantel**
sugar **el azúcar**

glass
el vaso

highchair
la silla para niños

Is Something Missing?

Can you bring me some pepper?
¿Podría traerme la pimienta?

I don't have a fork.
Falta un tenedor.

Can you please pass me the sugar?
¿Me puede pasar el azúcar?

spoon
la cuchara

knife
el cuchillo

How Was It?

The food is ... **La comida es / está ...**
  simple. **ligera.**
  hearty. **sustanciosa.**
  sweet. **dulce.**
  sour. **agria.**
  tasty. **sabrosa.**
  very spicy. **muy condimentada.**
  hot. **picante.**
  too hot. **demasiado picante.**

napkin
la servilleta

A *salad bowl* is *una ensaladera*.

The Menu

A complete Spanish menu consists of appetizers (*tapas* in Spain, *entremeses* in Latin America) followed by soup *(sopa, consomé)*, a main course *(el plato principal)*, and a dessert *(el postre)*.

You can also start with something to "pick at" (the Spanish say *algo para picar*). This is recommended at the seashore, where you will get several platters of seafood and shellfish that you eat with small skewers that are used for snacks at some cold buffets.

Like Spanish cuisine in general, dessert can be a real calorie bomb. Watch out for the two-layered cream cakes, which only the very hungry should tackle after a complete menu. As for drinks, you can enjoy mineral water *(agua mineral)*, which is available with or without carbonation *(natural/sin gas*, or *con gas*, respectively), or else you can order wine.

Wine is the national drink of all Spanish-speaking people, and you should pay special attention to Chilean, Spanish, and Argentinean brands.

cold appetizers
los entremeses fríos

hot appetizers
los entremeses calientes

soups
las sopas

salads
las ensaladas

egg dishes
los platos de huevos

fish
el pescado

shellfish
los mariscos

meat
la carne

poultry
la carne de ave

side dishes
las guarniciones

vegetables
las verduras

cheese
el queso

dessert
el postre

soft drinks
las bebidas sin alcohol

alcoholic beverages
las bebidas alcohólicas

hot beverages
las bebidas calientes

Appetizers and small snacks are often generally referred to as *tapas* (Spain) or *bocadillos* (America).

Breakfast

Breakfast in Latin America varies according to geography. Argentineans are fond of hearty beef sandwiches, Mexicans and Central Americans have a corn-based cuisine that also extends into breakfast. Tea *(té)* is as common as coffee with milk *(café con leche)*. Same as in the U.S., eggs are commonly served.

In Spain, every city is teeming with bars and cafés.

However, for those of us who are accustomed to a hearty breakfast *(el desayuno)*, disappointment awaits. The average Spaniard doesn't place much emphasis on breakfast, and the bars fill up early with workers who merely drink their *café solo* (black coffee) or a *café con leche* (café au lait) or *café cortado* (coffee with a dash of milk) and enjoy a croissant or roll. The Anglo-Saxon preference for a sturdy breakfast escapes them entirely.

a cup of coffee
una taza de café

a glass of milk
un vaso de leche

a slice of ham
una lonja de jamón

Specialties

Two fried eggs
dos huevos fritos

Toasted white bread
pan blanco tostado

Coffee with a dash of milk is also known as *café cortado*.

Drinks

coffee
el café

tea
el té

milk
la leche

orange juice
el zumo / jugo de naranja

cocoa **el cacao**
herbal tea **la tisana**

 Eggs

scrambled egg **los huevos revueltos**
poached egg **el huevo escalfado**
bacon and eggs **los huevos con tocino**

fried egg
el huevo frito

ham and eggs **los huevos con jamón**
omelet **la tortilla francesa**

soft-boiled egg
el huevo pasado por agua

hard-boiled egg **el huevo duro**

A soft-boiled egg is properly termed *un huevo pasado por agua*; a shorter expression is *un huevo tibio*.

Bread and Rolls

roll
el panecillo

white bread
el pan blanco

whole wheat bread
el pan integral

croissant
**la medialuna
/ el croissant**

toast
el pan tostado

bread **el pan**

wheat bread **el pan de trigo**

caraway seed bread **el pan con comino**

rye bread **el pan de centeno**

butter **la mantequilla**

honey **la miel**

crispbread / cracker **el pan sueco**

jam **la mermelada**

syrup **el jarabe**

rusks / zwieback **la galleta dulce**

Miscellaneous

fritters
las frituras

fried potatoes / hash browns
las patatas fritas

cornflakes
las hojuelas de maíz / los cornflakes

oatmeal / porridge
la papilla de avena / quáquer

cheese
el queso

müsli / granola
el müesli

fruit
la fruta

pancake
el crepe / la tortilla

ham
el jamón

bacon
el tocino

sweetener /
sugar
substitute
el endulzador / el dulcificante / el edulcorante

waffles
los wafles / los barquillos

sausage
el embutido

sausage
la salchicha

yogurt
el yogur

sugar
el azúcar

You will not find much dark, wholegrain bread in Spain; you may be able to locate some multi-grain bread.

Appetizers

artichokes **las alcachofas**
oysters **las ostras**
prawns **los camarones / las gambas**
cockles **los berberechos**
crab cocktail **el coctel de camarones**
crab **el cangrejo**
melon **el melón**
mussels **los mejillones**
smoked salmon **el salmón ahumado**
sardines **las sardinas**
clams **las almejas**

Soups

soup of the day **la sopa del día**
vegetable soup **la sopa de verdura**
noodle soup **la sopa de fideos**
tomato soup **la sopa de tomate**
chicken broth **el caldo de pollo**
beef broth **el caldo de ternera**

Salads

green salad **la ensalada de lechuga**
mixed salad / tossed salad **la ensalada mixta**
potato salad **la ensalada de papas / patatas**
egg salad **la ensalada con huevos**

Salad Dressings

Roquefort dressing **la salsa Roquefort**
vinaigrette dressing **la vinagreta**
Italian dressing **la salsa italiana**
French dressing **la salsa francesa**
Russian dressing **la salsa rusa**

Vinegar and Oil

olive oil **el aceite de oliva**
sunflower oil **el aceite de girasol**
balsamic vinegar **el vinagre balsámico**
herb vinegar **el vinagre de hierbas**
fruit vinegar **el vinagre de fruta**
wine vinegar **el vinagre de vino**
lemon vinegar **el vinagre de limón**
soy sauce **la salsa de soja**
mayonnaise **la mayonesa**

Tapas, small, imaginative creations, are the favorite snack in Spain.

From Ocean and Lake

eel **la anguila**
grayling **el tímalo**
perch **la perca**
bluefish **el pez azul**
flounder **el lenguado / la platija**
trout **la trucha**
golden perch **la acerina**
golden bream **la dorada**
shark **el tiburón**
pike **el lucio, el sollo**
halibut **el hipogloso / el halibut**
herring **el arenque**
codfish **el bacalao**
carp **la carpa**
salmon **el salmón**
mackerel **la caballa**
mullet **la lisa / el mújol**
ray / skate **la raya**
roe **las huevas de pescado**
red perch **la gallineta**
anchovies **las anchoas**
sardines **las sardinas**
haddock **el anón / el abadejo / el eglefino**
flounder **el lenguado / la platija**
swordfish **el pez espada**
sea bream **el besugo**
sea pike **la merluza / el róbalo**
anglerfish **el rape / el pejesapo**
sole **el lenguado**
turbot **el rodaballo / el turbo**
smelt **el eperlano / el esperinque**
salt cod **el bacalao**
tuna **el atún**
squid **el calamar / la sepia**
catfish **el barbo**
sturgeon **el sollo**
pike-perch **la lucioperca**

lobster
la langosta

prawn
**el camarón /
la gamba**

crab
el cangrejo

oyster **la ostra**
cockle **el berberecho**
jacob mussel **la ostra jacobea**
scallop **el escalope / la escalopa**
sea bass **la lubina**
octopus **el pulpo**
crawfish / crayfish **el langostino**
mussel **el mejillón**
sea urchin **el erizo de mar**
spider crab **la centolla**
clam **la almeja**

Two types of fish used in Spanish cuisine are *rodaballo* (turbot) and *lubina* (sea bass).

Types of Meat

mutton
el carnero

kid
el cabrito

veal
el becerro

goat
la cabra

rabbit
el conejo

Steaks

rare **a la inglesa**
medium **medio asado**
well done **bien hecho**

lamb
el cordero

Specialties

Cordero asado roast lamb
Chuletón de Avila veal steak
Cochinillo asado roast suckling piglet
Brochetas meat skewered with vegetables
Pinchitos morunos spicy meat on a spit

beef
la vaca

pork
el cerdo

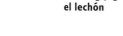

suckling pig
el lechón

A suckling piglet is also called *un cochinillo*.

Cuts of Meat

steak **el bistec**
round steak **la pierna**
sweetbread **las mollejas**
tip **la espadilla**
fillet steak **el filete de solomillo**
neck **el pescuezo**
leg **la pierna**
brain **los sesos**
prime rib **el entrecote**
cutlet **la chuleta**
tripe **el mondongo / los callos**
liver **el hígado**
loin **el lomo**
loin steak **el filete de lomo**
kidneys **los riñones**
chunks **la nuez**
spare ribs **las chuletas**
roast beef **el rosbif**
saddle of lamb / chine of beef **el lomo**
rump steak **el asado de culata**
ham **el jamón**
deep-fried cutlet **el escalope**
tail **el rabo**
bacon **el tocino**
tongue **la lengua**
rib steak **el costillar**

Ways to Prepare

browned **dorado**
roasted **asado**
low cholesterol **bajo en colesterol**
low-fat **bajo en grasa**
deep fried **frito sumergido**
for diabetics **para diabéticos**
baked **cocido en el horno**
fried **frito**
steamed **cocido al vapor**
stuffed **relleno**
grilled **a la parrilla**
chopped / ground **picado**
cooked **cocido**
smoked **ahumado**
shaken / stirred **revuelto**
braised **dorado a fuego moderado**

stewed **estofado**
larded **mechado**
glazed **garrapiñado**
goulash **el gulasch**
meat loaf **el picadillo**
low-calorie **bajo en calorías**
breadcrumb-fried **empanado**
raw **crudo**
tangy **fuerte**

Grilled is also termed *a la plancha*; *grilled fish* is thus *pescado a la plancha*.

Poultry

duck
el pato

chicken
la gallina

goose
el ganso

turkey
el pavo

pigeon
la paloma

Wild Game

pheasant
el faisán

hare
la liebre

stag
el ciervo

partridge
la perdiz

deer
el ciervo

wild duck
el ánade

boar
el jabalí

chicken **el pollo**
capon **el capón**
guinea fowl **la gallina de Guinea**
young fattened hen **la pularda**
quail **la codorniz**

grilled chicken **el pollo asado**

Venison is not very common in Spain and South America.

Potatoes

french fries **las papas / patatas fritas hervidas en aceite**

roasted potatoes **las papas / patatas fritas**

baked potatoes **las papas / patatas al horno**

potato salad **la ensalada de papas / patatas**

croquettes **las croquetas**

mashed potatoes **el puré**

pan-fried potatoes **las papas / patatas salteadas**

boiled potatoes **las papas / patatas cocidas**

sweet potatoes / yams **las papas / patatas dulces**

Noodles

flat noodles **los tallarines**

macaroni **los macarrones**

spaghetti **los espaguetis**

Rice

wild rice **el arroz salvaje**

cooked rice **el arroz cocido**

fried rice **el arroz frito**

whole-grain / brown rice **el arroz integral**

Bread

roll **el panecillo**

black bread **el pan negro**

whole wheat bread **el pan integral**

white bread **el pan blanco**

corn **el maíz**

wheat **el trigo**

rye **el centeno**

barley **la cebada**

oat **la avena**

Fried grated potatoes are not part of Spanish cuisine.

Vegetables

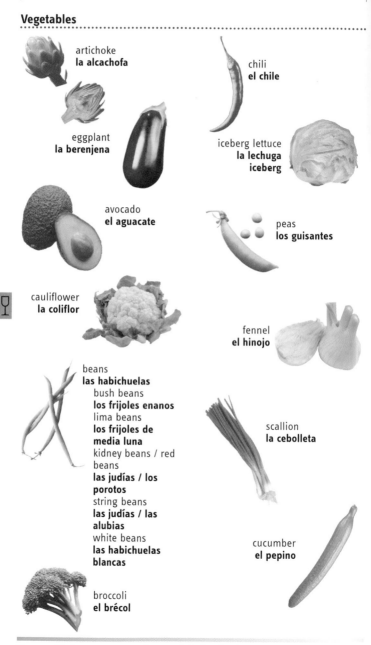

artichoke
la alcachofa

chili
el chile

eggplant
la berenjena

iceberg lettuce
**la lechuga
iceberg**

avocado
el aguacate

peas
los guisantes

cauliflower
la coliflor

fennel
el hinojo

beans
las habichuelas
   bush beans
   los frijoles enanos
   lima beans
   **los frijoles de
   media luna**
   kidney beans / red
   beans
   **las judías / los
   porotos**
   string beans
   **las judías / las
   alubias**
   white beans
   **las habichuelas
   blancas**

scallion
la cebolleta

cucumber
el pepino

broccoli
el brécol

You are likely to encounter the word *judías* for *beans* on menus in Spain. In
Latin America they will be *habichuelas* or *porotos*.

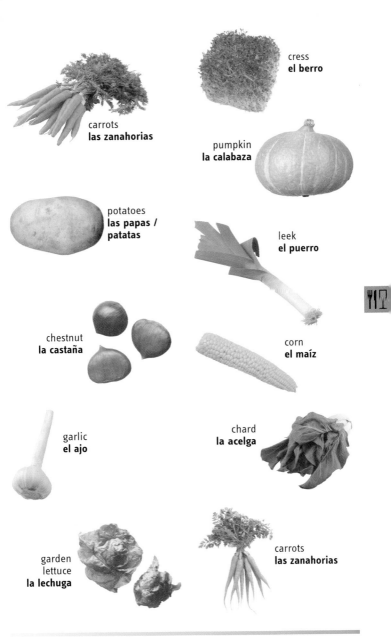

cress
el berro

carrots
las zanahorias

pumpkin
la calabaza

potatoes
**las papas /
patatas**

leek
el puerro

chestnut
la castaña

corn
el maíz

garlic
el ajo

chard
la acelga

garden
lettuce
la lechuga

carrots
las zanahorias

You can get French fries by ordering *patatas fritas* (Spain) or *papas fritas* (America).

Vegetables

okra
el quingombó

beet
la remolacha / la betarraga

pepper
el pimentón

brussel sprouts
las coles de Bruselas

chili pepper /
bell pepper
el ají / los pimientos picantes

red beets
los nabos rojos

mushrooms
los hongos / las setas

red cabbage
la lombarda

radish
el rábano

turnips
los nabos

Mushrooms are generally known as *champiñones*.

asparagus
los espárragos

zucchini
los calabacines

spinach
las espinacas

tiny green peas
los guisantes

celery
el apio

onions
las cebollas

tomatoes
los tomates

watercress **el berro**
chicory **la achicoria**
endive **la escarola**
paprika **la páprika**
chick peas **los garbanzos**
cabbage **la col**
lentils **las lentejas**
sauerkraut **el chucrut**
vipers grass **la escorzonera / el salcifí negro**
celery **el apio**
rutabaga **el nabicol**

white cabbage
la col blanca

savoy cabbage
la col rizada

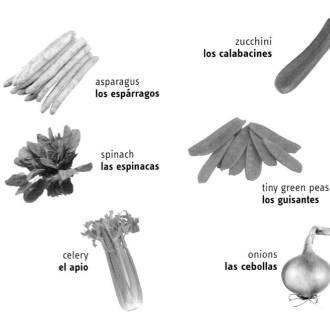

The general term for cabbage is *la berza* (Spain) or *el repollo* (South America).

Herbs and Spices

basil
la albahaca

sage
la salvia

dill
el eneldo

thyme
el tomillo

ginger
el jengibre

cinnamon
la canela

mint
la menta

oregano
el orégano

parsley
el perejil

rosemary
el romero

vinegar **el vinagre**
tarragon **el estragón**
capers **las alcaparras**
chervil **el perifollo**
caraway **el comino**
bay leaves **las hojas de laurel**
marjoram **la mejorana**
horseradish **el rábano picante**
nutmeg **la nuez moscada**
clove **el clavo de especia**
pepper **la pimienta**
saffron **el azafrán**
salt **la sal**
chive **el cebollino**
mustard **la mostaza**
vanilla **la vainilla**
sugar **el azúcar**

Spanish people are generally not fond of horseradish or meat sauces containing any amount of sugar.

Cheese

fresh cheese
el queso fresco

grated cheese
el queso rallado

sheep's milk cheese
el queso de leche de oveja

goat's milk cheese
el queso de leche de cabra

About a hundred years ago, thousands of Swiss and German farmers emigrated to Latin America. Today, their ancestors prosper from the highlands of Costa Rica to the southern regions of Chile, and their cheeses continue tickling Spanish taste buds.

One complication, however, is the variety of names that the same cheese receives in different countries. If you see an interesting cheese, our advice is to point with the finger and say *un cuarto de kilo, por favor* (one quart of a kilo, please).

Spain produces many cheeses, many of which are not well known beyond the country's borders. Some specialties include *cabrales*: a mold-ripened cheese from Asturias; *cendrat, montsec*: creamy goat cheese from Cataluña; *ibores*: goat cheese from Extremadura; *majorero*: ripened goat cheese from the Canary Islands; *manchego*: hard cheese made from sheep's milk; *serena*: an expensive specialty made from the milk of Merino sheep, produced only in the spring.

Fruit

pineapple
la piña

apple
la manzana

apricot
el albaricoque

banana
el plátano

pears
las peras

blackberries
las zarzamoras

strawberries
las fresas

The term *bananas* is also used in many South American countries.

Fruit

figs
los higos

cherries
las cerezas

pomegranate
la granada

kiwi fruit
el kiwi

grapefruit
la toronja

coconut
el coco

blueberries
los arándanos

lime
la lima

raspberries
las frambuesas

mango
el mango

persimmon
el caqui

melon
el melón

carambola
la carambola

Gooseberries are also called *grosellas espinosas.*

orange
la naranja

watermelon
la sandía

papaya
la papaya

lemon
el limón

peach
el melocotón

plum
la ciruela

pomelo
el pomelo

grape
la uva

dates **los dátiles**
chestnuts **las castañas**
elderberries **los saúcos**
currants **las grosellas**
cactus fruit **el higo chumbo**
litchee **el litchi**
tangerine **la mandarina**
mulberries **las moras**
mirabelle / yellow plum **la ciruela amarilla**
medlar **el níspero**
passion fruit **la pasionaria**
cranberries **los arándanos agrios**
quince **el membrillo**
rhubarb **el ruibarbo**
raisins **las pasas**
gooseberry **la grosella silvestre / la uva espina**
tamarind **el tamarindo**

A *plum* is *una ciruela*, but plum pudding is *el budín de pasas*.

Nuts

peanut
el cacahuate

pecan nut
la pacana / la nuez lisa

hazelnut
la avellana

pistachios
los pistachos

coconut
el coco

walnuts
las nueces

almond
la almendra

Brazil nuts **las nueces del Brasil**

pine nuts **los piñones**

sunflower seeds **las semillas de girasol**

The Spanish term *cacahuate* comes from the Native American language *Náhuatl*.

Cakes

apple flan / pie **la tarta de manzanas**

cheesecake **la tarta de queso fresco**

blueberry pie **la tarta de arándanos**

carrot cake **el pastel de zanahorias**

cherry pie **la tarta de cerezas**

lemon cake **el pastel de limón**

fruit pie / tart **la tarta de fruta**

cookie **la galleta**

chocolate cake **el pastel de chocolate**

vanilla cream pie **el pastel de vainilla**

cream **la nata**

Desserts

ice cream
el helado

assorted ice creams
el helado mixto

ice cream cone
el cucurucho

ice cream in a cup
la copa de helado

ice cream on a stick
helado de paleta

coffee with ice cream
el café helado

flavor
el sabor

with cream
con nata

vanilla pudding
el flan de vainilla

almond pudding
el flan de almendras

chocolate pudding
el flan de chocolate

bread pudding
el flan de pan

A very rough description of typical local dishes and snacks in Latin America would say that they are strongly influenced by corn in the north of the continent, by rice in the middle, and by wheat in the south.

Mexican *tacos*, *tamales* and *fajitas* are well known to most of us, although we should be aware that the "Mexican" dishes served in U.S. fast-food chains and many restaurants are not quite the same as their counterparts south of the Rio Grande.

A dish without rice in Colombia is a rare dish indeed, and what would be Argentinean cuisine without huge slabs of beef? And, always try the seafood of Peru and Chile.

Natural ice is *el hielo*; ice cream is *el helado*.

Snacks

The classical snack of Spain is *tapas*, small tidbits of which many bars offer three or four dozen types to choose from: meat and vegetable pâtés, slices of ham and cheese, small meat balls, seafood, fish, and other delicious items. People drink a glass of wine or sherry with them.

Tapas often introduce a substantial meal, and in fact they often replace a full meal. It's a ritual, especially in the large cities, to go from bar to bar and try to find the best tapas.

Pizza

Pizza has been known as an inexpensive snack in Naples for 200 years. Pizza's worldwide conquest began in 1895 when a homesick Neapolitan living in New York opened the first pizzeria. As late as the 1960s the rest of Italy knew of pizza only through hearsay.

Pizza Margherita tomatoes, mozzarella, basil

Pizza alla napolitana tomatoes, mozzarella, anchovies, oregano, olive oil

Pizza calabrese tomatoes, tuna, anchovies, olives, capers

Pizza alle vongole tomatoes, oregano, mussels, parsley, garlic

Pizza quattro stagioni tomatoes, mozzarella, mushrooms, baked ham, artichoke hearts

Pizza al prosciutto tomatoes, mozzarella, baked ham

Pizza con funghi tomatoes, mozzarella, mushrooms, garlic, parsley

Pizza alla siciliana tomatoes, mozzarella, paprika, salami, mushrooms

Pizza alla Pugliese tomatoes, mozzarella, onions

Pizza Romana tomatoes, mozzarella, anchovies, capers, olives

Pizza alla diavola tomatoes, mozzarella, salami, pepperoni

Pilla alla "Re Ferdinando" tomatoes, mozzarella, crab, garlic, parsley

Pizza puttanesca tomatoes, mozzarella, bacon, olives, capers, anchovies

Calzone folded-over pizza with ham, mozzarella, often with ricotta

Pizza is popular in Spain and South America.

What Would You Like?

a cup of coffee
una taza de café

a cup of tea
una taza de té

a glass of orange juice
un vaso de jugo / zumo de naranja

a bottle of milk
una botella de leche
hot milk
la leche caliente
cold milk
la leche fría

a can of soda
una lata de refresco

Coffee

coffee **el café**
with milk **con leche**

with sugar **con azúcar**
with cream **con crema**
with foamed milk **capuchino**
black **solo**
small **pequeño**
medium **medio**
large **grande**
decaffeinated coffee **el café descafeinado**
espresso **el exprés**
cappuccino **el capuchino**
mocha **el moca**

Tea

black tea **el té negro**
mint tea **el té de menta**
fennel tea **el té de hinojo**
chamomile tea **el té de manzanilla**
fruit tea **el té de fruta**
herbal tea **la tisana**
flavored tea **el té aromatizado**
unflavored tea **el té no aromatizado**
with lemon **con limón**

In Spanish, Coca-Cola is shortened to *Coca*.

Refreshments

mineral water **el agua mineral**

carbonated **con gas**

noncarbonated **sin gas**

fruit juice **el jugo / zumo de fruta**

orange juice **el jugo / zumo de naranja**

grape juice **el jugo / zumo de uva**

tomato juice **el jugo / zumo de tomate**

soda / soft drink **la limonada**

Miscellaneous

cocoa **el cacao**

milk **la leche**

hot / cold chocolate **el chocolate frío / caliente**

Beer

beer **la cerveza**

on tap **la cerveza de barril**

low alcohol **baja en alcohol**

nonalcoholic **sin alcohol**

bottle **la botella**

can **la lata**

Liquors

without ice **sin hielo**

with ice **con hielo**

vodka **el vodka**

whiskey **el whiski**

liqueur **el licor aromático**

spirits **los licores**

Specialties

In Latin America you must taste Chilean and Argentinean wines. Most supermarkets carry a wide selection at very, very low prices. Peru produces an excellent *pisco*, rum is the drink of Central America, and Mexican tequila has conquered the universe. Buy a few bottles of the best when you are returning home and you will extend your vacationing experience.

Spain, truly a wine-drinking country, makes wonderful Brandy de Jerez, which is brandy from the sherry region, aged in sherry casks. Well known brands are Carlos I, Gran Capitán, Conde de Osborne, and Lepanto.

If you want real fruit juice, you have to order *un zumo* or *un jugo*; otherwise you will get *una naranjada*, which is a fruit punch.

Wine and Champagne

Can I please see the wine list?
¿Podría traerme la carta de vinos?

cork
el corcho

corkscrew
el sacacorchos

I would have like to have a bottle of wine.
Quisiera una botella de vino.

Which will go best with the meal?
¿Cuál va mejor con la comida?

cooler
el champanero

Is this a good year?
¿Es una cosecha buena?

Can I taste the wine?
¿Puedo probar el vino?

The wine is corky.
El vino sabe a corcho.

The wine is not cold enough.
El vino no está frío.

Can you please cool the wine?
¿Podría enfriar el vino, por favor?

wine-growing area **la zona vitivinícola**

rosé **el vino rosado**

red wine **el vino tinto**

vineyard **la viña**

vintage **la vendimia**

wine tasting **la degustación del vino**

white wine **el vino blanco**

full-bodied **de mucho cuerpo**

light **suave**

fruity **afrutado**

dry **seco**

sweet **dulce**

In other Romance languages *red wine* always involves the color red; Spanish is an exception by calling it *vino tinto*.

Wine-Producing Regions

Spain is still underestimated as a wine producing nation. That may be a result of insufficient marketing or the slow change from mass- to quality production.

Rioja, Spain's best wine (similar to French Bordeaux) is well known outside the country. Note that the best Rioja is a red wine, but there is also

nominación de origen calificada (DOC).

Among the table wines the lowest grade is the *vino de mesa* (from unclassified areas, or ones of different classification, without any specified vintage); then there are *vino camarcal* and *vino de la tierra* (from particular, defined regions).

a white Rioja. Both are produced in the Ebro Valley.

Wine is also made in the countryside around Barcelona in the Tarragona region, in la Mancha and far into the south near Sevilla.

Spain's wines are divided into two levels: table wines and quality wines. For the quality wines there are about forty *Denominaciones de origen* (DO), and so far the Rioja is the only *De-*

Particular specialties from Spain are *sidra*, an apple wine from Asturias and the Basque region, the *cava*, a sparkling wine from Cataluña produced by the Champagne method, and of course the sherry from Jerez. This is made from dry white wine with added alcohol. It is available in varieties from dry (the light-colored *fino* and the darker *amontillado*) to sweet (*oloroso*, *cream*, and *Pedro Ximénez*).

A glass of wine is always *una copa de* vino, and never *un vaso de vino*.

Shopping

What's Most Important

Do you have toothbrushes?
¿Tiene cepillos de dientes?

Where do I find a shoe store?
¿Dónde hay una zapatería?

working hours / open hours
los horarios de apertura

closed
cerrado

I would just like to look around.
Sólo quiero echar un vistazo.

How much does that cost?
¿Cuánto cuesta?

That is too expensive.
Es demasiado caro.

Do you have something cheaper?
¿Tiene algo más barato?

Can I try on the shoes?
¿Puedo probarme los zapatos?

That is too big.
Es demasiado grande.

That is too small.
Es demasiado pequeño.

Forget Something?

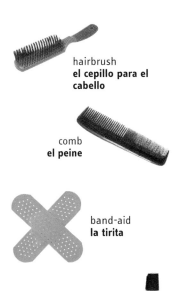

hairbrush
el cepillo para el cabello

comb
el peine

band-aid
la tirita

sunblock
la protección solar

underwear
la ropa interior

toothbrush
el cepillo de dientes

towel
la toalla

soap
el jabón

pajamas
el pijama

shoelaces
los cordones de zapatos

toothpaste
la pasta dentífrica

Es demasiado caro (It's too expensive) is an expression that you will use a lot.

Have you already been
served / waited on?
¿Le están atendiendo?

Thanks, I'm just
looking around.
**Gracias, estoy
echando un
vistazo.**

Can I help you?
**¿En qué puedo
servirle?**

Yes, I would like a pair of
pants.
**Quisiera unos
pantalones.**

Here, these are on
sale.
**Éstos están a
precio de oferta.**

Which size is
that?
¿Qué talla son?

That is size 38.
Son talla 38.

Ah, I think that is
too small.
**Creo que me van a
quedar chicos.**

Would you like to try
it on?
¿Desea probárselos?

Yes. Where are the
changing rooms?
**Sí. ¿Dónde están los
probadores?**

You can also use *oferta especial* for *sale* when you want to find something less
costly.

What You Often Need

Thanks, that is all.
Gracias, es todo.

I would like to have a pound of cherries.
Quisiera medio kilo de cerezas.

Do you have toothbrushes?
¿Tiene cepillos de dientes?

Where are your neckties?
¿Dónde están las corbatas?

What can you recommend?
¿Qué me recomienda?

Do you have any special offers?
¿Hay alguna oferta especial?

I have seen a pair of shoes in the display window.
He visto un par de zapatos en el escaparate.

I don't want to spend more than 60 euros.
No quiero gastar más de 60 euros.

I like them.
Me gustan.

I don't like them.
Estos no me gustan.

They are not exactly what I want.
Estos no son exactamente lo que estoy buscando.

Can you show me something else?
¿Podría enseñarme otro modelo?

How much does it cost?
¿Cuánto cuesta?

Where is the cashier?
¿Dónde está la caja?

I would like a receipt.
¿Me da un recibo, por favor?

Can you wrap it for me?
¿Me lo envuelve?

Can you deliver that to the hotel?
¿Podría mandármelo al hotel?

Do you deliver to foreign countries too?
¿También manda la mercancía al extranjero?

I would like to exchange this.
¿Podría cambiármelo?

I would like to make a complaint.
Quiero hacer una reclamación.

The product is defective.
El producto está defectuoso.

I would like my money back.
Quisiera que me devolviera el dinero.

I'll take them.
Me los llevo.

Could you give me a shopping bag?
¿Me da una bolsa?

The word for *complaint* is *la reclamación* or *el reclamo.*

What You Hear or Read

¿En qué puedo ayudarle?
Can I help you?

¿Ya le están atendiendo?
Have you already been served /
waited on?

¿Qué desea?
What would you like?

¿Cuál es su talla?
What is your size?

La liquidación / las rebajas
Sale

¿Desea algo más?
Will there be something else?

Lo siento, eso no lo tenemos.
We don't have that, unfortunately.

Son 12 euros.
That will be 12 euros.

¿Paga en efectivo o con tarjeta de crédito?
Are you paying in cash or by credit card?

¿Cuáles desea?
Which ones would you like?

In a Department Store

department
el departamento

elevator
el ascensor

entrance
la entrada

cash register / cashier
la caja

customer service
el servicio de atención al cliente

emergency exit
la salida de emergencia

escalator
la escalera mecánica

floor
el piso

toilets
los servicios higiénicos

stairways
las escaleras

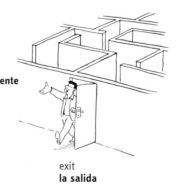

exit
la salida

The general term for *customer service* is *servicio posventa.*

Shops

souvenir shop **la tienda de regalos**

antique store **la tienda de antigüedades**

drugstore / pharmacy **la farmacia**

bakery **la panadería**

florist **la floristería**

bookshop **la librería**

computer store **la tienda de informática**

gourmet store **la tienda gastronómica**

shopping center **el centro comercial**

store **la tienda**

hardware **la ferretería**

electrical appliances store **la tienda de productos eléctricos**

bicycle shop **la tienda de bicicletas**

delicatessen **la rotisería / la fiambrería**

fish store **la pescadería**

flea market **el rastro**

photo store **la tienda de fotografía**

hairdresser shop / barber shop **la peluquería**

fresh produce stand **la verdulería**

household merchandise **los artículos domésticos**

jewelry store **la joyería**

department store **la tienda por departamentos**

clothing store **la tienda de ropa**

pastry shop **la pastelería**

cosmetics store **el salón de belleza**

art gallery **la galería de arte**

arts and crafts **la tienda de objetos artísticos**

dime store **la tienda de artículos baratos**

grocery store **la tienda de comestibles**

leather goods **los artículos de cuero**

market **el mercado**

butcher shop **la carnicería**

creamery / dairy **la lechería**

furniture store **la mueblería**

music store **la tienda de música**

fruit stand **la frutería**

eyewear store **la óptica**

perfumery **la perfumería**

fur store **la peletería**

pawnshop **la casa de empeño**

health food store **la tienda de alimentos naturales**

dry cleaners **la tintorería**

travel agency **la agencia de viajes**

appliance store **la tienda de electrodomésticos**

tailor shop **la sastrería**

stationery store **la papelería**

shoe store **la zapatería**

shoemaker **el zapatero**

toy store **la juguetería**

liquor store **la licorería**

sporting goods store **la tienda de artículos de deporte**

fabric store **la tienda de telas**

supermarket **el supermercado**

candy store **la confitería**

tobacco store **la tabaquería / el estanco**

pet shop **la tienda de animales**

car dealership **la agencia de automóviles**

car rental agency **la arrendataria de automóviles**

laundromat **la lavandería**

wine store **la tienda de vinos**

newsstand **el quiosco**

You may also find the electronics shop under the heading *electrodomésticos*.

Colors

■	black **negro**	■	green **verde**
□	white **blanco**	■	blue **azul**
■	gray **gris**	■	pink **rosa**
■	red **rojo**	■	orange **anaranjado**
	yellow **amarillo**	■	purple **lila**

Designs

colored / colorful
de colores

checkered
a cuadros

mottled
mezclado

printed / patterned
con dibujos

knobby
con motas

light
claro

dark
oscuro

high-contrast
con mucho contraste

low-contrast
con poco contraste

matte / dull
mate

glossy / shiny
brillante

polka-dotted
a lunares

 vertically striped
con rayas verticales

 horizontally striped
con rayas horizontales

 black-and-white
en blanco y negro

Spanish uses the same word for *of course, naturally,* and *light-colored: claro.*

At the Market

Cherries, beautiful cherries!
¡Cerezas, hay cerezas buenísimas!

They look nice.
Tienen buena pinta.

Would you like a taste?
¿Quiere probarlas?

Mmm, delicious. Give me one pound, please.
Mm, están riquísimas. Deme medio kilo, por favor.

What is that?
¿Qué es eso?

Viper's grass.
Es escorzonera.

How do you eat it?
¿Qué se hace con ella?

You cook it like a vegetable.
Se cocina como verdura.

The term *pound* is not used in Spain; you ask for a half-kilo or 500 grams.

Foods

beer
la cerveza

pastries / baked goods
los pasteles

bread
el pan

vegetables
las verduras

roll
el panecillo

coffee
el café

ice cream
el helado

cheese
el queso

fish
el pescado

canned food
las conservas

meat
la carne

seafood
los mariscos

In Mexico, rolls are called *bolillos*.

organic food **los alimentos naturales**

butter **la mantequilla**

vinegar **el vinagre**

beverages **las bebidas**

spices **los condimentos**

semolina **la sémola**

honey **la miel**

cake **la torta / el pastel / el bizcocho**

margarine **la margarina**

jam **la mermelada**

mayonnaise **la mayonesa**

flour **la harina**

milk products / dairy products **los productos lácteos**

oil **el aceite**

chocolate bonbons **los bombones de chocolate**

curd **el requesón**

rice **el arroz**

salt **la sal**

sour cream **la nata ácida**

whipped cream **la crema batida**

chocolate **el chocolate**

mustard **la mostaza**

candies **los dulces**

yogurt **el yogur**

sugar **el azúcar**

→ Also see FISH AND SHELLFISH, p. 117; TYPES OF MEAT, p.118; POULTRY, p. 120; VEGETABLES, p. 122; FRUITS, p. 127; and NUTS, p. 130

nuts
las nueces

fruit
la fruta

salad
la ensalada

tea
el té

wine
el vino

noodles
la pasta

sausages
los embutidos

Another term for whipped cream is *la nata batida*.

shopping
basket
**la cesta de
compras**

shopping cart
el carro de compras

shopping bag
**la bolsa de
compras**

Quantities

100 grams
100 gramos

a pound
medio kilo

a kilo
un kilo

a piece
un pedazo

a slice
una rebanada

a liter
un litro

a packet
un paquete

a bottle
una botella

a can
una lata

a glassful / a glass of ...
un vaso

Sales Conversations

I would like to have some butter.
Quiero mantequilla.

Do you have flour, too?
¿También hay harina?

A bit more, please.
Un poco más, por favor.

Can I taste it?
¿Puedo probarlo?

Is it OK if it's a little over?
¿No importa si es un poco más?

Anything else?
¿Desea algo más?

Thanks, that is all.
No gracias, es todo.

There are lots of mom and pop stores in Spain; a sure sign is the label *co-mestibles*.

Drugs and Cosmetics

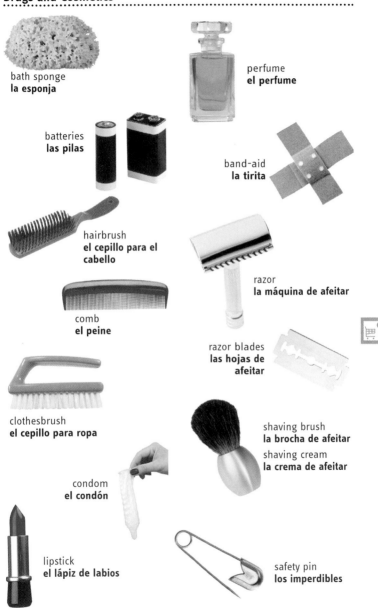

bath sponge
la esponja

perfume
el perfume

batteries
las pilas

band-aid
la tirita

hairbrush
el cepillo para el cabello

razor
la máquina de afeitar

comb
el peine

razor blades
las hojas de afeitar

clothesbrush
el cepillo para ropa

shaving brush
la brocha de afeitar

shaving cream
la crema de afeitar

condom
el condón

lipstick
el lápiz de labios

safety pin
los imperdibles

A razor blade is also called, in elaborate detail, *una hoja de afeitar*.

Drugs and Cosmetics

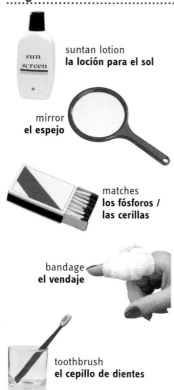

suntan lotion
la loción para el sol

mirror
el espejo

matches
**los fósforos /
las cerillas**

bandage
el vendaje

toothbrush
el cepillo de dientes

eye shadow **la sombra de ojos**
mouthwash **el agua dentífrica**
nail file **la lima para uñas**
nail polish **el esmalte de uñas**
nail polish remover **el quitaesmalte**
nail scissors **las tijeras para las uñas**
tissue / kleenex **el pañuelo de papel**

tweezers **las pinzas**
powder **los polvos de maquillaje**
cleaners / cleaning products **los
productos de limpieza**
rouge **el colorete**
sponge **la esponja**
soap **el jabón**
scrubbing brush **el cepillo para
fregar**
dishwashing liquid **el detergente**
tampons **los tampones**
handkerchiefs **los pañuelos**
toilet paper **el papel higiénico**
face cloth **el guante para la ducha**
laundry detergent **el detergente para
la lavadora**
absorbent cotton **el algodón
hidrófilo**
mascara **el rímel**
toothpaste **la pasta dentífrica**
dental floss **la seda dental**

concealer **el corrector**
eyebrow pencil **el lápiz de cejas**
sanitary napkin **la toallita sanitaria**
deodorant **el desodorante**
disinfectant **el desinfectante**
stain remover **el quitamanchas**
shampoo **el champú**
hand cream **la crema para las
manos**
insecticide **el insecticida**
body lotion **la crema para el cuerpo**

Like many other women in southern countries, Spanish women use lots of makeup.

For Children and Babies

ball
la pelota

sand pail
el balde / cubo de playa

kite
la cometa

nipples
el pezón / la tetina

shovel
la pala

bottle
el biberón

pacifier
el chupete

watering can
la regadera

child's bed
la cama del niño

swimming ring
el flotador

toy
el juguete

balloon
el globo

travelling bed
la cuna de viaje

baby cream **la crema para bebés**

swimsuit **el traje de baño / el bañador**

infant food / baby food **el alimento para bebé**

water wings **las nadaderas**

swimming goggles / diving goggles
las gafas de buceo

diapers **los pañales**

Spanish and South American people are very fond of children.

Tobacco Products

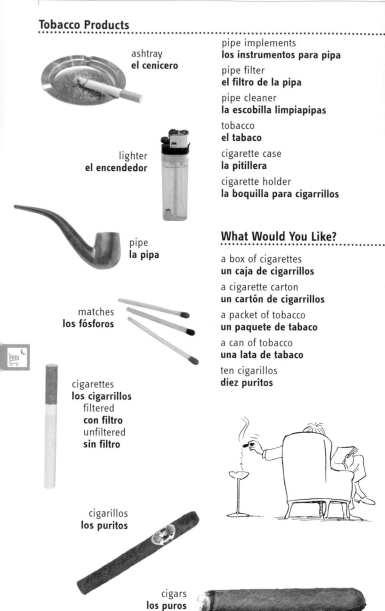

ashtray
el cenicero

lighter
el encendedor

pipe
la pipa

matches
los fósforos

cigarettes
los cigarrillos
filtered
con filtro
unfiltered
sin filtro

cigarillos
los puritos

cigars
los puros

pipe implements
los instrumentos para pipa

pipe filter
el filtro de la pipa

pipe cleaner
la escobilla limpiapipas

tobacco
el tabaco

cigarette case
la pitillera

cigarette holder
la boquilla para cigarrillos

What Would You Like?

a box of cigarettes
un caja de cigarrillos

a cigarette carton
un cartón de cigarrillos

a packet of tobacco
un paquete de tabaco

a can of tobacco
una lata de tabaco

ten cigarillos
diez puritos

Spain and Latin America resemble the United States in the 1970s: everybody knows that smoking is unhealthy, but too many continue smoking.

Clothing

I am looking for a skirt.
Busco una falda.

I am looking for something to go with it.
Busco algo que haga juego con esto.

Can I try that on?
¿Puedo probármelo?

I'll take that.
Me lo llevo.

I don't like that.
No me gusta.

I don't like the color.
El color no me gusta.

Where is the changing room? / dressing room?
¿Dónde está el probador?

Do you have a mirror?
¿Tiene un espejo?

The sleeves are too long.
Las mangas están demasiado largas.

Can you alter them?
¿Podría arreglarlas, por favor?

How long will the alteration take?
¿Cuánto tiempo tarda en arreglarlas?

What You Hear

¿Cuál es su talla?
What is your size?

¿Quiere probárselo?
Would you like to try it on?

¿Quiere que se lo arreglemos?
Should we alter it?

¿De qué color?
Which color?

Sizes

I wear size 38. **Mi talla es 38.**

small **pequeña**

medium **media**

large **grande**

extra large **muy grande**

Do you have a larger / smaller one?
¿Tiene algo más grande / pequeño?

That fits well. **Me queda bien.**

That doesn't fit. **No me queda bien.**

That is too ... **Está demasiado ...**
    small. **pequeño.**
    big. **grande.**
    tight / narrow. **ceñido.**
    loose / wide. **holgado.**
    short. **corto.**
    long. **largo.**

If you have momentarily forgotten the formula for "Do you have ..." you can also say ¿Hay ...? ("Is there any ...")

Articles of Clothing

swimsuit
el traje de baño / el bañador

trunks
el traje de baño / el bañador

bikini
el bikini

bowtie
la corbata de lazo

gloves
los guantes

hat
el sombrero

tie
la corbata

cap
el gorro

scarf
la bufanda

baseball cap
la gorra

Size Conversions

Men's Suits

Spain/L.A.	USA
46	36
48	38
50	40
52	42
54	44
56	46
58	48
60	50

Women's Clothing

Spain/L.A.	USA
38	10
40	12
42	14
44	16
46	18
48	20

Men's Shirts

Spain/L.A.	USA
36	14
37	14 1/2
38	15
39/40	15 1/2
41	16
42	16 1/2
43	17
44	17 1/2
45	18

In our new century, fashions have become truly international. People in Montevideo dress exactly like people in Manchester.

umbrella
el paraguas

handkerchief
el pañuelo

socks
los calcetines

underpants
los calzoncillos

hooded jacket / windbreaker / parka
el anorak / la parka

suit **el traje**

bathrobe **el albornoz**

blazer **el blazer**

blouse **la blusa**

brassiere / bra **el sostén**

belt **el cinturón**

scarf **la bufanda**

shirt **la camisa**

pants **los pantalones**

suspenders **los tirantes**

sports jacket **la chaqueta deportiva**

jacket **la chaqueta**

dress **el vestido**

outfit **el traje**

coat **el abrigo**

housecoat **la bata**

nightshirt **el camisón**

sweater / pullover **el suéter / el jersey**

raincoat **el impermeable**

skirt **la falda**

pajamas **el pijama**

apron **el delantal**

shorts **el pantalón corto**

panties **las bragas**

stockings **las medias**

tights **las medias de malla**

t-shirt **la camiseta**

undershirt **la camiseta**

slip / petticoat **las enaguas**

waistcoat **el chaleco**

The Spanish word for *suit* is *el traje*.

Sewing

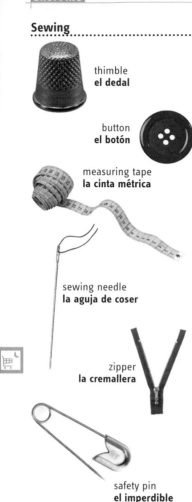

thimble
el dedal

button
el botón

measuring tape
la cinta métrica

sewing needle
la aguja de coser

zipper
la cremallera

safety pin
el imperdible

sleeve **las mangas**
thread **el hilo**
elastic **el elástico**
collar **el cuello**
cuffs **los puños**
pin **el alfiler**

Fabrics

What material is this made from?
¿De qué material está hecho?

I would like something in cotton.
Quisiera algo de algodón.

Is that machine-washable?
¿Se puede lavar en la lavadora?

Can one put this in the dryer?
¿Se puede secar en la secadora?

Does that shrink when washed?
¿Encoge al lavarlo?

wrinkle-free / no ironing
no necesita plancha

lining
el forro

cambric / batiste **la batista**
cotton **el algodón**
corduroy **la pana**
felt **el fieltro**
flannel **la franela**
terrycloth **la tela de toalla**
worsted **de lana peinada**
crepe **el crespón / el crepé**
synthetic fiber **la fibra sintética**
leather **el cuero / la piel**
linen **el lino**
microfiber **la microfibra**
poplin **la popelina**
velvet **el terciopelo**
satin **el raso**
silk **la seda**
wool **la lana**

Poplin is either *popelina* or *popelín*.

Leather Goods

gloves
los guantes

handbag
el bolso

suitcase
la maleta

tote bag
la bolsa de viaje

Dry Cleaning, Laundromat

Please clean this garment.
Me puede lavar esta prenda, por favor.

Which type of cleaning do you recommend?
¿Qué tipo de limpieza me recomienda?

I would like ...
Quiero ...
   dry-cleaning.
   la limpieza en seco.
   gentle cleaning.
   limpieza delicada.
   thorough cleaning.
   limpieza completa.

How much will that be?
¿Cuánto cuesta?

How long will it take?
¿Cuánto tiempo tardará?

When can I pick it up again?
¿Cuándo puedo venir a recogerlo?

Can you send me the garment?
¿Podría enviarme la prenda?

Here is my address.
Aquí tiene mi dirección.

---

briefcase **el maletín**

wallet / billfold **la cartera**

purse **el monedero**

belt **el cinturón**

artificial leather **el cuero / la piel sintética**

leather jacket **la chaqueta de cuero**

leather coat **el abrigo de cuero**

shoulder bag **la bolsa en bandolera**

suede **la gamuza**

washing machine **la lavadora**

dryer **la secadora**

spin-dryer **la centrifugadora**

coins **las monedas**

rinse **enjuagar**

spin-dry **centrifugar**

hot wash **lavar a alta temperatura**

delicate / gentle wash **el programa para lavado de ropa delicada**

spin-dry **el programa con centrifugado**

colored laundry **la ropa de color**

hot-water wash **la ropa blanca**

Dry cleaning is lavado en seco.

Shoes

I wear size 7.
Calzo el 7.

The shoes pinch.
Los zapatos me aprietan.

The shoes are ...
Los zapatos están ...
  too narrow.
  demasiado estrechos.
  too wide.
  demasiado anchos.
  too small.
  demasiado pequeños.
  too big.
  demasiado grandes.

Shoes with a...
Zapatos de ...
  flat heel.
  tacón bajo.
  high heel.
  tacón alto.

Can you resole the shoes?
¿Puede ponerle suelas nuevas a los zapatos?

I need new heels.
Necesito tapillas nuevas.

When will the shoes be ready?
¿Cuándo estarán listos los zapatos?

heel **el tacón**
bath slippers **las chanclas**
rubber boots **las botas de goma**
slippers **las zapatillas**

children's shoes **los zapatos para niños**
sandals **las sandalias**
shoelace **el cordón**
shoe brush **el cepillo para zapatos**
shoe cream / shoe polish **la crema para zapatos**
shoes **los zapatos**
sole **la suela**
boot **la bota**
track shoe **el zapato de deporte**
leather sole **la suela de cuero**
rubber sole **la suela de goma**
walking shoes / hiking boots **los zapatos de excursión**

Where Does It Pinch?

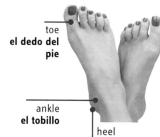

toe
el dedo del pie

ankle
el tobillo

heel
el talón

Size Conversions

Men's Shoes		Women's Shoes	
Spain/L.A.	**USA**	**Spain/L.A.**	**USA**
39	6 1/2	36	5 1/2
40	7 1/2	37	6
41	8 1/2	38	7
42	9	39	7 1/2
43	10	40	8 1/2
44	10 1/2	41	9
45	11		
46	11 1/2		

I wear a size 7 shoe is also *Calzo el 7.*

In the Sporting Goods Shop

swimsuit / bathing suit
el traje de baño / el bañador

trunks
el traje de baño / el bañador

golf clubs
los palos de golf

golf bag
la bolsa de golf

ball
la pelota

dumbbell
la pesa

basketball
el baloncesto

backpack / knapsack
la mochila

bikini
el bikini

snorkel
el esnórquel

soccer ball
la pelota de fútbol

fins
las aletas

golf ball
la pelota de golf

sun umbrella / parasol
la sombrilla

Spanish people say that they like *to play at sports*, whereas Anglo-Saxons *work at sports*.

In the Sporting Goods Shop

diving goggles /
diving mask
**las gafas de
buceo**

tennis ball
la pelota de tenis

tennis racket
la raqueta de tenis

ping-pong ball
la pelota de ping-pong

ping-pong paddle
la raqueta de ping-pong

walking shoes / hiking shoes
los zapatos de excursión

fishing rod
la caña de pescar

bathing cap
el gorro de baño

hiking boots / climbing boots
los zapatos de montaña

shuttlecock
el volante

badminton rackets
los raquetas de bádminton

inline skates / rollerblades
los patines en línea

thermal mattress
la colchoneta aislante

air mattress
el colchón neumático

sleeping bag
el saco de dormir

ice skates
los patines de hielo

water wings
las nadaderas

skateboard
la plancha de patín

tennis shoes / sneakers
los zapatos de tenis

track shoes / sneakers
**las zapatillas / los zapatos de
deporte**

hooded jacket / windbreaker / parka
el anorak / la parka

→ Also see TYPES OF SPORTS, p. 179;
AT THE BEACH, p. 183; WATER SPORTS,
p. 186; DIVING, p. 187; HIKING AND
CLIMBING, p. 191

Water wings are also called *flotties*.

Housewares

drainer
el colador

pail / bucket
el cubo

broom
la escoba

lighter
el encendedor

silverware /
tableware
los cubiertos

griddle / frying
pan
la sartén

bottle opener
**el abridor / el
destapador**

meat knife
**el cuchillo para
carne**

ironing
board
**la tabla de
planchar**
iron
la plancha

fly swatter
el matamoscas

can opener
el abrelatas

A bucket is also called *un balde* or *una cubeta* in South America.

Housewares

hair dryer
el secador de cabello

brush
la escobilla

dishes
la vajilla
dishrack
el escurreplatos

coffee grinder /
coffee mill
el molinillo de café

jug / pitcher
la jarra

watering can
la regadera

dustpan
la pala

glass
el vaso / la copa

candle
la vela

light bulb
la bombilla

candlestick
el candelero

In South America one word for dishes is *los trastes.*

chain
la cadena

ladder
la escalera de mano

washing brush
el cepillo para lavar

magnet
el imán

saucepan /
pot
la cacerola

knife
el cuchillo

corkscrew
el sacacorchos

creamer /
milk jug
**el cazo de
leche**

kitchen sponge
la esponja de platos

kerosene lamp /
hurricane lamp
**la lámpara de
petróleo**

insulated box
la nevera

cleaning rag
**el trapo para
limpiar**

You can use the word *la olla* to mean a conventional cooking pot.

Housewares

whisk
el batidor

vacuum cleaner
la aspiradora

stirring spoons
los cucharones

matches
**los fósforos /
las cerillas**

plunger
el destapador

cup
la taza

scissors
las tijeras

plate
el plato

string
el cordón

pot
la olla

mirror
el espejo

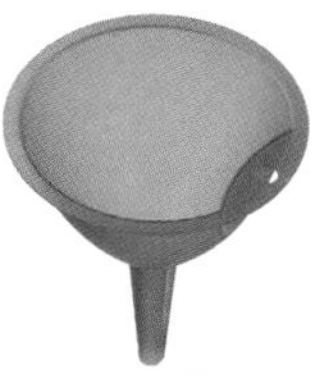

funnel
el embudo

The word for *scissors, las tijeras*, is always used in the plural.

padlock
el candado

hose
la manguera

scale
la báscula

rolling pin
el rodillo

hot water bottle /
bed warmer
**la bolsa de agua
caliente**

lemon
squeezer
el exprimidor

clothespin
la pinza de ropa

trash bag **la bolsa de basura**

aluminum foil **el papel de aluminio**

cup **el vaso**

twine **el cordel / el bramante**

plastic wrap **la película transparente**

paper napkins **las servilletas de
papel**

plastic bag **la bolsa de plástico**

laundry basket
la cesta de ropa

scrubbing brush **el cepillo para
fregar**

flashlight **la linterna**

pocket knife / jacknife **la navaja**

immersion heater **el calentador de
inmersión**

thermos **el termo**

fan / ventilator **el ventilador**

clothesrack **el tendedero**

clothesline
la cuerda para ropa

Another word for *scale* is *la balanza*.

Tools

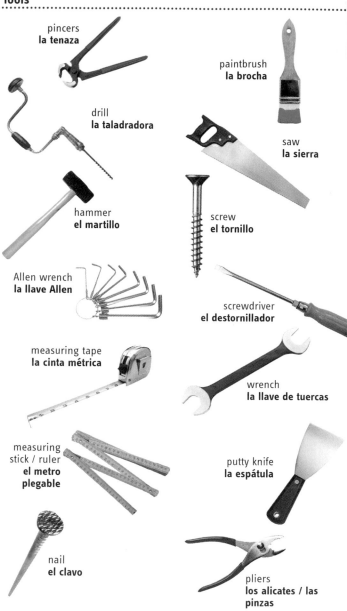

pincers
la tenaza

paintbrush
la brocha

drill
la taladradora

saw
la sierra

hammer
el martillo

screw
el tornillo

Allen wrench
la llave Allen

screwdriver
el destornillador

measuring tape
la cinta métrica

wrench
la llave de tuercas

measuring
stick / ruler
**el metro
plegable**

putty knife
la espátula

nail
el clavo

pliers
**los alicates / las
pinzas**

In some countries screwdriver is *el atornillador* ("screwer") and in others it is *el destornillador* ("unscrewer").

Camping Equipment

grill
la parrilla

butane gas
el gas butano

gas stove
el hornillo de gas

cooler
la nevera

hammock
la hamaca

tent peg
la estaca

charcoal
el carbón

deck chair
la tumbona

folding chair
la silla plegable

folding table
la mesa plegable

air mattress
el colchón neumático

air pump
la bomba de aire

mosquito net
el mosquitero

propane
el gas propano

sleeping bag
el saco de dormir

water jug
el bidón de agua

kerosene lamp /
hurricane lamp
**la lámpara de
petróleo**

tent
la tienda

tent pole
el palo de tienda

string
el cordón

→ Also see IN THE CAMPGROUND,
p. 100

The word *carboncillo* is also used for *charcoal* for grilling.

The Bookshop

Where can I find a bookstore?
¿Dónde hay una librería?

Do you also have books in English?
¿Tiene también libros en inglés?

I am looking for a novel. **Busco una novela.**

postcards **las tarjetas postales**

illustrated book / coffee-table book
el libro de fotografías

picture book **el libro ilustrado**

stamps **las estampillas / los sellos**

stationery / writing paper **el papel de cartas**

technical book **el libro técnico**

wrapping paper / gift wrap **el papel de regalo**

children's book **el libro infantil**

cookbook **el libro de cocina**

mystery / detective novel **la novela policíaca**

map **el mapa**

short novel / novella **la novela corta**

guidebook **la guía**

nonfiction **el libro de documentación**

science fiction **la ciencia ficción**

map of the city **el mapa de la ciudad**

dictionary **el diccionario**

magazine **la revista**

newspaper **el diario / el periódico**

calendar **el calendario**

Writing Implements

pencil
el lápiz

paper clips
los sujetapapeles

colored pen
el lápiz de color

fountain pen
la pluma fuente

ruler
la regla

notepad
el bloc de notas

Postcards are properly referred to as *las tarjetas postales* or simply *postales*.

notebook
el cuaderno

thumbtacks
las chinches

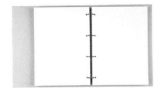

loose-leaf notebook
el cuaderno de anillos

scissors
las tijeras

string
el cordón

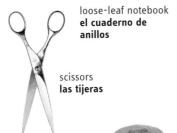

twine
el bramante / el cordel

pencil sharpener
el sacapuntas

labels
las etiquetas

felt tip pen
el rotulador

paper clips
las grapas

glue
el pegamento

ballpoint pen
el bolígrafo

eraser
la goma de borrar

stationery
el papel de cartas

stationery / office supplies
los artículos de papelería

adhesive tape
la cinta adhesiva

pocket calculator
la calculadora de bolsillo

playing cards
los naipes

ink
la tinta

Chinches means *thumbtacks*, but it also means *lice*.

Painting Supplies

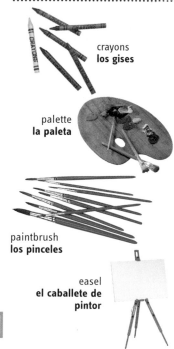

crayons
los gises

palette
la paleta

paintbrush
los pinceles

easel
el caballete de pintor

watercolors **las acuarelas**

watercolor paper **el papel para acuarela**

fixative **el fijador**

canvas stretcher / frame **el marco del lienzo**

charcoal pencil **el carboncillo**

chalk **la tiza**

canvas **el lienzo**

watercolor crayons / chalk **el giso o tiza para pintar**

oil paint **la pintura al óleo**

oil pastel **el pastel al óleo**

pastel **el pastel**

sketch pad **el bloc de dibujo**

In the Photography Shop

I am looking for a ...
Busco ...
  reflex camera.
  una cámara réflex.
  35-mm camera.
  una cámara de 35 mm.
  digital camera.
  una cámara digital.
  wide-angle / panorama camera.
  una cámara panorámica.

I would like to spend about 100 euros.
No quiero gastar más de 100 euros.

Is the guarantee valid internationally?
¿La garantía es válida a nivel internacional?

I need passport pictures.
Necesito fotos de pasaporte.

What Is Broken?

Something is wrong with my camera.
La cámara no funciona bien.

The film is jammed.
La película está trabada.

Can you repair it?
¿Puede repararlo?

How much will it cost?
¿Cuánto me costará?

How long will it take?
¿Cuánto tardará en repararlo?

exposure meter / light meter
el exposímetro

distance meter
el telémetro

shutter
el obturador

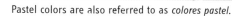

Pastel colors are also referred to as *colores pastel.*

Accessories

film
la película

lens
el lente / el objetivo

battery
la pila / la batería

flash
el flash

camera bag
la bolsa para el equipo de fotografía

automatic shutter release / self-timer
retardador de disparo

lens shade
el parasol

tripod
el trípode

telephoto lens
el teleobjetivo

uv-filter
el filtro de rayos UV

wide-angle lens
el objetivo gran angular

zoom lens
el zoom / el objetivo de distancia focal variable

Films

I would like ...
Necesito una ...
  black and white film.
  película en blanco y negro.
  color-negative film.
  película en colores.
  slide film / transparency film.
  película para diapositivas.

100 / 200 / 400 ASA.
de 100 / 200 / 400 ASA.

36 exposures.
de 36 fotografías.

daylight film
la película para luz natural

artificial light film
la película para luz artificial

Can you put the film into the camera?
¿Podría cargarme la cámara?

developing
el revelado

printing
la copia

format
el formato

slide frames
el marco para diapositivas

The roll of film is *el carrete*; the film itself is *la película*.

Developing Film

Please develop this
film.
**Revele esta película,
por favor.**

Do you also want a
print of each
picture?
**¿Quiere también
una copia de cada
foto?**

Yes, size 4 by 6.
**Sí, en tamaño
10 por 15.**

Glossy or matte?
¿De alto brillo o mate?

Glossy. When can I pick
up the pictures?
**De alto brillo. ¿Cuándo
puedo pasar a recoger las
fotografías?**

The day after tomorrow.
Pasado mañana.

To develop in all other senses of the word is *desarrollar*.

Video Cameras

I would like to buy a video camera.
Quiero comprar una cámara de vídeo.

It should not cost more than 300 dollars.
Que no cueste más de 300 dólares.

Does the camera have a worldwide warranty?
¿La cámara tiene garantía a nivel internacional?

Is this a discontinued model?
¿Es un modelo discontinuado?

Is this the most current model from this company?
¿Es el modelo más actual de la compañía?

For my videocamera I would like ...
Para mi vídeocamara quisiera ...
  film.
  una película adecuada.
  batteries.
  baterías.
  a charger.
  un cargador.
  a halogen light.
  una luz halógena.

Camcorders, DVD

VCR
el VCR / la videograbadora

videocassette
el videocasete

DVD player
el VCR / el lector DVD

Do you have cassettes for the PAL system too?
¿También hay cassettes para el sistema PAL?

Can it also run on 220 volts?
¿Es posible cambiar el voltaje a 220 voltios?

Or do I need a transformer for it?
¿O necesito un transformador?

The word *pila* is also used for a small battery.

Electronic Devices

adapter
el adaptador

plug
el enchufe

battery
la batería

alarm clock
el despertador

iron
la plancha

razor
la máquina de afeitar

flashlight
la linterna

extension cord
el cordón prolongador

hair dryer
el secador de pelo

light bulb
la bombilla

fuse
el fusible

socket
la toma de corriente

Instead of *toma de corriente* you can also say *enchufe* for *plug*.

Stereo

CD player
el lector portátil de CD

remote control
el control remoto / el mando a distancia

headphones
los auriculares

speakers
los parlantes / los altavoces

MP3 recorder / player
la grabadora / lectora de MP3

DVD player
el lector DVD

stereo system
el equipo estéreo

cassette recorder
la grabadora de casete

system components
los componentes del sistema

radio
la radio

digital recording
la grabación digital

tuner-amplifier
el amplificador-sintonizador

Computer

screen
la pantalla

keyboard
el teclado

RAM **la memoria principal**

operating system **el sistema operativo**

CD-writer **la grabadora de CD**

CD-ROM drive **la unidad de CD-ROM**

hard disk **el disco duro**

graphics card **la tarjeta gráfica**

laser printer **la impresora láser**

laptop **el laptop / la computadora portátil**

modem **el módem**

network cable **el cable de red**

network card **la tarjeta de red**

paper **el papel**

processor **el procesador**

scanner **el escáner**

sound card **la tarjeta de sonido**

control unit **la unidad de control**

web **la red**

inkjet printer **la impresora por chorro de tinta**

toner **el tóner**

internet **el internet**

video card **la tarjeta de vídeo**

If you want to pronounce CD in Spanish, you say CEH DEH.

At the Optician's

My frames are broken.
La montura se ha roto.

No problem, I can solder that.
No importa, se puede soldar.

Can I wait for it?
¿Puedo esperar aquí?

I'm sorry, it won't be ready until tomorrow.
Lo siento, no estará lista hasta mañana.

Don't you have an extra pair of glasses?
¿No tiene gafas de sustitución?

In some South American countries glasses are called *lentes*.

earpiece
la varilla

glass
el lente / el cristal

frame
el marco / la montura

The glass is broken.
El lente cristal se ha roto.

sunglasses
las gafas de sol

binoculars
los gemelos / los prismáticos

My glasses are broken.
Mis gafas se han roto.

Can you repair it?
¿Podría usted reparármelas?

How long will it take?
¿Cuánto tiempo durará la reparación?

magnifying glass
la lupa

Can I wait for it?
¿Puedo esperar aquí?

contact lenses
el / la lente de contacto
   hard lenses
   lentillas duras
   soft lenses
   lentillas suaves

vision
la visión

short-sighted
miope

far-sighted
hipermétrope

glasses case
el estuche para las gafas

cleaner
el limpiador de gafas

A case (such as a glasses case) is *un estuche*.

At the Watchmaker's

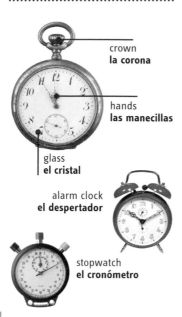

crown
la corona

hands
las manecillas

glass
el cristal

alarm clock
el despertador

stopwatch
el cronómetro

My watch / clock isn't working.
Mi reloj no funciona.

My watch / clock is running fast.
Mi reloj se adelanta.

My watch / clock is running slow.
Mi reloj se atrasa.

Can you repair it?
¿Puede reparármelo?

How long will it take?
¿Cuánto tiempo tardará?

wristband
la correa de pulsera

watch
el reloj de pulsera

pocket watch
el reloj de bolsillo

wall clock
el reloj de pared

waterproof
impermeable

Jeweler

I am looking for a gift. **Busco un regalo.**

It is for a man / a woman. **Es para hombre / mujer.**

Do you have something less expensive? **¿Hay algo más barato?**

What material is that? **¿Qué material es?**

Which gem is that? **¿Qué piedra es?**

pendant **el pendiente**

badge / pin **el alfiler**

bracelet **el brazalete / la pulsera**

brooch **el broche**

necklace **el collar**

tie pin **el alfiler de corbata**

cufflinks **los gemelos**

pearl necklace / string of pearls **el collar de perlas**

ring **el anillo**

earrings **los pendientes**

amethyst **la amatista**

amber **el ámbar**

diamond **el diamante**

stainless steel **el acero inoxidable**

ivory **el marfil**

gold **el oro**
    goldplated **dorado**

coral **el coral**

copper **el cobre**

onyx **la ónix**

pearl **la perla**

platinum **el platino**

ruby **el rubí**

sapphire **el zafiro**

silver **la plata**
    silver plated **plateado**

emerald **la esmeralda**

Another word for the hands of a watch is *las agujas* (needles).

Hair Stylist

hair gel
el gel para el cabello

elastic
la cinta elástica para el cabello

hairpins
las horquillas

barrette
el pasador

hairspray
la laca

hair conditioner
la crema suavizante

shampoo
el champú

curler
el rizador

hair dye / hair color
el tinte para el cabello

color rinse / tint
el tinte

hairbrush
el cepillo para el cabello

comb
el peine

perm
la permanente

sideburns
las patillas

curls
los rizos

center part
la raya mediana

part
la raya

mustache
el bigote

dandruff
la caspa

strands
los mechones

wig
la peluca

eyebrows
las cejas

beard
la barba

Dandruff shampoo is *champú anticaspa*.

How Would You Like It?

Are you free, or do I have to make an appointment?
¿Puedo ir cuando quiera o tengo que pedir una cita?

A wash and set, please.
Por favor, láveme el cabello y póngame rulos.

Please color my hair.
Por favor pínteme el cabello.

I want my hair to stay long.
Quiero dejarme el cabello largo.

Please cut off only the ends.
Por favor, córteme sólo las puntas.

Somewhat shorter than that.
Un poco más corto.

My ears should stay covered.
Las orejas tienen que quedar cubiertas.

Yes, that's right.
Sí, así está bien.

Would you please trim my beard?
¿Puede recortarme la barba?

A shave, please.
Me afeita, por favor.

color
teñir

blow-dry
secar

set
poner rulos

wash
lavar

tint
teñir

tease / back-comb
cardar

Which Hair Stylist?

modern
moderno

very short
muy corto

sporty
juvenil

A toupee is also called *un postizo.*

178 ciento setenta y ocho

Beach, Sports, and Nature

What's Happening?

darts
los dardos

fishing
la pesca

hang-gliding
el aladelta

baseball
el béisbol

basketball
el baloncesto

ice hockey
el hockey sobre hielo

billiards
el billar

boxing
el boxeo

Bowling is popular in Spain.

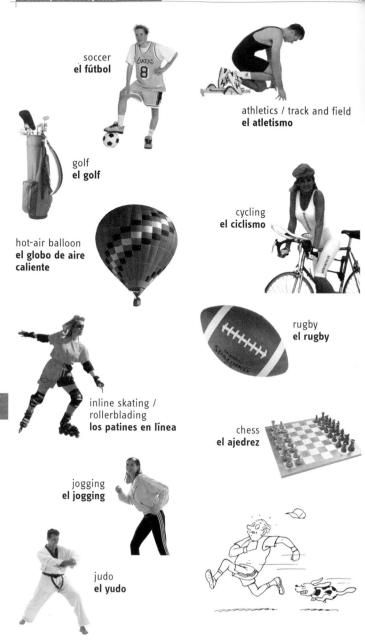

soccer
el fútbol

athletics / track and field
el atletismo

golf
el golf

cycling
el ciclismo

hot-air balloon
el globo de aire caliente

rugby
el rugby

inline skating / rollerblading
los patines en línea

chess
el ajedrez

jogging
el jogging

judo
el yudo

The Spanish have very competitive handball teams, especially in the Basque country and Cataluña.

skiing
esquiar

snowboard
el monoesquí

diving
el submarinismo

tennis
el tenis

ping-pong / table tennis
el ping-pong

aerobics **los ejercicios aeróbicos**

car racing **la carrera de coches**

badminton **el bádminton**

mountaineering / mountain climbing **el alpinismo**

ice-skating **el patinaje sobre hielo**

skydiving / parachute jumping **el paracaidismo**

football **el fútbol americano**

gymnastics **la gimnasia**

handball **el balonmano**

canoeing **el piragüismo**

karate **el karate**

bowling **el boliche**

cricket **el críquet**

horse racing **la carrera de caballos**

bicycle racing **el ciclismo**

regatta **la regata**

riding / horseback riding **la equitación**

wrestling **la lucha**

rowing **el remo**

swimming **la natación**

sailing **la vela**

squash **el squash**

weight lifting **el levantamiento de pesas**

surfing **el surf**

gymnastics **la gimnasia**

volleyball **el voleibol**

hiking **el excursionismo**

water polo **el water-polo**

waterskiing **el esquí acuático**

windsurfing
el windsurf

→ Also see IN THE SPORTING GOODS SHOP, p. 157

Spanish has adopted a lot of English expressions, such as *squash*.

Renting

I would like to rent a tennis racquet.
Quiero alquilar una raqueta de tenis.

What does it cost ...
¿Cuánto cuesta ...
  per hour?
  por hora?
  per day?
  al día?
  per week?
  a la semana?

That is too expensive for me.
Es demasiado caro.

Must I leave a deposit?
¿Tengo que depositar una fianza?

Instruction

I would like to take a tennis course.
Quisiera hacer un curso de tenis.

Are sailing courses offered here?
¿Se ofrecen cursos de vela aquí?

I have never practiced diving.
Nunca he practicado el submarinismo.

I am a beginner.
Soy principiante.

I am advanced.
Tengo experiencia.

Creative Vacations

cooking course **el curso de cocina**

painting course **el curso de pintura**

language course **el curso de idiomas**

dance **el baile**

theater **el teatro**

At the Beach

Where is the nearest beach?
¿Dónde está la playa más cercana?

Where can I rent a sun umbrella?
¿Dónde puedo alquilar una sombrilla?

How much is the rental of a chaise longue per day?
¿Cuánto cuesta una tumbona al día?

I am looking for a nudist beach.
Busco una playa de nudistas.

Is it high or low tide?
¿La marea está alta o baja?

How deep is the water?
¿Qué profundidad tiene el agua?

What's the water temperature?
¿Qué temperatura tiene el agua?

Are there any dangerous currents?
¿Hay corrientes peligrosas?

Is there a lifeguard on the beach?
¿Tiene un salvavidas la playa?

What do the flags mean?
¿Qué significan las banderas?

Notices and Signs

¡Prohibido bañarse!
Swimming prohibited!

Aviso de tormenta
Storm warning

¡Peligroso!
Danger!

Bañarse sólo a propio riesgo
Swimming at your own risk

Sólo nadadores
Only for swimmers

Prohibido tirarse
Diving prohibited

¡Corriente peligrosa!
Dangerous current!

Playa privada
Private beach

La vela is *the sail*; for *sailing* you can also say *la navegación a vela*.

At the Beach

swimsuit
el traje de baño

flippers
las aletas

trunks /
swimming trunks
el bañador

crab
el cangrejo

flip-flops
las chancletas

beach chair
la tumbona

bath towel
la toalla

motorboat
**la lancha de
motor**

ball
la pelota

bikini
el bikini

In Spain you can also say *motora* for a *motorboat*.

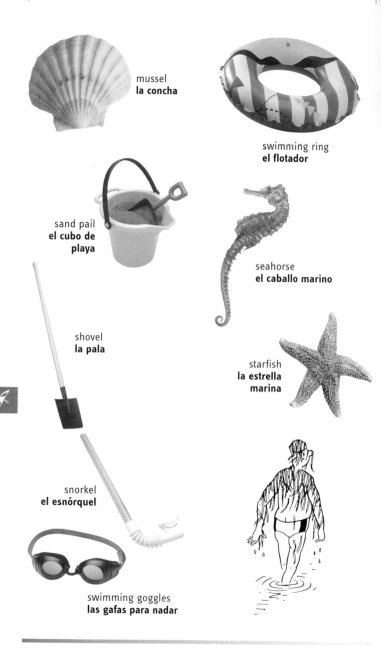

mussel
la concha

swimming ring
el flotador

sand pail
**el cubo de
playa**

seahorse
el caballo marino

shovel
la pala

starfish
**la estrella
marina**

snorkel
el esnórquel

swimming goggles
las gafas para nadar

The word for *sand* is *la arena*.

sunglasses
las gafas para el sol

suntan lotion
la loción para el sol

sunburn
la quemadura por el sol

sunstroke
la insolación

sun umbrella
la sombrilla

diving goggles / mask
las gafas de buceo

water polo
el polo acuático

seaweed **las algas**

beach cabin / cabana **la caseta para cambiarse**

boat **el bote**

boat rental **el alquiler de botes**

surf **el oleaje**

dune **la duna**

low tide **la marea baja**

shuttlecock **el volante**

rocky shoreline **la costa rocosa**

river **el río**

high tide **la marea alta**

pebble beach **la playa de arena gruesa**

air mattress **el colchón neumático**

sea **el mar**

non-swimmers **no nadadores**

canoe **la canoa / la piragua**

jellyfish **la medusa**

lifeguard **el salvavidas**

rowboat **el bote de remos**

sand **la arena**

sandy beach **la playa de arena**

shadow **la sombra**

swimmer **el nadador**

water wing **la nadadera**

ocean **el océano**

flip-flops **las chancletas**

beach towel **la toalla de playa**

current **la corriente**

surfboard **la tabla de surf**

pedal boat **el hidropedal**

pollution **la contaminación**

waterski **el esquí acuático**

wave **la ola**

The Spanish word *insolación* meaning *sunstroke* also is used simply to designate the effects of the sun.

Indoor and Outdoor Swimming Pools

I would like two tickets, please.
Quiero dos entradas, por favor.

Is there also a weekly pass /
multiple-entry pass?
**¿Hay también billetes semanales /
abonos?**

There is a discount for ...
¿Hay descuento para ...
  children?
  niños?
  teenagers?
  jóvenes?
  students?
  estudiantes?
  the handicapped?
  minusválidos?
  senior citizens?
  personas de edad?
  groups?
  grupos?

Where are the changing cabins?
**¿Dónde están las casetas para
cambiarse?**

Do you have lockers?
¿Hay cajas de seguridad?

Is the use of the sauna included in
the price?
**¿El uso de la sauna está incluido en
el precio?**

Does everyone have to wear a
bathing cap?
¿Es obligatorio ponerse el gorro?

Is there also a restaurant by the
swimming pool?
**¿Hay también algún restaurante al
lado de la piscina?**

What is the water temperature
today?
¿Qué temperatura tiene el agua hoy?

Do they keep the same water
temperature at all times?
**¿Mantienen la misma temperatura
del agua todos los días?**

How do you purify the water, with
chlorine or ozone?
**¿Limpian el agua con cloro o con
ozono?**

Do you use salt water or fresh
water?
**¿La piscina es de agua salada o de
agua dulce?**

Water Sports

kayak **el kayak**
canoe **la canoa / la piragua**
motorboat **la lancha de motor**
oars **los remos**
canoe **la canoa / la piragua**
rudder **el timón**
rowboat **el bote de remos**
rubber dinghy **la lancha inflable**
diving **el submarinismo**
pedal boat **el hidropedal**
waterskiing **el esquí acuático**
surfing **el surf**
windsurfing **hacer surf a vela**

Wind Surfing

sail **la vela**
mast **el mástil**
boom **la botavara**
surfboard **la tabla de surf**
centerboard **la orza de deriva**
auxiliary board **la orza auxiliar**
foot strap **las cinchas**

A paddle can also be called *un zagual* or *un canalete* in Spain.

Diving

I would like to go deep-sea diving.
Quisiera practicar el submarinismo.

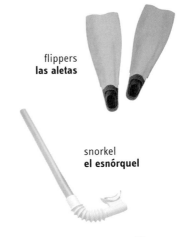

flippers
las aletas

snorkel
el esnórquel

I would like go cave-diving.
Quisiera hacer submarinismo en cuevas.

I have diving certification.
Tengo licencia submarinista.

I would like to get a diving certificate.
Quisiera sacar la licencia submarinista.

diving mask
las gafas de buzo

How much does it cost to get a diving certificate?
¿Cuánto cuesta sacar la licencia submarinista?

How long does it take to get a diving certificate?
¿Cuánto tiempo se necesita para sacar la licencia submarinista?

Will this diving certificate be accepted internationally?
¿Esta licencia vale a nivel internacional?

weight belt **el cinturón de plomo**

decometer **el decómetro**

compressed-air bottles **las bombonas de aire comprimido**

wetsuit **el traje de buceo**

diving watch **el reloj de buzo**

depth gauge **el batímetro / el profundímetro**

Diving goggles are also called *un visor*.

Sailing

I have a Class B sailing license.
Tengo licencia de navegación de vela de clase B.

I would like get a sailing license.
Quisiera sacar la licencia de navegación de vela.

Do you organize sailing trips that last several days?
¿Organiza usted excursiones de vela de varios días?

How much are they?
¿Cuánto cuestan?

When can we cast off?
¿Cuándo podemos zarpar?

Has anybody else registered?
¿Hay más gente inscrita?

I would like to sail in offshore waters.
Quisiera navegar cerca de la costa.

I am interested in sailing in the open sea.
Tengo interés en navegar en alta mar.

knots
los nudos

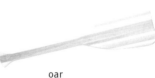

oar
el remo

life preserver
el flotador

life jacket
el chaleco salvavidas

There is a difference between an oar used for propulsion *(un remo)* and an oar used for steering *(un timón)*.

mast
el mástil

mainsail
la vela mayor

jib
el foque

main boom
el mástil principal

forecastle
el camarote de proa

tiller
la barra del timón

stern
la popa

rudder
el timón

mainsheet
la escota mayor

bow
la proa

centerboard
la orza de deriva

anchor **el ancla**
port **a babor**
leeward **a sotavento**
lighthouse **el faro**
windward **a barlovento**
motor **el motor**
starboard **a estribor**
rigging **el aparejo**

yawl **la lancha**
cruiser **el crucero**
trawler **la jabeguera**
schooner **la goleta**
yacht **el yate**

There are a side keel *(una orza lateral)* and a central keel *una orza central.*

Fishing

I would like to go fishing.
Quisiera salir a pescar.

Do I need a fishing license?
¿Necesito un permiso para poder pescar?

What does the license cost per day / per week?
¿Cuánto cuesta la licencia por día / por semana?

Where can I get a license?
¿Dónde puedo adquirir la licencia?

I am interested in deep-sea fishing.
Tengo interés en la pesca en alta mar.

How much would a fishing trip cost?
¿Cuánto cuesta participar en una excursión de pesca?

Whom should I contact?
¿A quién puedo dirigirme?

I am particularly interested in catching ...
Tengo especial interés en la pesca con ...

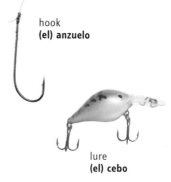

hook
(el) anzuelo

lure
(el) cebo

Which types of fish can be caught?
¿Qué tipo de peces puedo pescar?

Can we sail to other fishing grounds too?
¿Podemos ir también a otros caladeros?

fishing reel **el carrete**
fishing line **el sedal**
fishing rod **la caña de pescar**
weights / sinker **la plomada**
float **el flotador**

→ Also see FISH AND SHELLFISH, p. 117

El corcho is another word for a fishing bobber.

Hiking

Do you have a hiking map?
¿Tiene usted un mapa de las rutas de excursión?

Are the trails well marked?
¿Están bien señalados los caminos?

Is the route easy / difficult?
¿Es una excursión sencilla / pesada?

Is the route suitable for children?
¿La excursión es adecuada para niños?

Approximately what altitude is reached?
¿A qué altura se llega aproximadamente?

Where do I have to register for the hike?
¿Dónde tengo que apuntarme para la excursión?

Is there anything special to watch out for on the hike?
¿Hay que prestar especial atención a algo durante la excursión?

About how long will take me to go to ...?
¿Cuánto tiempo me tardará aproximadamente en llegar a ...?

Is the water drinkable?
¿El agua es potable?

In this area, am I allowed to ...
¿En esta zona está permitido ...
   spend the night in a tent?
   dormir en una tienda de campaña?
   light a fire?
   encender fuego?

Do I need any special permit for this area?
¿Hace falta un permiso especial para entrar en esta zona?

Where do I get the permit?
¿Dónde puedo conseguir el permiso?

Is that the right way to ...?
¿Es éste el camino a ...?

Can you show me the way on the map?
¿Puede enseñarme el camino en el mapa?

I have gotten lost.
Me he perdido.

How far is it still to ...?
¿Falta mucho para llegar a ...?

Climbing

I am looking for climbing spots in the area.
Busco lugares para alpinismo en esta región.

Where can I rent the necessary equipment?
¿Dónde puedo alquilar el equipo necesario?

Do you have guides?
¿Hay guías?

How much does a guide cost per day?
¿Cuánto cuesta un guía al día?

Do you have a guide who speaks English?
¿Hay guías que hablen inglés?

Spanish people don't go hiking as much as people in Nordic countries do.

Equipment

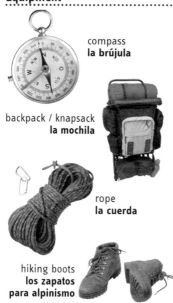

compass
la brújula

canteen
la cantimplora

backpack / knapsack
la mochila

reflective blanket **la manta aislante / térmica**

helmet **el casco**

ice ax **el hacha de hielo**

rope
la cuerda

climbing belt **la cuerda de trepar**

climbing boots **las botas de alpinismo**

emergency kit **el estuche de emergencia**

hiking boots
los zapatos para alpinismo

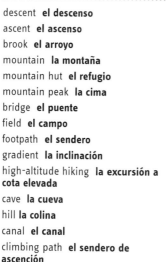

crampons **los trepadores**

flashlight **la linterna**

tent **la tienda de campaña**

Important Vocabulary

descent **el descenso**

ascent **el ascenso**

brook **el arroyo**

mountain **la montaña**

mountain hut **el refugio**

mountain peak **la cima**

bridge **el puente**

field **el campo**

footpath **el sendero**

gradient **la inclinación**

high-altitude hiking **la excursión a cota elevada**

cave **la cueva**

hill **la colina**

canal **el canal**

climbing path **el sendero de ascención**

climbing track **la cuesta**

cliff **el precipicio**

nature park **el parque natural**

sanctuary / reservation **la reserva**

pass **el paso**

mountain spring **el manantial**

degree of difficulty **el nivel de dificultad**

lake **el lago**

cable railway **el funicular**

one-day hike **la excursión de un día**

valley **el valle**

pond **el estanque**

trail **la trocha**

waterfall **la cascada**

vineyard **la viña**

meadow **la pradera**

Mountain climbing is not widely practiced in Spain or Latin America.

Nature

maple
el arce

laurel
el laurel

tree
el árbol

daisy
la margarita

beech
el haya

narcissus
el narciso

oak
el roble

carnation
el clavel

hibiscus
el hibisco

orchid
la orquídea

chestnut
el castaño

rose
la rosa

lily
la azucena

sunflower
el girasol

lime tree
el tilo

pine cone
la piña

The same word is used in Spanish for a channel of water and a television station: *un canal*.

Winter Sports

I would like to go skiing.
Quisiera esquiar.

I would like to learn skiing.
Me gustaría aprender a esquiar.

Do you have deep-snow runs?
¿Hay pistas de nieve sin preparar?

I am a beginner.
Soy principiante.

I am an experienced skier.
Soy un esquiador con experiencia.

Can you recommend a ski instructor?
¿Me puede recomendar un instructor de esquí?

Where can I rent / buy ski equipment?
¿Dónde puedo alquilar / comprar equipo de esquí?

What are the current snow / skiing conditions?
¿Cuáles son las condiciones actuales de la nieve y el esquí?

How difficult are the ski runs?
¿Qué nivel de dificultad tienen las pistas?

downhill skiing **el esquí alpino**

binding **las fijaciones**

cross-country skiing **el esquí a campo traviesa**

ski lift **el telesquí**

ski run **la pista**

sled **el trineo**

ice skates **los patines**

ski **el esquí**

ski instructor **el instructor de esquí**

ski pass **la tarjeta de esquí**

ski boot **la bota de esquiar**

ski pole **el bastón de esquí**

snowboard **el monoesquí**

wax **la cera**

cable railway **el funicular**

chair lift **el telesilla**

Spectator Sports

Is there a soccer game this week?
¿Hay algún partido de fútbol esta semana?

Where do I get tickets?
¿Dónde puedo sacar las entradas?

I would like to buy a ticket for the game of ... against ...
Quisiera sacar una entrada para el partido del ... contra el ....

What is the admission fee?
¿Cuánto cuesta la entrada?

Which teams are playing?
¿Qué equipos juegan?

What is the score?
¿Cómo va el partido?

A tie / draw.
Empatado.

4 to 1 for the Atletico of Madrid.
4 a 1 para el Atlético de Madrid.

The Atletico of Madrid won.
El Atlético de Madrid ganó.

The Atletico of Madrid lost.
El Atlético de Madrid perdió.

Can you please explain the rules to me?
¿Podría explicarme las reglas, por favor?

referee
el árbitro

win
la victoria

loss / defeat
la derrota

If you mean a ski pass, you can also say *carnet de esquí*.

Culture and Entertainment

At the Tourist Office

Excuse me, can you please help me?
¿Perdone, me puede ayudar, por favor?

I am looking for the tourist office.
Busco la oficina de turismo.

Please may I have ...
Me da por favor ...

  a map.
  un mapa de la ciudad.
  a subway map.
  un mapa del metro.
  brochures.
  unos folletos.

Do you have information on ...
¿Me puede dar informaciones acerca de ...

  cultural events?
  las actividades culturales?
  city tours?
  las giras turísticas de la ciudad?
  sights?
  los lugares de interés?
  restaurants?
  los restaurantes?
  hotels?
  los hoteles?

I would like a calendar of events.
Quisiera un programa de actividades.

Are there any interesting events this week?
¿Hay algún espectáculo interesante esta semana?

What are the main sights?
¿Cuáles son los lugares de interés más importantes?

I would like to see ...
Me gustaría ver ...

I am particularly interested in art.
El arte me interesa mucho.

Are there English-speaking guides?
¿Hay guías que hablen inglés?

What does a city tour cost?
¿Cuánto cuesta una gira por la ciudad?

When does it begin?
¿A qué hora empieza?

What is included in the price?
¿Qué incluye el precio?

When will we be back?
¿A qué hora estaremos de regreso?

Can you get tickets for me?
¿Podría conseguirme las entradas?

Another expression for the tourist office is *la oficina de información turística.*

What Is There?

old city **el centro histórico**
antiques **las antigüedades**
archaeology **la arqueología**
architecture **la arquitectura**
excavations **las excavaciones**
exhibition **la exposición**
building **el edificio**
library **la biblioteca**
sculpture **la escultura**
botany **la botánica**
botanical gardens **el jardín botánico**
bridge **el puente**
castle **el castillo**
well **la fuente**
monument **el monumento**
shopping center **el centro comercial**
factory **la fábrica**
fortress **la fortaleza**
flea market **el rastro**
graveyard / cemetery **el cementerio**
gallery **la galería**
garden **el jardín**
birthplace **la casa natal**
painting **las pinturas / los cuadros**
geology **la geología**
history **la historia**

glass painting **la decoración del cristal**
grave **la tumba**
dock **el muelle**
caves **las cuevas**
city center **el centro de la ciudad**
ceramics **las cerámicas**
cliff **el escollo / la roca**
concert hall **la sala de conciertos**
art **el arte**
art gallery **la galería de arte**
handicrafts **la artesanía**

landscape **el paisaje**
literature **la literatura**
painting **la pintura**
market **el mercado**
fair **la feria**
furniture **el amoblado**
fashion **la moda**
coins **las monedas**
museum **el museo**
music **la música**
national park **el parque nacional**
reservation / sanctuary **la reserva natural**
opera **la ópera**
park **el parque**
planetarium **el planetario**
town hall **el ayuntamiento**
religion **la religión**
reservation **la reserva**
ruins **las ruinas**
canyon **el cañón / el desfiladero**
lake **el lago**
stadium **el estadio**
statue **la estatua**
dam **la represa / la presa**
wetland / swamp **el pantano**
theater **el teatro**
ceramics / pottery **la cerámica**
tower **la torre**
remains / ruins **los restos arqueológicos**
university **la universidad**
ornithology **la ornitología**
volcano **el volcán**
economy / finance **la economía**
skyscraper **el rascacielo**
desert **el desierto**
zoo **el parque zoológico**

The word *castillo* is used for both castle and fortress.

Churches and Monasteries

abbey **la abadía**
altar **el altar**
arch **el arco**
choir **el coro**
Christian **el cristiano**
Christianity **el cristianismo**
cathedral **la catedral**
choir loft **la galería del coro**
windows **las ventanas**
wing **el ala**
frieze **el friso**

dome **la cúpula**
nave **la nave**
mass **la misa**
Middle Ages **la edad media**
medieval **medieval**
center nave **la nave central**
Muslim **el musulmán**

priest **el sacerdote**
bell **la campana**
Gothic **el estilo gótico**
church service **la misa**
Jew **el judío**
pulpit **el púlpito**
chapel **la capilla**
cathedral **la catedral**
Catholic **el católico**
church **la iglesia**
steeple **el campanario**
cloister **el convento**
denomination **la creencia**
cross **la cruz**
cloisters **el claustro**
crypt **la cripta**

pilgrim **el peregrino**
main entrance **el portal**
Protestant **el protestante**
transept **la nave transversal**
relief **el relieve**
religion **la religión**
romanesque **el estilo románico**
rosette **el rosetón**
sacristy **la sacristía**
sarcophagus **el sarcófago**
side aisle **la nave lateral**
synagogue **la sinagoga**
font **la pila bautismal**
temple **el templo**
tower **la torre**
mural **el fresco**

The Catholic mass is *la misa*; the religious service for other religions is called *el oficio*.

In the Museum

When is the museum open?
¿A qué hora abre el museo?

How much is the admission?
¿Cuánto cuesta la entrada?

How much does a guided tour cost?
¿Cuánto cuesta un recorrido con guía?

Two admission tickets for adults, please.
Dos entradas para adultos, por favor.

Three admission tickets for children.
Tres entradas para niños.

Is there an English-language catalog?
¿Tienen catálogos en inglés?

Can I take photographs?
¿Está permitido sacar fotografías?

Is there a discount for ...
¿Hay descuentos para ...
    children?
    niños?
    groups?
    grupos?
    senior citizens?
    ancianos?
    students?
    estudiantes?
    handicapped?
    minusválidos?

What is the name of the ...
¿Cómo se llama ...
    architect?
    el arquitecto?
    artist?
    el artista?
    founder?
    el fundador?

Who has created ...
¿De quién es ...
    the painting?
    la pintura?
    the sculpture?
    la escultura?

    the music?
    la música?
    the exhibition?
    la exposición?

Do you have a poster / postcard of ... ?
¿Tiene pósters / postales de ... ?

Notices and Signs

Prohibido sacar fotografías
Photography prohibited

Guardarropa
Cloakroom

Cerrado
Closed

Cajas de seguridad
Lockers

Servicios
Toilets

Cerrado por restauración
Closed for renovation

What's It Like?

amusing **divertido**
impressive **impresionante**
astonishing **asombroso**
magnificent **maravilloso**
ugly **feo**
splendid **espléndido**
pretty **bonito**
romantic **romántico**
dreadful **horrible**
strange / unusual **raro**
great **fantástico**
uncanny **inquietante**

To express how *neat* something was, people also use the word *estupendo*.

What Is There?

ballet **el ballet**

discotheque / disco **la discoteca**

festival **el festival**

film **la película**

folklore **el folclor / el folklore**

jazz concert **el concierto de jazz**

cabaret **el cabaret**

concert **el concierto**

musical **el musical**

nightclub **el club nocturno**

opera **la ópera**

operetta **la opereta**

procession **la procesión**

casino **el casino**

theater **el teatro**

parade **el desfile**

circus **el circo**

What You Hear or Read

Lo siento, están agotadas todas las entradas.
I'm sorry, we are sold out.

La entrada, por favor.
Your ticket, please.

Este es su lugar.
Here is your seat.

el guardarropa
cloakroom

los servicios higiénicos
toilets

la salida
exit

Information

What is playing at the theater tonight?
¿Qué hay esta noche en el teatro?

Can you recommend a play?
¿Qué obra de teatro me recomienda?

What is playing at the cinema today?
¿Qué ponen hoy en el cine?

I would like to see a good musical.
Me gustaría ver un buen musical.

Where is ...
¿Donde está ...
    the cinema / movie theater?
    el cine?
    the theater?
    el teatro?
    the concert hall?
    la sala de conciertos?
    the opera?
    la ópera?

When does the performance begin?
¿A qué hora empieza la representación?

How long is the play?
¿Cuánto tiempo dura la obra?

When does the show end?
¿Cuándo términa?

Where is the cloakroom, please?
¿Dónde está el guardarropa, por favor?

How long is the intermission?
¿Cuánto tiempo dura la pausa?

Is evening attire necessary?
¿Es necesario ir vestido de etiqueta?

Another word for a woman's evening dress is *el traje de noche*.

Theater and Concerts

What type of play is this?
¿Qué tipo de obra es ésta?
  comedy
  la comedia
  tragedy
  la tragedia
  drama
  el drama

Who is the playwright?
¿De quién es la obra?

Who is the set designer?
¿De quién es la escenografía?

Who plays the leading role?
¿Quién es el protagonista?

Who are ...
¿Quiénes son ...
  the actors?
  los actores?
  the singers?
  los cantantes?
  the dancers?
  los bailarines?

Who is ...
¿Quién es ...
  the director?
  el director?
  the choreographer?
  el coreógrafo?
  the conductor?
  el director de orquesta?
  the author
  el autor?
  the star?
  la estrella?
  the orchestra?
  la orquesta?
  the composer?
  el compositor?

Can I rent binoculars?
¿Puedo alquilar un par de gemelos?

Buying Tickets

Do you still have tickets for today?
¿Quedan entradas para la función de hoy?

Do you have also discounted tickets?
¿Tienen entradas rebajadas?

How much does a seat cost in a ...
¿Cuánto cuesta una entrada ...
  lower price range?
  de precio más bajo?
  expensive price range?
  de precio más alto?

I would like a seat ...
Quiero un asiento ...
  in the orchestra.
  en la platea.
  iin the balcony.
  en la galería.
  in the middle.
  en el centro.
  with a good view.
  con buena vista.
  in the box.
  en el palco.

I would like to reserve three tickets.
Quisiera reservar tres entradas.

Discos and Nightclubs

Is there a place where we can have fun tonight?
¿Dónde se puede uno divertir por la noche?

Is there a disco around here?
¿Hay discotecas por aquí?

What does one wear?
¿Cómo tengo que vestirme?

Are there young / older people there?
¿Hay gente joven o ya mayor allá?

Would you like to dance?
¿Baila conmigo?

May I invite you?
¿Me permite invitarla?

Can I take you home?
¿Me permite acompañarla a casa?

The cheapest tickets to the theater are for *el paraíso* (Spain) or *la galería* (America).

Offices and Institutions

bank **el banco**

library **la biblioteca**

embassy **la embajada**

city hall **el municipio**

immigration authority **el departamento de extranjería**

fire department **los bomberos**

lost and found **la oficina de objetos perdidos**

consulate **el consulado**

hospital **el hospital**

police **la policía**

police station **estación de policía / cuartel de policía / la comisaría**

post office **correos**

town hall **el ayuntamiento**

environmental protection agency **el departamento del medio ambiente**

Where can I find the nearest police station?
¿Dónde está la estación de policía más cercana?

When do the banks open?
¿Cuándo abren los bancos?

When are you open?
¿A qué hora abre?

Are you also open on Saturdays?
¿Abren también los sábados?

Closed
Cerrado

I am looking for ...
Busco ...

The Right Address

Another word for *town hall* is *la municipalidad*.

At the Post Office Counter

Where is the nearest post office?
¿Dónde está la oficina de correos más cercana?

What are the working hours?
¿Cuál es el horario de apertura?

Where is the nearest mailbox?
¿Dónde hay un buzón aquí cerca?

What color is it?
¿De qué color es?

How much does a letter cost ...
¿Cuánto cuesta enviar una carta ...
  to the United States?
  a los Estados Unidos?
  to Australia?
  a Australia?
  to New Zeland?
  a Nueva Zelanda?

How long does a letter take to ... ?
¿Cuánto tiempo tarda la carta en llegar a ...?

Please give me a 70-cent stamp.
Deme una estampilla / un sello de 70 céntinos, por favor.

Can you help me fill this out?
¿Podría ayudarme a rellenarlo?

Next day delivery, please.
Para envío mañana, por favor.

Can I send a fax from here?
¿Puedo enviar un fax desde aquí?

Can I insure this parcel?
¿Puedo asegurar este paquete?

sender **el remitente**

address **la dirección**

stamp **la estampilla / el sello**

printed matter **el impreso**

express mail **la carta urgente**

registered mail **el correo certificado**

recipient **el destinatario**

acknowledgment **el acuse de recibo**

fax **el fax**

charge **la tarifa**

money order **el giro postal**

weight **el peso**

airmail **el correo aéreo**

COD **contra reembolso**

small parcel **el paquete pequeño**

parcel **el paquete**

postage **el franqueo / el porte**

remittance **el giro postal**

postcard **la tarjeta postal**

general delivery **en lista de correos**

zip code **el código postal**

counter **la ventanilla**

telegram **el telegrama**

telex **el télex**

insurance **el seguro**

customs declaration **la declaración de aduana**

 ## Telegrams

I would like to send a telegram.
Quiero enviar un telegrama.

How much does it cost per word?
¿Cuánto cuesta una palabra?

Will the telegram arrive today?
¿Llegará hoy el telegrama?

Picking Up Mail

Is there any mail for me?
¿Ha llegado correo para mí?

My name is ...
Mi nombre es ...

Your ID, please.
Su documento de identidad, por favor.

A shorter word for *registered mail* is *certificado.*

The Bank

Where is the nearest bank?
¿Dónde está el banco más cercano?

I would like to cash a traveler's check.
Quisiera hacer efectivo un cheque de viajero.

What is the exchange rate today?
¿A cuánto está el tipo de cambio hoy?

I would like to withdraw 400 dollars with my credit card.
Quiero sacar 400 dólares con mi tarjeta de crédito.

I am having problems with your automatic teller. Would you please help me?
Tengo problemas con el cajero automático. ¿Me puede ayudar, por favor?

The automatic teller has taken my credit card.
El cajero automático no me devuelve mi tarjeta de crédito.

I would like to make a transfer.
Quisiera hacer un giro.

I would like to open an account.
Quisiera abrir una cuenta.

Can you give me the customer service number of my credit card company?
¿Podría darme el número del servicio de atención al cliente de la compañía de mi tarjeta de crédito?

My credit card was stolen.
Me han robado la tarjeta de crédito.

I would like to have my card stopped.
Quiero bloquear mi tarjeta de crédito.

In Latin America and Spain you can pay using major credit cards, at least in the larger cities and in tourist areas.

The prices of dollars and euros fluctuate daily in America, and checking your newspaper is a good idea.

Spain is part of the European Union, and its currency is now the euro. The coin denominations are 1, 2, 5, 10, 20, and 50 cents and 1 and 2 euro. Bills are 5, 10, 20, 50, 100, 200, and 500 euro.

It's always a good idea to keep a small supply of coins available, especially for taxis and public transportation.

cash **el dinero en efectivo**

PIN (personal identification number) **el número secreto**

remittance **el giro**

automatic teller (ATM) **el cajero automático**

money exchange **el cambio de divisa**

cash register / cashier **la caja**

change **el dinero suelto**

credit card **la tarjeta de crédito**

coins **las monedas**

working hours **los horarios de apertura**

traveler's check **el cheque de viajero**

counter **la ventanilla**

check **el cheque**

bills / notes **los billetes**

transfer **la transferencia / el giro**

currency **la divisa**

exchange rate **el tipo de cambio**

exchange bureau **la oficina de cambio**

La caja can mean both *cash register* and *box*.

Help! Thief!

My car was broken into.
Han forzado mi coche.

Where did it happen?
¿Dónde le ha sucedido?

There in the parking lot.
En el estacionamiento / aparcamiento.

When did it happen?
¿A qué hora pasó eso?

Between 11 a.m. and 12 noon.
Entre las once y la una de la tarde.

What was stolen?
¿Qué le han robado?

All our luggage.
Todo nuestro equipaje.

Your ID, please.
Su documento de identidad, por favor

That was also stolen.
También me lo han robado.

A parking lot is sometimes also called *un aparcamiento.*

At the Police Station

Help!
¡Socorro!

Where is the nearest police station?
¿Dónde está la estación de policía más cercana?

I would like to do make a complaint.
Quisiera poner una denuncia.

I would like to report an accident.
Quiero reportar un accidente.

Does anyone here speak English?
¿Hay alguien que hable inglés?

I don't understand you.
No le entiendo.

I would like a lawyer.
Quiero hablar con un abogado.

I need an interpreter.
Necesito un intérprete.

Please inform my consulate.
Notifique al consulado de mi país, por favor.

Please inform me of my rights.
Por favor infórmeme qué derechos tengo.

I need a report for my insurance agency.
Necesito un certificado para mi agencia de seguro.

I am not responsible.
No ha sido culpa mía.

What Happened?

I have lost my purse.
He perdido el monedero.

My money has been stolen.
Me han robado el dinero.

My car was broken into.
Han forzado mi coche.

I have been cheated.
Me han engañado.

I have been molested.
Me han acosado sexualmente.

I have been robbed.
Me han desvalijado.

I have been attacked / mugged.
Me han asaltado.

My son is missing.
Mi hijo ha desaparecido.

I have been raped.
Me han violado.

If only *sexual harassment* is involved, the term is *importunación sexual*.

What Was Stolen?

ID **el documento de identidad**
car **el automóvil / el auto / el coche**
car documents **los papeles del auto**
wallet **la cartera**
camera **la cámara**
purse **el monedero**
luggage **el equipaje**
handbag **el bolso**
credit card **la tarjeta de crédito**
check **el cheque**
watch **el reloj**

Lost and Found

Where is the lost and found office?
¿Dónde está la oficina de objetos perdidos?

I have lost my watch.
He perdido mi reloj.

I have left my handbag somewhere.
He dejado olvidado mi bolso.

Has a suitcase been handed to you?
¿Ha sido entregada aquí una maleta?

Would you please get in touch with me?
¿Podría avisarme, por favor?

Here is my address.
Aquí tiene mi dirección.

Important Vocabulary

lawyer **el abogado**
complaint **la denuncia**
statement **la declaración**
right to remain silent **el derecho de recusación de declaración**
swindler / cheat **el estafador**

thief **el ladrón**
theft **el robo**
prison **la prisión**
legal proceedings **los procedimientos legales / la sesión judicial**
marriage fraud **la defraudación matrimonial**
report **el protocolo**
trial **el proceso**
drugs **las drogas / los estupefacientes**
judge **el juez**
district attorney **el fiscal**
pickpocket **el carterista**
mugging **el asalto**
crime **el delito**

rape **la violación**
arrest **el arresto**

Fiscal designates a district attorney; in another sense it refers to taxes.

First Aid

I fell down.
Me he caído.

I was hit by a car.
Me han atropellado.

I was attacked.
Me han asaltado.

I need a doctor.
Necesito un doctor.

Call an ambulance please.
Llame una ambulancia, por favor.

I have injured my arm.
Me he hecho daño en el brazo.

I cannot move my leg.
No puedo mover la pierna.

I have broken my arm.
Me he roto el brazo.

I am bleeding.
Estoy sangrando.

My blood type is ...
Mi grupo sanguíneo es ...

I have ...
Padezco de ...
  asthma
  asma
  diabetes
  diabetes
  hypertension
  hipertensión
  low blood pressure
  tensión baja

AIDS
SIDA

I am allergic to ...
Tengo alergia a ...
  mites
  los ácaros
  dust
  el polvo
  animal fur
  el pelo de los animales
  grass
  las hierbas / las plantas gramíneas
  pollen
  el polen

I am allergic to penicillin.
Soy alérgico a la penicilina.

I am pregnant.
Estoy embarazada.

What You Hear

¿Puedo ayudarle?
Can I help you?

¿Quiere que llame una ambulancia?
Should I call an ambulance?

Permanezca tranquilo.
Just lie there quietly.

¡Voy a pedir ayuda!
I will get help!

En seguida vienen a socorrerle.
Help is on the way.

Se ha desmayado.
You were unconscious.

El embarazo means *the pregnancy*; the word also is used for *embarrassment* and *awkwardness*.

Drugstore

Where is the nearest drugstore?
¿Dónde está la farmacia más cercana?

I need some medicine for diarrhea.
Necesito un remedio para la diarrea.

I need some bandages.
Necesito vendajes.

Can I wait for it?
¿Puedo esperar aquí?

This medication is only by prescription.
Este medicamento requiere receta médica.

How do I take the medicine?
¿Cómo debo tomarlo?

laxative **el laxante**

eye drops **el colirio**

sedative / tranquilizer **el sedante**

ointment for burns **la pomada para las quemaduras**

disinfectant **el desinfectante**

disposable needles / syringes **las jeringas desechables**

throat lozenges / cough drops **las pastillas para la garganta**

cough syrup **el jarabe para la tos**

insect repellent **el repelente de insectos**

nose decongestant **el descongestante nasal**

antihistamine **la antihistamina**

insulin **la insulina**

ear drops **las gotas para los oídos**

sleeping pills **las pastillas para dormir**

painkiller **el analgésico**

pregnancy test **la prueba del embarazo**

cotton **el algodón hidrófilo**

thermometer
el termómetro

condoms
condones

band-aids
las tiritas

hot-water bottle
la bolsa de agua caliente

Taking Medications

external **de uso externo**

internal **de uso interno**

dissolve in water **disolver en el agua**

on an empty stomach **en ayunas**

let it melt in the mouth **dejar deshacerse en la boca**

swallow without chewing **vía oral sin masticar**

before / after meals **antes / después de las comidas**

twice daily **dos veces al día**

every three hours **cada tres horas**

Use *medicamento, medicina* or *remedio* for any *medication*.

The Human Body

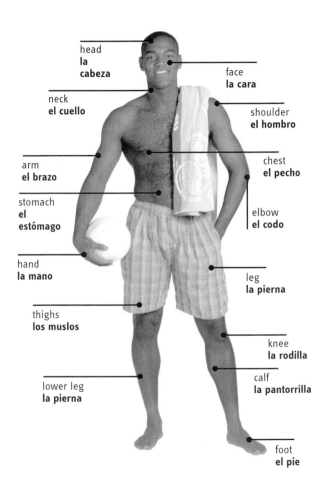

head
la cabeza

face
la cara

neck
el cuello

shoulder
el hombro

arm
el brazo

chest
el pecho

stomach
el estómago

elbow
el codo

hand
la mano

leg
la pierna

thighs
los muslos

knee
la rodilla

calf
la pantorrilla

lower leg
la pierna

foot
el pie

If someone has a belly, the word used is *una barriga*.

The Human Body

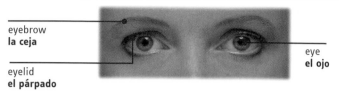

eyebrow
la ceja

eye
el ojo

eyelid
el párpado

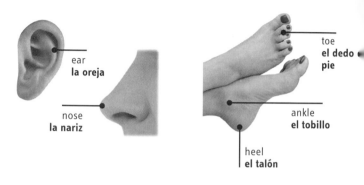

ear
la oreja

nose
la nariz

toe
el dedo del pie

ankle
el tobillo

heel
el talón

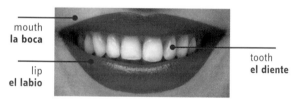

mouth
la boca

tooth
el diente

lip
el labio

finger
los dedos

middle finger
el dedo del corazón

ring finger
el dedo anular

forefinger
el dedo índice

little finger /
pinkie
**el dedo
meñique**

thumb
el dedo pulgar

wrist
la muñeca

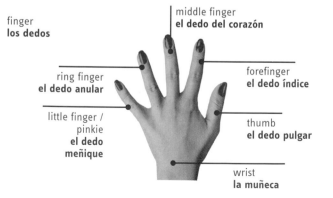

Amusingly, the toes are referred to as the *foot fingers*.

Parts of the Body

artery **la arteria**

bladder **la vejiga**

appendix **el apéndice**

blood **la sangre**

bronchial tubes **los bronquios**

intestine **el intestino**

gallbladder **la vesícula biliar**

brain **el cerebro**

joint **la articulación**

skin **la piel**

heart **el corazón**

hip **la cadera**

jaw **la mandíbula**

bone **el hueso**

liver **el hígado**

lung **el pulmón**

stomach **el estómago**

tonsils **las amígdalas**

muscle **el músculo**

neck **el cuello**

nerve **el nervio**

kidneys **los riñones**

rib **la costilla**

back **la espalda**

collarbone **la clavícula**

tendon **el tendón**

vein **la vena**

spinal column **la columna vertebral**

tongue **la lengua**

At the Doctor's

Is there a doctor here?
¿Hay un doctor aquí?

What are the office hours?
¿Cuál es el horario de consultas?

Can I come immediately?
¿Puedo ir inmediatamente?

Can the doctor see me at home?
¿Podría el doctor venir a verme en mi casa?

I have a pain.
Tengo dolor.

I feel weak.
Me siento débil.

I feel ...
Me siento ...
   sick
   mal
   dizzy
   mareado

I have a cough.
Tengo tos.

I take high blood pressure medicine.
Tomo medicinas para la hipertensión.

The name of the medication is ...
La medicina se llama ...

Can you prescribe a medicine for me?
¿Puede recetarme una medicina?

Do I need a prescription for it?
¿Necesito una receta para poder comprarla?

I have insurance.
Tengo seguro de enfermedad.

Here is my international insurance card.
Aquí tiene mi certificado internacional de seguro de salud.

Please give me the bill and a copy of your report.
Me da la factura y una copia del informe médico, por favor.

If you have circulation problems, you can also say, *tengo problemas de circulación.*

What the Doctor Says

¿Qué molestias tiene?
What is your problem?

¿Dónde le duele?
Where does it hurt?

¿Desde cuándo?
For how long?

¿Con qué frecuencia?
How often?

¿Dónde le duele?
Where does it hurt?

¿Le duele aquí?
Does this hurt?

Quítese la ropa, por favor.
Please undress.

Respire profundamente.
Take a deep breath.

Abra la boca.
Open your mouth.

Saque la lengua.
Stick out your tongue.

Tosa.
Cough.

Otra vez.
Once again.

¿Fuma?
Do you smoke?

¿Bebe alcohol?
Do you drink alcohol?

¿Padece de alergia?
Do you have any allergies?

¿Toma usted medicinas regularmente?
Do you take any medication regularly?

¿Toma píldoras anticonceptivas?
Are you taking the pill?

Le voy a recetar una medicina.
I will prescribe something for you.

Le voy a poner una inyección.
I will give you a shot.

¿Tiene usted un carnet de vacunación?
Do you have a vaccination certificate?

Es necesario suturar la herida.
The wound must be stitched.

Tenemos que sacarle una radiografía.
You must have an x-ray.

Tiene que consultar a un especialista.
You must see a specialist.

Tiene que operarse.
You must have an operation.

Tiene que permanecer unos días en cama.
You must stay in bed a few days.

Regrese mañana.
Come back tomorrow.

No es nada grave.
It is nothing serious.

No tiene nada.
There is nothing wrong with you.

Specialists

surgeon
el cirujano

gynecologist
el ginecólogo

ear, nose and throat specialist
el otorrinolaringólogo

internist
el internista

pediatrician
el pediatra

psychiatrist
el psiquiatra

urologist
el urólogo

An eye doctor is un *oftalmólogo*.

Illnesses

allergy **la alergia**

angina **la angina de pecho**

rash **el salpullido / el exantema**

lump / swelling **la hinchazón**

bite **la picadura / la mordedura**

boil **el furúnculo**

stomachache **el dolor abdominal**

flatulence **la flatulencia**

inflammation of the bladder **la cistitis**

appendicitis **la apendicitis**

hemorrhage **la hemorragia**

high blood pressure **la hipertensión**

bleeding **el sangramiento**

burn **la quemadura**

bronchitis **la bronquitis**

diabetes **la diabetes**

diphteria **la difteria**

diarrhea **la diarrea**

inflammation **la inflamación**

cold **el resfriado**

fever **la fiebre / la calentura**

concussion **la conmoción cerebral**

jaundice **la ictericia**

ulcer **la úlcera**

flu **la gripe**

sore throat **el dolor de garganta**

heart problems **los trastornos cardíacos**

heart attack **el infarto cardíaco**

hay fever **la alergia / la reacción alérgica**

cough **la tos**

infection **la infección**

insect bite **la picadura de insecto**

sciatica **la ciática**

whooping cough **la tos ferina**

fracture **la fractura**

headache **el dolor de cabeza**

cancer **el cáncer**

circulatory disorder **el trastorno circulatorio**

paralysis **la parálisis**

pneumonia **la pulmonía**

stomachache **el dolor de estómago**

tonsillitis **la amigdalitis**

measles **el sarampión**

migraine **la migraña / la jaqueca**

mumps **las paperas**

nosebleed **la hemorragia nasal**

smallpox **la viruela**

bruise **la contusión**

rheumatism **el reumatismo**

German measles **la rubeola**

backache **el dolor de espalda**

salmonella **la salmonela**

gash **la herida por corte**

head cold **el catarro**

chills **el escalofrío**

swelling **la tumefacción**

stitch in the side **la puntada / los dolores de costado**

heartburn **la acidez estomacal**

sunburn **la quemadura por el sol**

sunstroke **la insolación**

tetanus **el tétano**

nausea **la náusea**

burn **la quemadura**

poisoning **la intoxicación**

injury **la lesión**

sprain **la luxación**

constipation **el estreñimiento**

viral illness **la enfermedad viral**

chickenpox **la varicela**

wound **la herida**

strain **la distensión**

The medical term for heartburn is *acedía* or *acidez estomacal*.

What's the Matter?

I have cut myself.
Me he cortado.

I have been bitten by ...
Me ha picado un ...

I have something in my eye.
Tengo algo en el ojo.

My child fell down.
Mi hijo se ha caído.

My ankle is swollen.
Tengo hinchado el tobillo.

I have vomited.
He vomitado.

At the Gynecologist's

¿Está embarazada?
Are you pregnant?

¿Toma píldoras anticonceptivas?
Are you taking the pill? / Are you on the pill?

¿Cuándo fue su última menstruación?
When was your last period?

I am having my period.
Estoy menstruando.

I have not had a period for two months.
La última menstruación fue hace dos meses.

I think I am pregnant.
Creo que estoy embarazada.

I am pregnant.
Estoy embarazada.

I have menstrual pains.
Tengo dolores ocasionados por la menstruación.

I take the pill. / I'm on the pill.
Estoy tomando la píldora anticonceptiva.

pregnancy test **la prueba del embarazo**

abortion **el aborto**

inflammation of the bladder **la cistitis**

breast **el seno**

fallopian tubes **la trompa de Falopio**

miscarriage **el aborto no intencional**

uterus **el útero**

condom **el condón**

cramp **el calambre**

vaginitis **la vaginitis**

pregnancy **el embarazo**

intrauterine device **el DIU**

vagina **la vagina**

If you want to say that you have a cold, you say *tengo un resfriado.*

At the Dentist's

Is there a dentist here?
¿Hay algún dentista aquí?

I need an appointment urgently.
Necesito urgentemente una cita.

I have a toothache.
Tengo dolor de muelas.

I have lost a filling.
Se me ha caído el empaste.

I have broken a tooth.
Se me ha roto una muela.

My denture broke.
Se me rompió la dentadura postiza.

I would like a local anesthetic.
Quiero anestesia local.

Enjuague, por favor.
Rinse, please.

Le voy a empastar el diente.
I will fill your tooth.

Le voy a hacer un tratamiento provisional.
I'm only treating it temporarily.

¿Quiere que le ponga una inyección?
Would you like an injection?

Tengo que sacarle el diente.
I have to remove / pull the tooth.

abscess **el absceso**
anesthetic **la anestesia**
inflammation **la inflamación**
denture **la dentadura postiza**
dental surgeon **el ortodoncista**
crown **la corona / la funda**
nerve **el nervio**
filling **el empaste**

wisdom tooth **la muela del juicio**
root-canal work **el tratamiento de la raíz**
bridge (dental) **el puente dental**
gum **la encía**
toothache **el dolor de muela**
braces **la abrazadera dental**
root (of the tooth) **la raíz**

Another word for *filling* is *una emplombadura*; *el relleno*, on the other hand, designates the filling in a food item.

In the Hospital

Does anybody speak English here?
¿Hay alguien que hable inglés aquí?

Please speak more slowly.
Hable más despacio, por favor

I would like to be flown home.
Quiero regresar en avión.

I have repatriation insurance.
Tengo un seguro para la repatriación.

What do I have?
¿Qué tengo?

Do I have to have an operation?
¿Tengo que operarme?

How long do I have to stay in the hospital?
¿Cuánto tiempo tengo que quedarme en el hospital?

Can you please give me a pain killer?
¿Puede darme un analgésico, por favor?

Will you please inform my family.
¿Puede informar a mi familia, por favor?

bed **la cama**

bedpan **el orinal**

blood transfusion **la transfusión de sangre**

surgeon **el cirujano**

call-button **la campanilla**

male nurse **el enfermero**

nurse **la enfermera**

anesthesia **la anestesia**

operation **la operación**

wheelchair **la silla de ruedas**

injection **la inyección**

The needle used to give a shot is called *una jeringa*.

Business Travel

At the Reception Desk

I have made an appointment with Mr. Smith.
Tengo una cita con el Señor Smith.

Mr. Pérez is expecting me.
El Sr. Pérez me está esperando.

Would you please tell him I'm here.
¿Podría avisar que he llegado, por favor?

Here is my card.
Aquí tiene mi tarjeta de visita.

I am sorry, I am somewhat late.
Lo siento, he llegado un poco tarde.

At the Conference Table

...sends his regards to you.
Muchos recuerdos de parte del señor ...

Our company would be pleased to offer you the following.
Nuestra empresa quisiera presentarle la siguiente oferta.

Is that your final offer?
¿Es su mejor oferta?

I'm sorry, that's our limit.
Lo siento, ese es nuestro límite.

I think there is a misunderstanding.
Creo que hay un malentendido.

That is an interesting suggestion.
Es una sugerencia muy interesante.

Can you explain that in more detail?
¿Podría usted explicármelo más detalladamente?

What exactly are you thinking of?
¿Qué es lo que usted se imagina exactamente?

Let's summarize ...
En síntesis...

Let me put it like this.
Déjeme expresarlo de la manera siguiente.

Would you excuse me a moment?
¡Discúlpeme un momento!

I must discuss this with my company first.
Tengo que hablar primero con mi empresa.

We will think it over.
Lo pensaremos.

We will check that.
Lo verificaremos.

Could I make a phone call?
¿Puedo hacer una llamada?

Could we make another appointment for tomorrow?
¿Podríamos concertar otra cita para mañana?

We will stay in touch by phone.
Mantendremos el contacto por teléfono.

Thank you for the constructive discussion.
Muchas gracias por esta conversación tan constructiva.

I am very pleased with our negotiations.
Estoy muy satisfecho con nuestras negociaciones.

To our successful cooperation.
Por una colaboración exitosa.

In Spain and Latin America important business transactions are often conducted over a good meal.

Important Vocabulary

conclusion **la conclusión**

shares **las acciones**

offer **la oferta**

investment **la inversión**

import limitations / restrictions **las restricciones a la importación**

purchase price **el precio de compra**

euro **el euro**

European Union **la Unión Europea**

freight charges **los gastos de transporte**

guarantee **la garantía**

business partner **el socio**

business meeting **la cita de negocios**

law **la ley**

profit **el beneficio**

liability **la responsabilidad**

trade agreement **el acuerdo comercial**

profit margin **el margen de ganancias**

manufacturer **el fabricante**

fee **el honorario**

import **la importación**

colleague **el colega**

conditions **las condiciones**

conference **la conferencia**

cooperation **la cooperación**

expenses / costs **los gastos / costos**

retail / selling price **el precio de**

venta al público

supplier **el proveedor**

licensing fee **la tasa de licencia**

marketing **la mercadotecnia / el marketing**

sales tax **el IVA**

employee **el empleado**

price **el precio**

minutes (of a meeting) **el protocolo**

commission **la comisión**

discount / rebate **el descuento**

invoice **la factura**

taxes **los impuestos**

price per piece **el precio por unidad**

agenda **la orden del día**

royalties **las regalías**

transportation costs **los gastos de transporte**

takeover **la adquisición de una empresa por otra**

negotiation **la negociación**

loss **la pérdida**

insurance **el seguro**

representative / agent **el representante / el agente**

business card **la tarjeta profesional**

chairman **el presidente**

customs regulations **las disposiciones de aduana**

The word for *shipping charges* by ship or truck are *el flete.*

Corporate Structure

Corporation
la sociedad anónima / corporación

incorporated
constituido legalmente en corporación

board of trustees
el consejo de administración

chairman of the board
el presidente del consejo de administración

advisory board
el consejo consultivo

board of directors
la junta directiva

advertising / marketing manager
el jefe de la sección de publicidad / marketing

sales manager
el jefe de ventas

secretary
el secretario / la secretaria

assistant
el asistente / la asistente

chief executive officer (CEO), president
el presidente de la junta directiva

board member
el miembro de la junta directiva

general manager
el gerente de la empresa

executive vice president
el vicepresidente ejecutivo

divison manager
el jefe de división

department manager
el jefe de departamento

general manager
el gerente general

authorized officer
el apoderado

Spanish and North American companies are often structured in different ways.

Contracts

appendix **el anexo**

order **el pedido**

security **la fianza / la caución**

proprietorship **la propiedad / los derechos de propiedad**

place of fulfillment of contract **el lugar de cumplimiento**

deadline **el plazo**

guarantee **la garantía**

court of jurisdiction **la jurisdicción**

business conditions **las condiciones comerciales**

liability **la responsabilidad**

purchase contract **el contrato de compraventa**

delivery terms **las condiciones de entrega**

time of delivery **el plazo de entrega**

paragraph **el artículo**

appointment **la fecha**

signature **la firma**

agreement **el acuerdo**

contract **el contrato**

penalty **la multa / la sanción**

contract in writing **el contrato por escrito**

payment terms **las condiciones de pago**

Trade Fairs

I am looking for the stall of the company ...
Busco el stand de la empresa ...

We deal in ...
Nosotros negociamos con ...

We produce ...
Nosotros producimos ...

Here is my card.
Aquí tiene mi tarjeta de visita.

Can I give you a brochure?
¿Puedo darle un folleto?

Can I show it to you?
¿Me permite que se lo muestre?

Can you send me an offer?
¿Podría mandarme una oferta?

Do you have a catalog?
¿Tiene usted algún catálogo?

Can I arrange a meeting?
¿Puedo concertar una cita?

exit **la salida**

exhibitor **el expositor**

ID card **el documento de identificación**

entrance **la entrada**

invitation **la invitación**

technical visitors **el visitante especializado**

aisle **el pasillo**

hall **el pabellón**

catalog **el catálogo**

brand **la marca**

name badge **la placa de identificación**

press conference **la conferencia de prensa**

brochure **el folleto**

stall / stand **el stand**

floor **el piso**

trademark **la marca de fábrica**

The general sales and purchasing conditions are also referred to as *las condiciones generales de venta* or *las condiciones generales de compra*.

Glossary

English – Spanish

A

a little un poco
a, an un, uno, una
abbey abadía (f)
abortion aborto (m)
abscess absceso (m)
accident accidente (m)
acknowledgment acuse de recibo (m)
acquaintance conocido (m)
actor actor (m)
actress actriz (f)
ad anuncio (m)
adapter adaptador (m)
address dirección (f)
adhesive tape cinta adhesiva (f)
administration administración (f)
aerobics ejercicios aeróbicos (m)
afterward después
again de nuevo
agent agente (m/f)
agreement acuerdo (m)
air aire (m)
air mattress colchón neumático (m)
air pump bomba de aire (f)
air-conditioning climatizador (m)
airmail correo aéreo (m)
airport aeropuerto (m)
aisle pasillo (m)
aisle seat asiento junto al pasillo (m)
alarm clock despertador (m)
all todos
allergy alergia (f)
alley callejón (m)
almond almendra (f)
altar altar (m)
alter cambiar
although aunque
aluminum foil papel de aluminio (m)
amazing asombroso
ambulance ambulancia (f)
amusing divertido
anaesthetic anestesia (f)
anchor ancla (m)
anchovy anchoa (f)
and y
anesthesia anestesia (f)

angina angina de pecho (f)
anglerfish rape (m)
angry enojado
ankle tobillo (m)
annoyed molesto
anorak anorak (m)
answering machine contestador automático (m)
antihistamine antihistamina (f)
antique store tienda de antigüedades (f)
antiques antigüedades (f)
apartment apartamento (m)
appendicitis apendicitis (f)
appendix apéndice (m)
appendix (book) apéndice (m)
apple manzana (f)
apple flan flan de manzanas (m)
apple juice jugo de manzana (m)
apple pie tarta de manzanas (f)
appointment cita (f)
apricot albaricoque (m)
April abril
apron delantal (m)
archaeology arqueología (f)
architect arquitecto (m)
architecture arquitectura (f)
area code prefijo (m)
arm brazo (m)
armchair sillón (m)
army ejército (m)
arrest arresto (m)
arrival llegada (f)
arrival time hora de llegada (f)
art arte (m)
art gallery galería de arte (f)
artery arteria (f)
artichoke alcachofa (f)
artificial leather piel sintética (f)
artist artista (m)
arts and crafts store tienda de objetos artísticos (f)
as como

ascent ascenso (m)
ashtray cenicero (m)
ask preguntar
asparagus espárrago (m)
asthma asma (m)
at a, en
at night por la noche
August agosto
aunt tía (f)
Austria Austria
author autor (m)
authorized officer apoderado (m)
automatic teller (ATM) cajero automático (m)
autumn otoño (m)
avocado aguacate (m)
awesome impresionante

B

baby cream crema para bebés (f)
baby food alimento para bebé (m)
babysitting cuidado breve del niño (m)
backache dolor de espalda (m)
backfire encendido defectuoso (m)
backpack mochila (f)
backyard patio (m)
bacon tocino (m)
bad malo
badge insignia (f)
badminton badminton (m)
badminton rackets raquetas de badminton (f)
baggage carts carro de las maletas (m)
baggage claim devolución del equipaje (f)
baggage room depósito de equipaje (m)
bait cebo (m)
baked cocido en el horno
baker panadero (m)
bakery panadería (f)
balance equilibrio (m)
balcony balcón (m)
ball pelota (f)
ballet ballet (m)
balloon globo (m)
ballpoint pen bolígrafo (m)
balsamic vinegar vinagre balsámico (m)

banana plátano (m)
bandage vendaje (m)
band-aid tirita (f)
bank banco (m)
barley cebada (f)
barrette pasador (m)
baseball béisbol (m)
basil albahaca (f)
basketball baloncesto (m)
bath baño (m)
bath slippers chanclas (f)
bathing cap gorro de baño (m)
bathrobe albornoz (m)
bathroom baño (m)
bathtub bañera (f)
batiste batista (f)
battery batería (f)
bay leaf hoja de laurel (f)
beach playa (f)
beach cabin caseta para cambiarse (f)
beach patrol servicio de playa (m)
beach towel toalla de playa (f)
beans habichuelas (f)
beard barba (f)
beautiful hermoso
beauty salon salón de belleza (m)
because porque
bed cama (f)
bed sheet sábana (f)
bedpan orinal de cama (m)
bedroom dormitorio (m)
beech haya (m)
beef vaca (f)
beef broth caldo de ternera (m)
beer cerveza (f)
before antes de
beginner principiante (m,f)
believe creer
bell campana (f)
bellboy botones (m)
belt cinturón (m)
beverage bebida (f)
bicycle pump bomba para hinchar neumáticos (f)
bicycle racing ciclismo (m)
bicycle shop tienda de bicicletas (f)
bikini bikini (m)
bill cuenta (f)
billboard cartelera (f), anuncio (m)
billfold, wallet cartera (f)
billiards billar (m)
billion mil millones

binoculars prismáticos (m)
biologist biólogo (m)
birthplace lugar natal (f)
bite mordedura (f)
black negro
black bread pan negro (m)
black tea té negro (m)
black-and-white en blanco y negro
blackberries zarzamoras (f)
bladder vejiga (f)
blanket manta (f)
blazer blazer (m)
bleeding sangramiento (m)
blinker, flasher luz intermitente (f)
blood sangre (f)
blood transfusion transfusión de sangre (f)
blood type grupo sanguíneo (m)
blouse blusa (f)
blow-dry secar con secador
blue azul
blueberries arándanos (m)
bluefish pez azul (m)
boar jabalí (m)
board of trustees consejo de administración (m)
boarding pass tarjeta de embarque (f)
boat bote (m)
boat rental alquiler de lanchas (m)
body lotion loción para el cuerpo (f)
boil furúnculo (m)
bone hueso (m)
bookkeeper contable (m)
bookseller librero (m)
bookstore librería (f)
boot bota (f)
botanical gardens jardín botánico (m)
botany botánica (f)
bottle botella (f)
bottle opener destapador (m)
bow proa (f)
bowl plato hondo (m)
bowling boliche (m)
bowtie corbata de pajarita (f)
boxing boxeo (m)
bracelet pulsera (f)
braces abrazadera dental (f)
brain cerebro (m)

braised estofado
brake freno (m), frenar
brake cable cable de freno (m)
brake fluid líquido del freno (m)
brake light luz de parada (f)
brake lining forro del freno (m)
brand marca (f)
brassiere sostén (m)
Brazil nuts nueces del Brasil (f)
bread pan (m)
breadcrumb-fried empanado
break romper
breakdown avería (f)
breakdown assistance servicio de averías (m)
breakfast desayuno (m)
breast seno (m)
bridge puente (m)
briefcase maletín (m)
broccoli brécol (m)
brochure folleto (m)
broker corredor (m)
bronchial tubes bronquios (m)
bronchitis bronquitis (f)
brooch broche (m)
brook arroyo (m)
broom escoba (f)
brother hermano (m)
browned poco asado
bruise contusión (f)
brussel sprouts coles de Bruselas (f)
bucket cubo (m)
building edificio (m)
bumper parachoques (m)
bungalow casita de campo (f)
burn quemadura (f)
bush-beans judías (f)
business card tarjeta profesional (f)
business meeting cita de negocios (f)
business partner socio (m)
businessman comerciante (m)
busy signal señal de línea ocupada (f)
butane gas gas butano (m)
butcher carnicero (m)
butter mantequilla (f)
button botón (m)
buy comprar

C

cabaret cabaret (m)
cabbage col (f)
cabin camarote (m)
cable cable (m)
cable railway funicular (m)
cactus fruit higo chumbo (m)
cake pastel (m)
calendar calendario (m)
calf pantorrilla (f), becerro (m)
call-button campanilla (f)
camera cámara (f)
camera bag bolsa para el equipo de fotografía (f)
camper autocaravana (f)
campsite campamento (m)
can lata (f)
can opener abrelatas (m)
can, be able poder
canal canal (m)
cancer cáncer (m)
candies dulces (m)
candle vela (f)
candlestick candelero (m)
candy dulces (m)
canned food conservas (f)
canoe canoa (f), piragua (f)
canoeing piragüismo (m)
canvas lienzo (m)
canyon cañón (m)
cap gorro (m)
cap with visor gorra (f)
capers alcaparras (f)
capon capón (f)
cappuccino capuchino (m)
captain capitán (m)
car coche (m)
car documents papeles del coche (m)
car ferry transbordador de automóviles (m)
car number número del vagón (m)
car racing carrera de coches (f)
carambola carambola (f)
caraway seed bread pan con comino (m)
carburettor carburador (m)
card telephone teléfono de tarjeta (m)
carnation clavel (m)
carpenter carpintero (m)
carrot zanahoria (f)
car-train autotrén (m)

cash payment pago en efectivo (m)
cash register caja (f)
cashier cajero (m)
casino casino (m)
cassette recorder grabador de casete (m)
castle castillo (m)
cat gato (m)
catalog catálogo (m)
catfish barbo (m)
cathedral catedral (f)
Catholic católico (m)
cauliflower coliflor (f)
cave cueva (f)
CD player lector de CD (m)
CD-ROM drive unidad de CD-ROM (f)
CD-writer grabadora de CDs (f)
celery apio (m)
cell phone celular (m)
cellular móvil (m)
cemetery cementerio (m)
center nave nave central (f)
center part raya mediana (f)
centimeter centímetro (m)
central heating calefacción central (f)
ceramic cerámica (f)
ceramics cerámica (m)
chain cadena (f)
chainguard cubrecadenas (m)
chair silla (f)
chair lift telesilla (m)
chairman presidente (m)
chalk tiza (f)
chambermaid camarera (f)
change dinero suelto (m)
change, exchange cambio (m)
chapel capilla (f)
charcoal carbón (m)
charcoal pencil carboncillo (m)
chard acelga (f)
charge tarifa (f)
cheap barato
check cheque (m)
checkered a cuadros
checkroom consigna (f)
cheese queso (m)
chemist químico (m)
chemistry química (f)
cherry cereza (f)
chervil perifollo (m)
chess ajedrez (m)
chestnut castaño (m), castaña (f)

chick polluelo (m)
chicken pollo (m), gallina (f)
chicken broth caldo de pollo (m)
chickenpox varicela (f)
chick-pea garbanzo (m)
chicory achicoria (f)
child care cuidado del niño (m)
children niños (m)
children's book libro infantil (m)
children's playground parque infantil (m)
children's shoes zapatos para niños (m)
child's bed cama de niño (f)
chili chile (m)
chill escalofrío (m)
chimney chimenea (f)
chimney sweep deshollinador (m)
chive cebollino (m)
chocolate chocolate (m)
chocolate bonbon bombón de chocolate (m)
choir coro (m)
choir loft galería del coro (f)
Christian cristiano (m)
Christianity cristianismo (m)
Christmas Navidad (f)
church iglesia (f)
church service misa (f)
cigarette cigarrillo (m)
cigarette holder boquilla para cigarrillos (f)
cigarillos puritos (m)
cigars puros (m)
cinema cine (m)
cinnamon canela (f)
circulatory disorder trastorno de la circulación (m)
circus circo (m)
citizens' action acción cívica (f)
citizens' initiative iniciativa cívica (f)
civil servant funcionario (m)
clam almeja (f)
cleaning limpieza (f)
cleaning products productos de limpieza (m)
cleaning rag trapo para limpiar (m)
clearing despejo (m)

cliff precipicio (m)

climbing belt cuerda de trepar (f)

climbing boots botas de montaña (m), botas de alpinismo (f)

climbing path sendero de ascención (m)

cloakroom guardarropa (m)

cloister convento (m), claustro (m)

closed cerrado

clothes dryer secadora (f)

clothesbrush cepillo para ropa (m)

clothesline cuerda para la ropa (f)

clothespin pinza de ropa (f)

clothesrack tendedero (m)

clothing store tienda de ropa (f)

cloud nube (f)

cloudy nublado

clove clavel (m)

clutch embrague (m)

coal heating calefacción de carbón (f)

coalition coalición (f)

coast costa (f)

coat abrigo (m)

cockle berberecho (m)

cocoa cacao (m)

coconut coco (m)

COD contra reembolso

codfish bacalao (m)

coffee café (m)

coffee grinder molinillo de café (m)

coffee machine cafetera (f)

coffee with ice cream café helado (m)

coin moneda (f)

coin-operated telephone teléfono público de monedas (m)

cold resfriado (m), frío

collaborator colaborador (m)

collar cuello (m)

collarbone clavícula (f)

colleague compañero de trabajo (m)

collect call llamada de cobro revertido (f)

college universidad (f)

color color (m)

color rinse tinte temporal para el cabello (m)

colored de colores

colored laundry ropa de color (f)

colored pencil lápiz de color (m)

comb peine (m)

come venir

comedy comedia (f)

commission comisión (f)

commuter train tren de cercanías (m)

compact polvo de maquillaje (m)

compartment compartimiento (m)

compass brújula (f)

complaint denuncia (f)

compressed-air bottles bombonas de aire comprimido (f)

computer expert experto de informática (m)

computer store tienda de informática (f)

concealer corrector (m)

concert concierto (m)

concert hall sala de conciertos (f)

concussion conmoción cerebral (f)

condom condón (m)

condominium condominio (m)

conductor revisor (m)

conference conferencia (f)

congressman

connecting flight vuelo de enlace (m)

constipation estreñimiento (m)

constitution constitución (f)

construction worker albañil (m)

consulate consulado (m)

contact lens lente de contacto (f)

contract contrato (m)

convention convención (f)

cook cocinero (m)

cookbook libro de cocina (m)

cooked cocido

cookie galleta (f)

cooking course curso de cocina (m)

coolant enfriador (m)

cooler champanero (m), nevera (f)

cooperation cooperación (f)

copper cobre (m)

corduroy pana (f)

cork corcho (m)

corkscrew sacacorchos (m)

corn maíz (m)

cost costo (m)

cotton algodón (m)

cough tos (f)

cough drops pastillas para la garganta (f)

cough syrup jarabe para la tos (m)

counter ventanilla (f)

country road carretera regional (f)

county condado (m)

course tipo de cambio (m)

cousin primo (m)

cover cubierta (f)

cow vaca (f)

crab cangrejo (m)

cracker galleta (f)

craftsperson artesano (m)

cramp calambre (m)

crampons trepadores (m)

cranberries arándanos agrios (m)

crawfish langostino (m)

crayon gis (m)

cream nata (f)

creamer jarrita para crema (f)

credit card tarjeta de crédito (f)

crepe crespón (m)

cress berro (m)

crew tripulación (f)

crime delito (m)

croissant media luna (m)

croquettes croquetas (f)

cross cruz (f)

cross-country skiing esquí a campo traviesa (m)

crossroad encrucijada (f), cruce (m)

crosswalk zona peatonal (f)

crown funda dental (f)

cruise crucero (m)

crypt cripta (f)

cucumber pepino (m)

cufflinks gemelos (m)

cuffs puños (m)

culture cultura (f)

cup vaso (m), taza (f)

curd requesón (m)

curl rizo (m)

curler rizador (m)

currants grosellas (f)

currency divisa (f)

current corriente (f)

curtain cortina (f)
customer service servicio de atención al cliente (m)
customs aduana (f)
customs check inspección aduanera (f)
customs declaration declaración de aduana (f)
customs regulations disposiciones aduaneras (f)
cute mono
cutlet chuleta (f)
cycling ciclismo (m)
cylinder head culata (f)
daily diariamente
dairy products productos lácteos (m)
daisy margarita (f)
dam presa (f)
dance baile (m)
dandruff caspa (f)
dark oscuro
darling querido
dart dardo (m)
date fecha (f)
date of arrival día de llegada (m)
date of departure día de salida (m)
dates dátiles (m)
daughter hija (f)
daughter-in-law nuera (f)
day día (m)
day after tomorrow pasado mañana
day before yesterday anteayer
day ticket billete válido por un día (m)
deadline plazo (m)
deceive, cheat engañar
December diciembre
deck cubierta (f)
deck chair tumbona (f), silla de cubierta (f)
decorator decorador (m)
deep profundo
deep-fried cutlet escalope (m)
deer ciervo (m)
defeat derrota (f)
degree of difficulty nivel de dificultad (m)
delay retraso (m)
delicatessen tienda de comestibles finos (f)
delivery terms condiciones de entrega (f)
democracy democracia (f)
denomination creencia (f)

dental bridge puente dental (m)
dental floss seda dental (f)
dental technician técnico dental (m)
dentist dentista (m)
denture dentadura postiza (f)
deodorant desodorante (m)
department departamento (m)
department head jefe de departamento (m)
department store centro comercial (m)
departure salida (f)
departure time hora de salida (f)
deposit fianza (f)
depressed deprimido (m)
depth gauge batímetro (m)
descent descenso (m)
desert desierto (m)
desk escritorio (m)
dessert postre (m)
detective novel novela policíaca (f)
diabetes diabetes (f)
diagonally striped a rayas diagonales
dial tone señal de línea libre (f)
diamond diamante (m)
diaper pañal (m)
diarrhea diarrea (f)
dictionary diccionario (m)
diesel diésel/dieseloil (m)
digital recording grabación digital (f)
dill eneldo (m)
dime store tienda de artículos baratos (f)
dining car vagón-restaurante (m)
dinner cena (f)
diphteria difteria (f)
direct dialling selección directa (f)
discotheque, disco discoteca (f)
discount descuento (m)
discount price precio con descuento (m)
dish, plate plato (m)
dishes vajilla (f)
dishrack escurreplatos (m)
dishwasher lavaplatos (m)
dishwashing liquid detergente (m)
disinfectant desinfectante (m)

disposable needle jeringa desechable (f)
distance meter telémetro (m)
distributor distribuidor (m)
district attorney fiscal (m)
diving submarinismo (m)
diving goggles gafas de buceo (f)
diving license licencia submarinista (f)
diving watch reloj de buzo (m)
do hacer
dock muelle (m)
doctor médico (m)
doctor's assistant auxiliar de médico (f)
dog perro (m)
dome cúpula (f)
donkey burro/asno (m)
door puerta (f)
door handle tirador de puerta (m)
dope estupefacientes (m)
double bed cama matrimonial (f)
double cabin camarote doble (m)
double room habitación doble (f)
double-decker double cubierta, doble piso (f, m)
downhill skiing esquí alpino (m)
downtown centro de la ciudad (m)
dozen docena (f)
drama drama (m)
dreadful horrible
dress vestido (m)
drill taladradora (f)
drink beber
drinking water agua potable (m)
driver chófer (m)
drizzle llovizna (f)
druggist farmacéutico (m)
drugs drogas (f)
drugstore farmacia (f)
drum brake freno de tambor (m)
dry seco
dry cleaning tintorería (f)
dry goods mercería (f)
dry-cleaning limpieza en seco (f)
dryer secadora (f)
duck pato (m)
dull opaco

dumbbell pesa/haltera (f)
dune duna (f)
during the day durante el día
dustpan pala de basura (f)
dutiable sujeto a derechos de aduana
duty-free exento de derechos de aduana
DVD player lector DVD (m)
dynamo dínamo (f)

E
each cada
ear oreja (f)
ear of grain espiga (f)
ear, nose and throat specialist otorrinolaringólogo (m)
eardrops gotas para los oídos (f)
earlier más temprano
early temprano
earrings pendientes (m)
easel caballete de pintor (m)
Easter Pascua (f)
eat comer
economist economista (m)
economy economía (f)
eel anguila (f)
egg dishes platos de huevos (m)
eggplant berenjena (f)
elastic elástico (m), cinta elástica para el cabello (f)
elbow codo (m)
elderberries saúcos (m)
elections elecciones (f)
electric blanket manta eléctrica (f)
electric heating calefacción eléctrica (f)
electric range cocina/hornilla eléctrica (f)
electrical appliances store tienda electrodomésticos (f)
electrical cord cordón eléctrico (m)
electrician electricista (m)
electricity electricidad (f)
elevator ascensor (m)
embassy embajada (f)
emergency emergencia (f)
emergency brake freno de emergencia (m)
emergency exit salida de emergencia (f)
emergency flashers intermitentes de emergencia (f)

employee empleado (m)
empty vacío
enclosure anexo (m)
engineer ingeniero (m)
English language and literature filología inglesa (f)
enough suficiente
entrance entrada (f)
entrepreneur empresario (m)
envelope sobre (m)
eraser goma de borrar (f)
escalator escalera mecánica (f)
espresso exprés (m)
event suceso (m)
excavations excavaciones (f)
excellent excelente
excess baggage exceso de equipaje (m)
exchange bureau oficina de cambio (f)
exchange rate tipo de cambio (m)
exhaust tubo de escape (m)
exhibition exposición (f)
exhibitor expositor (m)
exit salida (f)
expense gasto (m)
expensive caro
export exportación (f)
exposure meter exposímetro (m)
express mail carta urgente (f)
express train tren rápido (m)
extension cord cordón prolongador (m)
external de aplicación exterior
extra (gas) gasolina súper (f)
extra costs gastos adicionales (m)
eye ojo (m)
eyebrow ceja (f)
eyebrow pencil lápiz de cejas (m)
eyelid párpado (m)
eyeshadow sombra de ojos (f)
eyewear store óptica (f)

F
fabric store tienda de telas (f)
face cara (f)

face mitt guante para la ducha (m)
factory fábrica (f)
fair feria (f)
fall caerse
fall in love enamorarse
fallopian tubes trompas de Falopio (f)
family ticket billete con tarifa familiar (m)
fantastic fantástico
far lejos
farm granja (f)
farmer agricultor (m)
far-sighted hipermétrope
fashion moda (f)
fast rápido
father padre (m)
father-in-law suegro (m)
faucet grifo (m)
fax fax (m)
February febrero
fee honorario (m)
feel sentir
felt fieltro (m)
felt tip pen rotulador (m)
fender guardabarros (m)
fennel hinojo (m)
ferry transbordador/ferry (m)
festival festival (m)
fever fiebre (f)
few poco
fiancé novio (m)
fiancée novia (f)
field campo (m)
fig higo (m)
fillet steak filete de solomillo (m)
filling empaste (m)
film película (f)
finance finanza (f)
find encontrar
finger dedo (m)
fins aletas (f)
fire fuego (m)
fire department bomberos (m)
first primero
fish pescado (m)
fish store pescadería (f)
fishing pesca (f)
fishing license permiso para pescar (m)
fishing line sedal (m)
fishing rod caña de pescar (f)
fixative fijador (m)
flannel franela (f)
flashbulb flash (m)
flasher destellador (m)

flashlight linterna (f)
flat noodles tallarines (m)
flatulence flatulencia (f)
flavor sabor (m)
flea market rastro (m)
flight vuelo (m)
flight number número de vuelo (m)
flight schedule horario de vuelo (m)
float veleta (f)
flood inundación (f)
floor piso (m)
florist floristería (f)
flounder platija (f), lenguado (m)
flour harina (f)
flu gripe (f)
fly swatter matamoscas (m)
fog niebla (f)
folding chair silla plegable (f)
folding table mesa plegable (f)
folklore folklore (m)
font pila bautismal (f)
foot pie (m)
footpath sendero (m)
for por, para
forefinger dedo índice (m)
foreigner extranjero (m)
forget olvidar
fork tenedor (m)
format formato (m)
fortress fortaleza (f)
fountain pen pluma fuente (f)
fracture fractura del hueso (f)
freight charges gastos de transporte (m)
freighter buque mercante (m)
french fries papas fritas (f)
fresh produce stand verdulería (f)
Friday viernes
fried frito
fried egg huevo frito (m)
fried potatoes papas fritas (f)
friend amigo (m)
frieze friso (m)
front axle eje delantero (m)
front wheel fork horquilla de rueda delantera (f)
frost helada (f)
fruit fruta (f)
fruit juice jugo de fruta (m)

fruit stand frutería (f)
fruit tart tarta de fruta (f)
fruit tea té de fruta (m)
fruity afrutado
frustrated frustrado
frying pan sartén (f)
fuel guage indicador de gasolina (m)
fuel injector pump inyector de combustible (m)
full lleno
full board pensión completa (f)
full-bodied de mucho cuerpo
funnel embudo (m)
fur shop peletería (f)
furniture muebles (m)
fuse fusible (m)

G . . . .
gallbladder vesícula biliar (f)
gallery galería (f)
garage garaje (m)
garbage basura (f)
garbage can cubo de basura (m)
garden jardín (m)
gardener jardinero (m)
garlic ajo (m)
gas gasolina (f)
gas can lata de gasolina (f)
gas cylinder bombona de gas (f)
gas pedal acelerador (m)
gas pump surtidor de gasolina (f)
gas station gasolinera (f)
gas stove cocina / hornillo de gas (m)
gash herida por corte (f)
gasket junta (f)
gate salida (f)
gear engranaje (m)
gearbox caja de cambios (f)
gearshift palanca del cambio (f), cambio de marchas (m)
general delivery en lista de correos
gentle wash programa para lavado de ropa delicada (m)
geology geología (f)
German measles rubeola (f)
Germany Alemania
get obtener
gift regalo (m)

gift wrap papel de regalo (m)
ginger jengibre (m)
give dar
glass vidrio (f)
glass painting decoración del cristal (f)
glasses case estuche para gafas (m)
glazed garrapiñado
glazier vidriero (m)
glove compartment guantera (f)
gloves guantes (m)
glue pegamento (m)
go ir
goat cabra (f)
goat's milk cheese queso de leche de cabra (m)
gold oro (m)
golden bream dorada (f)
golden perch acerina (f)
golf golf (m)
golf bag bolsa de golf (f)
golf ball pelota de golf (f)
golf clubs palos de golf (m)
good bueno
Good Friday Viernes Santo (m)
goose ganso (m)
gooseberry grosella silvestre (f)
gorgeous espléndido
Gothic gótico
goulash gulasch (m)
government gobierno (m)
gradient inclinación (f)
grain cereal (m)
gram gramo (m)
grandfather abuelo (m)
grandmother abuela (f)
grandson nieto (m)
grape uva (f)
grape juice jugo de uva (m)
grapefruit toronja (f)
graphics card tarjeta gráfica (f)
grave tumba (f)
gray gris
grayling tímalo (m)
great estupendo
green verde
green beans judías verdes (f)
green pepper pimiento (m)
green salad ensalada de lechuga (f)
greeting saludo (m)

grill parrilla (f)
grilled chicken pollo asado (m)
grilled, barbecued a la parrilla
grocery store tienda de comestibles (f)
ground, chopped picado
group card billete de tarifa de grupo (m)
guarantee garantía (f)
guesthouse room habitación en casa de huéspedes (f)
guidebook guía de viajes (f)
guinea fowl gallina de Guinea (f)
gum encía (f)
gymnastics gimnasia (f)
gynecologist ginecólogo (m)

H

haddock anón (m)
hail granizo (m)
hair pelo (m)
hair color color del cabello (m)
hair dye tinte para el cabello (m)
hairbrush cepillo para el cabello (m)
hairdresser peluquero (m)
hairdryer secador (m)
hairpins horquillas (f)
hair-setting lotion fijador para el cabello (m)
hairspray laca (f)
half medio, mitad
half board media pensión (f)
halibut hipogloso (m)
hall pabellón (m)
ham jamón (m)
hammer martillo (m)
hammock hamaca (f)
hand mano (f)
hand baggage equipaje de mano (m)
hand brake freno de mano (m)
hand cream crema para las manos (f)
hand towel toalla pequeña (f)
handbag bolso (m)
handball balonmano (m)
handicrafts artesanía (f)
handlebars manillar (m)
hands manecilla (f)

hanger percha (f)
hang-gliding aladelta (m)
harbor puerto (m)
harbor tour recorrido por el puerto (m)
hard disk disco duro (m)
hard-boiled egg huevo duro (m)
hardware ferretería (f)
hare liebre (f)
harvester segadora-trilladora (f)
hat sombrero (m)
have tener
hay heno (m)
hay fever alergio (f)
hazelnut avellana (f)
hazy brumoso
head cabeza (f)
head cold catarro (m)
headache dolor de cabeza (m)
headache pill pastilla para dolor de cabeza (f)
headlight faro del automóvil (m), luz delantera (f)
headphones auriculares (m)
health food store tienda de alimentos naturales (f)
hear oír
heart corazón (m)
heart attack infarto cardíaco (m)
heart problem trastorno cardíaco (m)
heartburn acidez estomacal (f)
heat calor (m)
heater calefactor (m)
heating calefacción (f)
heel tacón (m), talón (m)
hello buenos días
helmet casco (m)
help ayuda (f), ayudar
hemorrhage hemorragia (f)
herbal tea tisana (f)
here aquí, acá
herring arenque (m)
hibiscus hibisco (m)
high alta, alto
high blood pressure hipertensión (f)
high pressure presión alta (f)
high season temporada alta (f)
high tide marea alta (f)
highchair silla de niños (f)
high-contrast con mucho contraste

hike salir de excursión
hiking excursionismo (m)
hiking boots zapatos de excursión (m)
hill colina (f)
hip cadera (f)
history historia (f)
honey miel (f)
hood capó (m)
horn bocina (f)
horse caballo (m)
horse racing carrera de caballos (f)
horseback riding equitación (f)
horseradish rábano picante (m)
hose manguera (f)
hospital hospital (m)
hot caliente
hot water agua caliente (m)
hot water bottle bolsa de agua caliente (f)
hot water heater calentador (m)
hot-air balloon globo de aire caliente (m)
hotel hotel (m)
hotelier administrador de hotel (m)
hot-water wash lavado con agua caliente (m)
hour hora (f)
hourly cada hora
household merchandise artículos domésticos (m)
housewife ama de casa (m)
how long cuánto tiempo
how much cuánto
hub cubo (m)
humidity humedad (f)
hunger hambre (m)
hurricane huracán (m)
hurricane lamp quinqué (m)
husband marido (m)
hydrofoil acuaplano (m)

I

ice hielo (m)
ice ax hacha de hielo (m)
ice cream helado (m)
ice cream cone cucurucho (m)
ice cube cubito de hielo (m)
ice hockey hockey sobre hielo (m)
ice skates patines de hielo (m)

ice-skating patinaje sobre hielo (m)
ID documento de identidad (m)
if si
ignition encendido (m)
immersion heater calentador de inmersión (m)
immigration inmigración (f)
immigration authority departamento de extranjería (m)
import importación (f)
impressive impresionante
in en
in the afternoon por la tarde
in the evening por la tarde
in the morning por la mañana
industry industria (f)
infection infección (f)
inflammation inflamación (f)
inflammation of the bladder cistitis (f)
information información (m)
injection inyección (f)
injure herir
injury lesión (f)
ink tinta (f)
inkjet printer impresora por chorro de tinta (f)
inner tube cámara de aire (f)
insect bite picadura de insecto (f)
insecticide insecticida (m)
inside adentro
inside cabin camarote interno (m)
insulated bag nevera (f)
insulin insulina (f)
insurance seguro (m)
intermission entreacto (m)
internal interno
internet internet (m)
internist internista (m)
interpreter intérprete (m)
intestine intestino (m)
intra-uterine device DIU (m)
introduce presentar
investment inversión (f)
invitation invitación (f)
invoice factura (f)
iron plancha (f)
ironing board tabla de planchar (f)

J ....
jack gato (m)
jacket chaqueta (f)
jacknife, pocket knife navaja (f)
jam mermelada (f)
January enero
jaundice ictericia (f)
jaw mandíbula (f)
jazz jazz (m)
jellyfish medusa (f)
jetty embarcadero (m)
Jew judío (m)
jeweler joyero (m)
jogging jogging (m)
joint articulación (f)
journalist periodista (m)
judge juez (m)
judo yudo (m)
July julio
jumper cables cables de empalme para la puesta en marcha (m)
June junio

K ....
karate kárate (m)
kayak kayak (m)
kerosene lamp lámpara de querosén (f)
key llave (f)
keyboard teclado (m)
kid cabrito (m)
kidney riñón (m)
kidney beans judías (f)
kilo kilo (m)
kilometer kilómetro (m)
kingdom reino (m)
kitchen cocina (f)
kitchen rag estropajo (m)
kitchenette cocina pequeña (f)
kite cometa (f)
kiwi fruit kiwi (m)
knee rodilla (f)
knife cuchillo (m)
knobby con motas
knot nudo (m)
know saber

L ....
label etiqueta (f)
ladder escalera de mano (f)
lake lago (m)
lamb cordero (m)
lamp lámpara (f)
landing aterrizaje (m)
landlord alquilador (m)
landscape paisaje (m)
language course curso de idiomas (m)

larded mechado
large grande
laser printer impresora láser (f)
last stop estación final (f)
late tarde
later más tarde
laundromat lavandería (f)
laundry basket cesta de la ropa (f)
laundry detergent detergente para lavadora (m)
laurel laurel (m)
law ley (f)
lawyer abogado (m)
laxative laxante (m)
leather cuero (m)
leather coat abrigo de cuero (m)
leather goods artículos de piel (m)
leather jacket chaqueta de cuero (f)
leather sole suela de cuero (f)
leek puerro (m)
leeward sotavento
left izquierda
leg pierna (f)
legal proceedings sesión judicial (f)
lemon limón (m)
lemon squeezer exprimidor (m)
lens lente (m)
lens shade parasol (m)
lentils lentejas (f)
let dejar
letter carta (f)
letterhead membrete (m)
lettuce lechuga (f)
liability responsabilidad (f)
library biblioteca (f)
licensing fee tasa de licencia (f)
life guard salvavidas (m)
life jacket chaleco salvavidas (m)
life preserver salvavidas (m)
lifeboat bote salvavidas (m)
light luz (f)
light switch interruptor de luz (m)
lightbulb bombilla (f)
lighter encendedor (m)
lighthouse faro (m)
lightning relámpago (m)
like como, gustar
lily azucena (f)

lime lima (f)
lime tree tilo (m)
linen lino (m)
lip labio (m)
lipstick lápiz de labios (m)
liqueur licor (m)
liquor store licorería (m)
listen escuchar
liter litro (m)
literature literatura (f)
little poco
liver hígado (m)
living room sala (f)
loafer haragán (m)
lobster langosta (f)
local call llamada local (f)
lock cerradura (f)
locker consigna automática (f)
locksmith cerrajero (m)
locomotive locomotora (f)
loin lomo (m)
loin steak filete de lomo (m)
long largo
long-distance call conferencia interurbana (f)
look for buscar
loose holgado
loose-leaf notebook cuaderno de anillos (m)
loss pérdida (f)
lost-and-found office oficina de objetos perdidos (f)
low cholesterol bajo en colesterol
low pressure baja presión (f)
low season temporada baja (f)
low tide marea baja (f)
low-calorie bajo en calorías
low-contrast con poco contraste
lower leg pierna (f)
low-fat bajo en grasa
luggage, baggage equipaje (m)
lumbago lumbago (m)
lump bulto (m)
lunch almuerzo (m)
lung pulmón (m)

M............................
macaroni macarrones (m)
mackerel caballa (f)
magazine revista (f)
magnet imán (m)
magnifying glass lupa (f)

mailbox buzón (m)
main entrance portal (m)
mainland tierra firme (f)
male nurse enfermero (m)
manager gerente (m), director (m)
mango mango (m)
manufacturer fabricante (m)
many muchos
map mapa (m)
map of the city mapa de la ciudad (m)
maple arce (m)
March marzo
margarine margarina (f)
marjoram mejorana (f)
market mercado (m)
marketing marketing (m)
married casado
mascara rímel (m)
mashed potatoes puré (m)
mason albañil (m)
master maestro (m)
match fósforo (m)
material material (m)
matte mate
mattress colchón (m)
maximum (values) valores máximos (m)
May mayo
mayonnaise mayonesa (f)
mayor's office alcaldía (f)
meadow prado (m)
measles sarampión (m)
measuring stick metro plegable (m)
measuring tape cinta métrica (f)
meat carne (f)
meat knife cuchillo para carne (m)
meatloaf picadillo (m)
mechanic mecánico (m)
medication medicamento (f)
medicine medicina (f)
medieval medieval
medium medio (m)
medlar níspero (m)
meet conocer
meeting place punto de encuentro (m)
melon melón (m)
menu menú (m)
merchant mercader (m)
meter metro (m)
microfiber microfibra (f)
microwave microondas (m)
Middle Ages edad media (f)

middle finger dedo del corazón (m)
midnight medianoche (f)
midwife partera (f)
migraine jaqueca (f)
milk leche (f)
milk jug cazo para la leche (m)
millimeter milímetro (m)
mineral water agua mineral (m)
minibar minibar (m)
minimum values valores mínimos (m)
minister sacerdote (m)
mint menta (f)
minute minuto (m)
mirror espejo (m)
miscarriage aborto no intencional (m)
mixed salad ensalada mixta (f)
mocha moca (f)
modem módem (m)
moderately warm calor moderado
Monday lunes (m)
money dinero (m)
money exchange cambio de divisa (m)
money order giro postal (m)
month mes (m)
monument monumento (m)
mooring atracadero (m)
more más
mosquito net mosquitero (m)
motel motel (m)
mother madre (f)
mother-in-law suegra (f)
motor motor (m)
motor vehicle mechanic mecánico de automóviles (m)
motorboat motolancha (f)
mottled mezclado
mountain montaña (f)
mountain climbing alpinismo (m)
mountain hut refugio (m)
mountain peak cima (f)
mountain spring manantial (m)
mouth boca (f)
mouthwash agua dentífrica (m)
movie película (f)
much mucho
mudguard guardabarros (m)

mug jarra (f)
mugging asalto (m)
mulberries moras (f)
mullet lisa (f)
mumps paperas (f)
mural fresco (m)
muscle músculo (m)
museum museo (m)
mushroom hongo (f)
music música (f)
music store tienda musical (f)
musical musical (m)
musician músico (m)
Muslim musulmán (m)
mussel ostra (f), mejillón (m)
must deber
mustache bigote (m)
mustard mostaza (f)
mutton carnero (m)
mystery misterio (m)

N

nail clavo (m)
nail file lima para uñas (f)
nail polish esmalte de uñas (m)
nail polish remover quita-esmalte (m)
nail scissors tijeras para uñas (f)
name badge placa de identificación (f)
napkin servilleta (f)
narcissus narciso (m)
narrow estrecho (m)
national highway carretera nacional (f)
nature park parque natural (m)
nausea náusea (f)
nave nave (f)
neck cuello (m)
necklace collar (m)
negotiation negociación (f)
nephew sobrino (m)
nerve nervio (m)
network cable cable de red (m)
network card tarjeta de red (f)
new nuevo
New Year's day Año Nuevo
New Year's eve Noche Vieja
news noticias (f)
newspaper periódico (m)
newsstand quiosco (m)
niece sobrina (f)

night table mesita de noche (f)
nightclub club nocturno (m)
nightshirt camisón (m)
nipple pezón (m)
no no
no ironing no necesita plancha
non-fiction libro de documentación (m)
non-smoking section sección de no fumadores
non-swimmers no nadadores
noodle soup sopa de fideos (f)
noodles pasta (f)
noon mediodía (m)
nose nariz (f)
nosebleed hemorragia nasal (f)
notary notario (m)
notebook cuaderno (m)
notepad bloc de notas (m)
nothing nada
November noviembre (m)
now ahora
nurse enfermera (f)
nut nuez (f), tuerca (f)
nutmeg nuez moscada (f)

O

oak roble (m)
oars remos (m)
oat avena (f)
oatmeal, porridge papilla de avena (f)
occupied ocupado
ocean océano (m)
ocean view vista al mar (f)
October octubre (m)
octopus pulpo (m)
off season fuera de temporada (f)
offer oferta (f)
office hours horario de consulta (m)
office supplies papelería (f)
official oficial (m)
oil aceite (m)
oil filter filtro del aceite (m)
oil paints pintura al óleo (f)
ointment for burns pomada para las quemaduras (f)
okra quingombó (m)
old viejo (m)

old city centro histórico (m)
olive oil aceite de oliva (m)
omelet tortilla de huevos (f)
on en, sobre
one-week ticket billete semanal (m)
onions cebollas (f)
only sólo
open hours horarios de apertura (m)
opera ópera (f)
operation operación (f)
operetta opereta (f)
opinion opinión (f)
or o
orange naranja (f)
orange juice jugo de naranja (m)
orchid orquídea (f)
order pedir
oregano orégano (m)
organic food alimentos naturales (m)
ornithology ornitología (f)
orthodontist ortodoncista (m)
other otros, otras
out (of) de
outfit traje (m)
outside afuera
outside cabin camarote exterior (m)
outstanding excelente
oyster ostra (f)
ozone ozono (m)

P

pacifier chupete (m)
padlock candado (m)
pain dolor (m)
painkiller analgésico (m)
paintbrush pincel (m)
painter pintor (m)
painting pintura (f), cuadro (m)
painting course curso de pintura (m)
pair par (m)
pajamas pijama (m)
palette paleta (f)
pancake panqueque (m)
panhandler mendigo (m)
panties bragas (f)
pants pantalones (m)
papaya papaya (f)
paper papel (m)
paper clips sujetapapeles (m), grapas (f)

paper napkins servilletas de papel (f)
paragraph párrafo (m)
paralysis parálisis (f)
paramedic paramédico (m)
parcel paquete (m)
park parque (m)
parking fee tarifa de estacionamiento (f)
parking garage garaje de estacionamiento (m)
parking lot vending machine boletera de estacionamiento (f)
parking place estacionamiento (m)
parliament parlamento (m)
parsley perejil (m)
part (hair) raya (f)
partridge perdiz (f)
pass paso (m)
passenger pasajero (m)
passion fruit pasionaria (f)
passport pasaporte (m)
pastel pastel (m)
pastels pinturas al pastel (f)
pastries pasteles (m)
pastry shop pastelería (f)
patterned con dibujos
pawnbroker casa de empeño (f)
pay phone teléfono público (m)
payment terms condiciones de pago (f)
pea guisante (m)
peach melocotón (m)
peanut cacahuate (m)
pear pera (f)
pearl perla (f)
pearl necklace collar de perlas (m)
pebble beach playa de arena gruesa (f)
pecan nut pacana (f)
pedal pedal (m)
pedal boat hidropatín (m)
pediatrician pediatra (m)
pencil lápiz (m)
pencil sharpener sacapuntas (m)
pendant pendiente (m)
pepper pimienta (f), pimentón (m)
perch perca (f)
perfume perfume (m)
perfumery perfumería (f)
perm permanente (f)

persimmon caqui (m)
pharmacy farmacia (f)
pheasant faisán (m)
philosophy filosofía (f)
phone call llamada telefónica (f)
phone card tarjeta telefónica (f)
photo store tienda de fotografía (f)
photographer fotógrafo (m)
physics física (f)
pickpocket carterista (m)
picture book libro ilustrado (m)
pie tarta (f)
pig cerdo (m)
pigeon paloma (f)
pike lucio (m)
pilgrim peregrino (m)
pillow almohada (f)
PIN número secreto (m)
pin alfiler (m)
pincers tenazas (f)
pine cone piña (f)
pine nut piñón (m)
pineapple piña (f)
ping-pong ball pelota de ping-pong (f)
ping-pong racket raqueta de ping-pong (f)
ping-pong, table tennis ping-pong (m)
pink rosado
pinkie dedo meñique (m)
pipe pipa (f)
pipe cleaner escobilla limpiapipas (f)
pipe filter filtro de pipa (m)
pipe implements instrumentos para pipa (m)
pistachio pistache (m)
piston pistón (m)
place lugar (m)
plane ticket pasaje (m)
planetarium planetario (m)
plastic bag bolsa de plástico (f)
plastic wrap película transparente (f)
platform andén (m)
platinum platino (m)
playing cards naipes (m)
please por favor
pliers tenazas (f)
plug enchufe (m)
plug, stopper tapón (m)
plum ciruela (f)

plumber plomero (m)
pneumonia pulmonía (f)
poached egg huevo escalfado (m)
pocket calculator calculadora de bolsillo (f)
poisoning intoxicación (f)
police policía (f)
police station estación de policía (f)
policeman policía (m)
political refugee refugiado político (m)
politics política (f)
polka-dotted a lunares
pollution contaminación (f)
pomegranate granada (f)
pomelo pomelo (m)
pond estanque (m)
poplin popelina (f)
port babor (m)
porter mozo de estación (m), cargadero (m)
post office correos (m)
post office box (P.O. Box) apartado postal (m)
postage franqueo (m)
postcard tarjeta postal (f)
pot olla (f)
potato papa / patata (f)
pottery alfarería (f)
poultry carne de ave (f)
pound libra (f)
powder (snow) nieve-polvo (f)
power corriente (f)
prawn gambas (f)
preferably preferentemente
pregnancy embarazo (m)
pregnancy test prueba del embarazo (f)
pregnant embarazada
pre-season pretemporada (f)
president presidente (m)
press prensa (f)
press conference conferencia de prensa (f)
pretty bonito
previously antes
price precio (m)
priest sacerdote (m)
printed impreso
printed matter impreso (m)
prison prisión (f)
private beach playa privada (f)
procession procesión (f)

processor procesador (m)
production producción (f)
professor profesor (m)
profit beneficio (m)
programmer programador (m)
prom baile de gala (m)
propane propano (m)
prostitute prostituta (f)
Protestant protestante (m)
psychiatrist psiquiatra (m)
psychologist psicólogo (m)
psychology psicología (f)
public school escuela pública (f)
public service servicio público (m)
publishing house editorial (f)
puddle charco (m)
pulpit púlpito (m)
pumpkin calabaza (f)
purchase contract contrato de compraventa (m)
purchase price precio de compra (m)
purple lila
purse monedero (m)
putty knife espátula (f)
quail codorniz (f)
quarter cuarto (m)
quarterback jugador de defensa (m)
quiet tranquilo
quince membrillo (m)

R
rabbit conejo (m)
racing bike bicicleta de carreras (f)
radiator radiador (m)
radio radio (f)
radish rábano (m)
railroad ferrocarril (m)
railway station estación de ferrocarril (f)
rain llover, lluvia (f)
raincoat impermeable (m)
raisin pasa (f)
RAM memoria principal (f)
rape violar
rape violación (f), salpullido (m)
raspberries frambuesas (f)
raw crudo
ray raya (f)
razor máquina de afeitar (f)
razor blades hojas de afeitar (f)
read leer

rear parte trasera (f)
rear axle eje trasero (m)
rear windshield luneta trasera (f)
rearview mirror retrovisor (m)
rebate descuento (m)
receipt recibo (m)
receiver auricular (m)
reception recepción (f)
reception desk registro (m)
recipient destinatario (m)
recommend recomendar
red rojo
red beets nabos rojos (m)
red cabbage lombarda (f)
red perch gallineta (f)
red wine vino tinto (m)
reduction reducción (f)
referee árbitro (m)
reflector reflector (m)
refrigerator refrigerador (m)
regatta regata (f)
regional regional
registered mail correo certificado (m)
regular gas gasolina normal (f)
relief relieve (m)
religion religión (f)
remains restos (m)
remittance giro postal (m)
remote control mando a distancia (m)
rent alquilar
rental fee cuota de arriendo (f)
repair reparar
repair kit bote de parches (m)
repeat repetir
report reportaje (m)
representative representante (m), diputado (m)
reservation reserva (f)
reserve reservar
restaurant restaurante (m)
restroom excusado (m)
retail store tienda al por menor (f)
retired person jubilado (m)
retraining readaptación profesional (f)
return flight vuelo de vuelta (m)
rev counter tacómetro (m)
rheumatism reumatismo (m)
rhubarb ruibarbo (m)

rib costilla (f)
rice arroz (m)
ride pasear
right derecha
right to remain silent derecho de recusación de declaración (f)
rim llanta (f)
ring anillo (m)
ring finger dedo anular (m)
rinse enjuagar
river río (m)
river boat trip viaje por el río (m)
roast asado (m)
roast beef rosbif (m)
rob desvalijar
robe bata (f)
rocky shoreline costa rocosa (f)
roe hueva de pescado (f)
roll panecillo (m)
rollerblades patines (m)
rollerblading patinar
rolling pin rodillo (m)
romanesque estilo románico (m)
romantic romántico
roofer tejador (m)
room habitación (f)
room number número de la habitación (m)
room service servicio de habitaciones (m)
rooster gallo (m)
root (of the tooth) raíz (f)
root canal work tratamiento de la raíz (m)
rope cuerda (f)
rose rosa (f)
rosemary romero (m)
rosette rosetón (m)
rouge colorete (m)
round steak pierna (f)
round-trip viaje de ida y vuelta (m)
round-trip ticket billete de ida y vuelta (m)
rowboat bote de remos (m)
rowing remar
rubber boots botas de goma (f)
rubber dinghy lancha inflable (f)
rubber raft balsa de goma (f)
rubber sole suela de goma (f)
rudder timón (m)

rugby rugby (m)
ruin ruina (f)
ruler regla (f)
rump steak asado de culata (m)
rusks, zwieback galleta dulce (f)
rutabaga nabicol (f)
rye bread pan centeno (m)

S

sacristy sacristía (f)
saddle sillín (m)
saddle (of lamb) lomo (m)
saddlebag alforja (f)
safe caja fuerte (f)
safety pin imperdible (m)
saffron azafrán (m)
sage salvia (f)
sail vela (f)
sailboat barco de vela (m)
sailing navegación de vela (f)
sailing licence licencia de navegación de vela (f)
sailor marinero (m)
salad ensalada (f)
salesperson vendedor (m)
salmon salmón (m)
salmonella salmonela (f)
salt sal (f)
salt cod bacalao (m)
salutation saludo (m)
same mismo
sanctuary santuario (m)
sand arena (f)
sand pail cubo de playa (m)
sandals sandalias (f)
sandy beach playa arenosa (f)
sanitary napkin toallita higiénica (f)
sarcophagus sarcófago (m)
sardine sardina (f)
satin raso (m)
Saturday sábado
sauerkraut chucrut (m)
sauna sauna (f)
sausage embutido (m)
savoy cabbage col rizada (f)
saw sierra (f)
say decir
scales báscula (f)
scallion cebolleta (f)
scallop escalope / escalopa (m,f)
scanner escáner (m)
scarf chal (m)
sciatica ciática (f)
scientist científico (m)

scissors tijeras (f)
scrambled egg huevo revuelto (m)
screen pantalla (f)
screw tornillo (m)
screwdriver destornillador (m)
scrubbing brush cepillo para fregar (m)
sculpture escultura (f)
sea mar (m)
sea bass lubina (f)
sea bream besugo (m)
sea pike merluza (f)
sea urchin erizo de mar (m)
seahorse caballo marino (m)
seasick mareado
season ticket billete estacional (m)
seat asiento (m)
seat belt cinturón de seguridad (m)
seaweed algas (f)
second segundo
second hand store tienda de artículos usados (f)
security fianza (f)
security check control de seguridad (m)
see ver
self-timer, automatic shutter release retardador de disparo (m)
sell vender
semolina sémola (f)
sender remitente (m)
senior citizen persona madura (f)
September septiembre (m)
sequoia secuoya (f)
sewing kit avíos de costura (m)
sewing needle aguja de coser (f)
shadow sombra (f)
shampoo champú (m)
shares acciones (f)
shark tiburón (m)
shatter trizar
shaving brush brocha de afeitar (f)
shaving cream crema de afeitar (f)
sheep oveja (f)
sheep's milk cheese queso de leche de oveja (m)
sheet ice hielo resbaladizo (m)
shellfish mariscos (m)

sheriff alguacil (m)
shiny, glossy brillante
shirt camisa (f)
shit mierda (f)
shock absorber amortiguador (m)
shoe zapato (m)
shoe brush cepillo para zapatos (m)
shoe polish crema para zapatos (f)
shoe store zapatería (f)
shoelaces cordones (m)
shoemaker zapatero (m)
shopping bag bolsa de compras (f)
shopping basket cesta de compras (f)
shopping cart carro de compras (f)
shopping center centro comercial (m)
shore excursion excursión por la costa (f)
short corto
short circuit cortocircuito (m)
short novel novela corta (f)
shorts pantalón corto (m)
short-sighted miope
shoulder hombro (m)
shoulder bag bolsa en bandolera (f)
shovel pala (f)
shower ducha (f)
showers chaparrón (m)
shutter persiana (f)
shuttlecock volante (m)
sick enfermo
side aisle nave lateral (f)
side dishes guarniciones (f)
sideburns patillas (f)
sideview mirrors espejos exteriores (m)
sidewalk acera (f)
signature firma (f)
silk seda (f)
silver plata (f)
silverware cubiertos (m)
single soltero
single bed cama individual (f)
single cabin camarote individual (m)
sinker plomada (f)
sister hermana (f)
size tamaño (m)
skate patín (m)
skateboard tabla de patín (f)

sketch pad bloc de dibujo (m)
ski esquí (m)
ski boots bota de esquiar (f)
ski instructor instructor de esquí (m)
ski lift telesquí (m)
ski pass tarjeta de esquí (f)
ski pole bastón de esquí (m)
ski run pista de esquí (f)
skiing esquiar
skilled worker obrero especializado (m)
skin piel (f)
skirt falda (f)
sky diving paracaidismo (m)
skyscraper rascacielos (m)
sled trineo (m)
sleeper coche-litera (m)
sleeping bag saco de dormir (m)
sleeping car coche-cama (m)
sleeping pills pastillas para dormir (f)
sleet nieve granizada (f)
sleeve manga (f)
slide frame marco para diapositivas (m)
slip enagua (f)
slippers zapatillas (f)
slot machine máquina tragamonedas (f)
slow lento
small pequeño
small parcel paquete pequeño (m)
smallpox viruela (f)
smell oler
smelt eperlano (m)
smoke fumar
smoked ahumado
smoked salmon salmón ahumado (m)
smoking section sección de fumadores
sneakers zapatillas (m)
snorkel esnórquel (m)
snow nieve (f), nevar
snow chains cadenas antideslizantes (f)
snowboard monoesquí (m)
soap jabón (m)
soccer fútbol (m)
soccer ball pelota de fútbol (f)

socket toma de corriente (f)
socks calcetines (m)
soda soda (f)
soft drink refresco (m)
soft-boiled egg huevo pasado por agua (m)
sole lenguado (m), suela (f)
some algún
son hijo (m)
son-in-law yerno (m)
sore throat dolor de garganta (m)
sorry perdón
sound card tarjeta de sonido (f)
soup sopa (f)
sour cream nata ácida (f)
souvenir shop tienda de regalos (f)
soy sauce salsa de soja (f)
spaghetti espaguetis (m)
spare parts piezas de recambio (f)
spare ribs chuletas (f)
spare wheel rueda de recambio (f)
spark plug bujía (f)
speak hablar
speaker altavoz (m)
specialist especialista (m)
speedometer velocímetro (m)
spice condimento (m)
spider crab centolla (f)
spinach espinaca (f)
spinal column columna vertebral (f)
spin-dry centrifugar
spin-dryer centrifugadora (f)
spirits alcohol (m)
splendid magnífico
spoke (wheel) rayo (m)
sponge esponja (f)
spoon cuchara (f)
sport deporte (m)
sporting goods store tienda de artículos de deporte (f)
sprain luxación (f)
spring primavera (f)
square plaza (f)
square kilometer kilómetro cuadrado (m)
square meter metro cuadrado (m)
squash squash (m)
squid calamar (m)
stadium estadio (m)

stag ciervo (m)
stain remover quitamanchas (m)
stainless steel acero inoxidable (m)
stairways escaleras (f)
stamp estampilla, sello (f, m)
starboard estribor (m)
starfish estrella marina (f)
starter motor de arranque (m)
statement declaración (f)
stationery artículos de papelería (m), papel de cartas (m)
statue estatua (f)
steak bistec (m)
steal robar
steamed rehogado
steamer barco de vapor (m)
steeple campanario (m)
steering dirección (f)
steering wheel volante (m)
stereo system equipo estéreo (m)
stern popa (f)
stew guisar
still todavía
stirred revuelto
stirring spoon cucharón (m)
stitch in the side dolores de costado (m)
stockings calcetines largos (m)
stomach estómago (m)
stomachache dolor abdominal (m), dolor de estómago (m)
stop parada (f)
stopover parada (f), **stopover** escala (f)
stopwatch cronómetro (m)
storm tormenta (f)
straight ahead siempre recto
strain distensión (f)
strainer colador (m)
strand mechón (m)
strange raro
straw paja (f)
strawberry fresa (f)
street calle (f)
street number número de casa (m)
streetcar tranvía (m)
string cordón (m)
string beans judías verdes (f)

strong fuerte
student alumno (m), estudiante (m)
stuffed relleno
sturgeon sollo (m)
subway metro (m)
suckling pig lechón (m)
suction pump bomba de succión (f)
suede gamuza (f)
sugar azúcar (m)
sugar substitute sustituto del azúcar (m)
suit traje (m)
suitcase maleta (f)
suite suite (f)
summer verano (m)
sun sol (m)
sun glasses gafas para el sol (f)
sun umbrella, parasol sombrilla (f)
sunblock protección solar (f)
sunburn quemadura por el sol (f)
Sunday domingo (m)
sunflower girasol (m)
sunflower oil aceite de girasol (m)
sunflower seeds semillas de girasol (f)
sunrise salida del sol (f)
sunroof techo corredizo (m)
sunset puesta del sol (f)
sunstroke insolación (f)
super excelente
supermarket supermercado (m)
supplier proveedor (m)
surcharge suplemento del billete (m)
surf oleaje (m)
surfboard tabla de surf (f)
surfing surf (m)
surgeon cirujano (m)
suspenders tirantes (m)
swab citología (f)
swamp pantano (m)
sweater suéter (m)
sweet dulce
sweet potatoes patatas dulces (f)
sweetbread mollejas (f)
sweetener dulcificante (m)
swell marejada (f)
swelling tumefacción (f), hinchazón (f)
swimmers nadadores
swimming goggles gafas para nadar (f)

swimming pool piscina (f)
swimming ring flotador (m)
swimming trunks traje de baño (m)
swindler estafador (m)
switchboard cuadro de conexión manual (m)
swollen hinchado
swordfish pez espada (m)
synagogue sinagoga (f)
synthetic fiber fibra sintética (f)
syringe jeringa (f)
syrup jarabe (m)

T......................

table mesa (f)
tablecloth mantel (m)
tail rabo (m)
taillight luz trasera (f)
tailor sastre (m)
take tomar
takeoff salida (f)
tamarind tamarindo (m)
tampons tampones (m)
tangerine mandarina (f)
tangy picante
tank tanque (m)
tarragon estragón (m)
taste degustar
tax impuesto (m)
tax advisor asesor fiscal (m)
taxi driver taxista (m)
tea té (m)
teacher maestro (m)
teaspoon cucharilla (f)
technical book libro técnico (m)
telegram telegrama (m)
telephone teléfono (m)
telephone booth cabina telefónica (f)
telephone connection conexión telefónica (f)
telephone directory guía telefónica (f)
telephone line línea telefónica (f)
telephone number número de teléfono (m)
telephoto lens teleobjetivo (m)
television televisión (f)
telex télex (m)
tell contar
temple templo (m)
tendon tendón (m)
tennis tenis (m)
tennis ball pelota de tenis (f)

tennis racket raqueta de tenis (f)
tent tienda (f)
tent peg estaca (f)
tent pole palo de la tienda (m)
terrace terraza (f)
terrific maravilloso
terry cloth tejido de rizo (m)
tetanus tétano (m)
thank you gracias
that one ese, esa
thaw deshielo (m)
theater teatro (m)
theft robo (m)
then entonces
there allá, allí
therefore por eso
thermometer termómetro (m)
thermos termo (m)
thief ladrón (m)
thigh muslo (m)
thimble dedal (m)
think pensar
thirst sed (f)
this one éste, ésta
thread hilo (m)
through por
thumb dedo pulgar (m)
thumb tacks chinches (f)
thunder trueno (m)
thunderstorm tormenta (f)
Thursday jueves
thyme tomillo (m)
ticket billete (m)
ticket counter taquilla (f)
ticket inspector inspector (m)
tie corbata (f)
tie pin alfiler de corbata (m)
tight ceñido
tights medias (f)
time of delivery plazo de entrega (m)
timetable, schedule horario (m)
tip propina (f)
tire neumático (m)
tired cansado
tissue pañuelo de papel (m)
toast pan tostado (m)
toaster tostador (m)
tobacco tabaco (m)
tobacco store estanco (m)
today hoy
toe dedo del pie (m)
toilet paper papel higiénico (m)

tomato juice zumo de tomate (m)
tomatoes tomates (m)
tomorrow mañana
ton tonelada (f)
tongue lengua (f)
tonsil amígdala (f)
tonsillitis amigdalitis (f)
too much demasiado
tool herramienta (f)
tooth diente (m)
toothache dolor de muelas (m)
toothbrush cepillo de dientes (m)
toothpaste pasta dentífrica (f)
tornado ciclón (m)
tow remolcar
towel toalla (f)
tower torre (f)
towing cable cable para remolcar (m)
towing service servicio de grúa (m)
town hall ayuntamiento (m)
toy juguete (m)
toy store juguetería (f)
track andén (m)
track and field atletismo (m)
track shoes zapatos de deporte (m)
tractor tractor (m)
trademark marca de fábrica (f)
traffic light semáforo (m)
tragedy tragedia (f)
trailer caravana (f)
trainee aprendiz (m)
tranquilizer, sedative sedante (m)
transept nave transversal (f)
transfer hacer transbordo, giro
transit travesía (f)
transmission transmisión (f)
transportation costs gastos de transporte (m)
trash bag bolsa de basura (f)
travel agency agencia de viaje (f)
traveler's check cheque de viajero (m)
traveling bag bolsa de viaje (f)
travelling crib cuna de viaje (f)

tree árbol (m)
trial proceso (m)
trillion billón
tripe mondongo (m)
tripod trípode (m)
trout trucha (f)
trunk maletero (m)
try on probar
t-shirt camiseta (f)
Tuesday martes
tuna atún (m)
turbot rodaballo (m)
turkey pavo (m)
turn signals intermitente (m)
turnips nabos (m)
turnpike autopista (f)
tuxedo esmoquin (m)
TV televisor (m)
tweezers pinzas (f)
twine bramante (m)
typhoon tifón (m)

U............................
ugly feo
ulcer úlcera (f)
umbrella paraguas (m)
uncanny inquietante
uncle tío (m)
unconscious desmayado
underpants calzoncillos (m)
undershirt camiseta (f)
understand entender
underwear ropa interior (f)
unit unidad (f)
United States Estados Unidos
university universidad (f)
unleaded sin plomo
unusual inusual
urologist urólogo (m)
uterus útero (m)

V............................
vacation apartment apartamento de vacaciones (m)
vacation house casa de vacaciones (f)
vacation spot lugar turístico (m)
vacuum cleaner aspiradora (f)
vagina vagina (f)
vaginitis vaginitis (f)
valley valle (m)
valuables objetos de valor (m)
valve válvula (f)

vanilla vainilla (f)
v-belt correa en cuña (f)
VCR videograbadora (f)
vegetable soup sopa de verdura (f)
vegetables verduras (f)
vein vena (f)
velvet terciopelo (m)
ventilator, fan ventilador (m)
vertically striped a rayas verticales
very muy
vest chaleco (m)
veterinarian veterinario (m)
videocassette videocasete (m)
vinegar vinagre (m)
vineyard viña (f)
vintage vendimia (f)
viper's grass escorzonera (f)
viral illness enfermedad viral (f)
vision visión, agudeza de la vista (f)
vodka vodka (m)
volcano volcán (m)
volleyball voleibol (m)
voltage voltaje (m)
vote voto (m)

W............................
waffle barquillo (m)
waiter camarero (m)
waiting room sala de espera (f)
wall clock reloj de pared (m)
walnut nuez (f)
wardrobe armario (m)
warm caliente
warning triangle triángulo de emergencia (m)
washbasin lavabo (m)
washing machine lavadora (f)
washroom cuarto de aseo (m)
wastepaper basket papelera (f)
watch reloj de pulsera (m), reloj (m)
watchmaker relojero (m)
water agua (m)
water bottle botella de agua (f)
water jug bidón de agua (m)
water polo polo acuático (m)

water pump bomba de agua (f)
water supply suministro de agua (m)
water wings nadaderas (f)
watercolor acuarela (f)
watercolor crayon gis de acuarela (m)
watercolor paper papel para acuarela (m)
watercress berro (m)
waterfall cascada (f)
watering can regadera (f)
watermelon sandía (f)
waterproof impermeable
waterskiing esquí acuático (m)
wave ola (f)
wax cera (f)
wax-bean frijol (m)
weak débil
Wednesday miércoles
weekend fin de semana (m)
weight pesa (f)
weight belt cinturón de plomo (m)
well pozo (m)
wetsuit traje de buceo (m)
what qué
wheat trigo (m)
wheel rueda (f)
wheelchair silla de ruedas (f)
when cuándo
where dónde
whipped cream crema batida (f)
whisk batidor (m)
white blanco
white beans habichuelas blancas (f)

white bread pan blanco (m)
white cabbage col blanco (f)
white wine vino blanco (m)
Whitsun Pentecostés (m)
who quién
wholewheat bread pan integral (m)
whooping cough tos ferina (f)
why por qué
wide ancho
wife esposa (f)
wig peluca (f)
wild duck ánade (m)
win victoria (f)
wind viento (m)
windbreaker parca (f)
window ventana (f)
window pane cristal de la ventana (m)
window seat asiento junto a la ventana (m)
windshield parabrisas (m)
windshield wiper limpiaparabrisas (m)
windsurfing windsurf (m)
windward barlovento (m)
wine vino (m)
wine list carta de vinos (f)
wine store tienda de vinos (f)
winter invierno (m)
wisdom tooth muela del juicio (f)
with con
without sin
wool lana (f)
work trabajar
worker obrero (m)

working hours horas de trabajo (f)
worsted estambre (m)
wound herida (f)
wrapping paper papel para envolver (m)
wrench llave (f), llave de tuercas (f)
wrestling lucha (f)
wrinkle-free inarrugable
wrist muñeca (f)
wristband correa de pulsera (f)
write escribir
write down apuntar
wrong equivocado

X.........................
X-ray radiografía (f)

Y.........................
yacht yate (m)
year año (m)
yellow amarillo
yellow pages páginas amarillas (f)
yellow plum ciruela amarilla (f)
yes sí
yesterday ayer
yogurt yogur (m)
young joven
young fattened hen pularda (f)
youth hostel albergue juvenil (m)

Z.........................
zip code código postal (m)
zipper cremallera (f)
zoo parque zoológico (m)
zoology zoología (f)
zucchini calabacines (m)

Spanish – English

A

a cuadros checkered
a la parrilla grilled, barbecued
a lunares polka-dotted
a rayas diagonales diagonally striped
a rayas verticales vertically striped
a, en at
abadía (f) abbey
abogado (m) lawyer
aborto (m) abortion
aborto no intencional (m) miscarriage
abrazadera dental (f) braces
abrelatas (m) can opener
abrigo (m) coat
abrigo de cuero (m) leather coat
abril April
absceso (m) abscess
abuela (f) grandmother
abuelo (m) grandfather
accidente (m) accident
acción cívica (f) citizens' action
acciones (f) shares
aceite (m) oil
aceite de girasol (m) sunflower oil
aceite de oliva (m) olive oil
acelerador (m) gas pedal
acelga (f) chard
acera (f) sidewalk
acerina (f) golden perch
acero inoxidable (m) stainless steel
achicoria (f) chicory
acidez estomacal (f) heartburn
actor (m) actor
actriz (f) actress
acuaplano (m) hydrofoil
acuarela (f) watercolor
acuerdo (m) agreement
acuse de recibo (m) acknowledgment
adaptador (m) adapter
adentro inside
administración (f) administration
administrador de hotel (m) hotelier
aduana (f) customs

aeropuerto (m) airport
afrutado fruity
afuera outside
agencia de viaje (f) travel agency
agente (m/f) agent
agosto August
agricultor (m) farmer
agua (m) water
agua caliente (m) hot water
agua dentífrica (m) mouthwash
agua mineral (m) mineral water
agua potable (m) drinking water
aguacate (m) avocado
aguja de coser (f) sewing needle
ahora now
ahumado smoked
aire (m) air
ajedrez (m) chess
ajo (m) garlic
aladelta (m) hang-gliding
albahaca (f) basil
albañil (m) mason, construction worker
albaricoque (m) apricot
albergue juvenil (m) youth hostel
albornoz (m) bathrobe
alcachofa (f) artichoke
alcaldía (f) mayor's office
alcaparras (f) capers
alcohol (m) spirits
Alemania Germany
alergia (f) allergy
alergio (f) hay fever
aletas (f) fins
alfarería (f) pottery
alfiler (m) pin
alfiler de corbata (m) tie pin
alforja (f) saddlebag
algas (f) seaweed
algodón (m) cotton
alguacil (m) sheriff
algún some
alimento para bebé (m) baby food
alimentos naturales (m) organic food
allá, allí there
almeja (f) clam
almendra (f) almond

almohada (f) pillow
almuerzo (m) lunch
alpinismo (m) mountain climbing
alquilador (m) landlord
alquilar rent
alquiler de lanchas (m) boat rental
alta, alto high
altar (m) altar
altavoz (m) speaker
alumno (m) student
ama de casa (m) housewife
amarillo yellow
ambulancia (f) ambulance
amígdala (f) tonsil
amigdalitis (f) tonsillitis
amigo (m) friend
amortiguador (m) shock absorber
ánade (m) wild duck
analgésico (m) painkiller
ancho wide
anchoa (f) anchovy
ancla (m) anchor
andén (m) track, platform
anestesia (f) anaesthetic, anesthesia
anexo (m) enclosure
angina de pecho (f) angina
anguila (f) eel
anillo (m) ring
año (m) year
Año Nuevo New Year's day
anón (m) haddock
anorak (m) anorak
anteayer day before yesterday
antes previously
antes de before
antigüedades (f) antiques
antihistamina (f) antihistamine
anuncio (m) billboard, ad
apartado postal (m) post office box (P.O. Box)
apartamento (m) apartment
apartamento de vacaciones (m) vacation apartment
apéndice (m) appendix (book), appendix
apendicitis (f) appendicitis
apio (m) celery

apoderado (m) authorized officer
aprendiz (m) trainee
apuntar write down
aquí, acá here
arándanos (m) blueberries
arándanos agrios (m) cranberries
árbitro (m) referee
árbol (m) tree
arce (m) maple
arena (f) sand
arenque (m) herring
armario (m) wardrobe
arqueología (f) archaeology
arquitecto (m) architect
arquitectura (f) architecture
arresto (m) arrest
arroyo (m) brook
arroz (m) rice
arte (m) art
arteria (f) artery
artesanía (f) handicrafts
artesano (m) craftsperson
articulación (f) joint
artículos de papelería (m) stationery
artículos de piel (m) leather goods
artículos domésticos (m) household merchandise
artista (m) artist
asado (m) roast
asado de culata (m) rump steak
asalto (m) mugging
ascenso (m) ascent
ascensor (m) elevator
asesor fiscal (m) tax advisor
asiento (m) seat
asiento junto a la ventana (m) window seat
asiento junto al pasillo (m) aisle seat
asma (m) asthma
asombroso amazing
aspiradora (f) vacuum cleaner
aterrizaje (m) landing
atletismo (m) track and field
atracadero (m) mooring
atún (m) tuna
aunque although
auricular (m) receiver
auriculares (m) headphones
Austria Austria
autocaravana (f) camper

autopista (f) turnpike
autor (m) author
autotrén (m) car-train
auxiliar de médico (f) doctor's assistant
avellana (f) hazelnut
avena (f) oat
avería (f) breakdown
avíos de costura (m) sewing kit
ayer yesterday
ayuda (f) help
ayudar help
ayuntamiento (m) town hall
azafrán (m) saffron
azúcar (m) sugar
azucena (f) lily
azul blue

B.........................
babor (m) port
bacalao (m) codfish, salt cod
badminton (m) badminton
baile (m) dance
baile de gala (m) prom
baja presión (f) low pressure
bajo en calorías low-calorie
bajo en colesterol low cholesterol
bajo en grasa low-fat
balcón (m) balcony
ballet (m) ballet
baloncesto (m) basketball
balonmano (m) handball
balsa de goma (f) rubber raft
banco (m) bank
bañera (f) bathtub
baño (m) bath, bathroom
barato cheap
barba (f) beard
barbo (m) catfish
barco de vapor (m) steamer
barco de vela (m) sailboat
barlovento (m) windward
barquillo (m) waffle
báscula (f) scales
bastón de esquí (m) ski pole
basura (f) garbage
bata (f) robe
batería (f) battery
batidor (m) whisk
batímetro (m) depth gauge
batista (f) batiste

beber drink
bebida (f) beverage
becerro (m) calf
béisbol (m) baseball
beneficio (m) profit
berberecho (m) cockle
berenjena (f) eggplant
berro (m) watercress, cress
besugo (m) sea bream
biblioteca (f) library
bicicleta de carreras (f) racing bike
bidón de agua (m) water jug
bigote (m) mustache
bikini (m) bikini
billar (m) billiards
billete (m) ticket
billete con tarifa familiar (m) family ticket
billete de ida y vuelta (m) round-trip ticket
billete de tarifa de grupo (m) group card
billete estacional (m) season ticket
billete semanal (m) one-week ticket
billete válido por un día (m) day ticket
billón trillion
biólogo (m) biologist
bistec (m) steak
blanco white
blazer (m) blazer
bloc de dibujo (m) sketch pad
bloc de notas (m) notepad
blusa (f) blouse
boca (f) mouth
bocina (f) horn
boletera de estacionamiento (f) parking lot vending machine
boliche (m) bowling
bolígrafo (m) ballpoint pen
bolsa de agua caliente (f) hot water bottle
bolsa de basura (f) trash bag
bolsa de compras (f) shopping bag
bolsa de golf (f) golf bag
bolsa de plástico (f) plastic bag
bolsa de viaje (f) traveling bag
bolsa en bandolera (f) shoulder bag

bolsa para el equipo de fotografía (f) camera bag
bolso (m) handbag
bomba de agua (f) water pump
bomba de aire (f) air pump
bomba de succión (f) suction pump
bomba para hinchar neumáticos (f) bicycle pump
bomberos (m) fire department
bombilla (f) lightbulb
bombón de chocolate (m) chocolate bonbon
bombona de gas (f) gas cylinder
bombonas de aire comprimido (f) compressed-air bottles
bonito pretty
boquilla para cigarrillos (f) cigarette holder
bota (f) boot
bota de esquiar (f) ski boots
botánica (f) botany
botas de alpinismo (f) climbing boots
botas de goma (f) rubber boots
botas de montaña (m) climbing boots
bote (m) boat
bote de parches (m) repair kit
bote de remos (m) rowboat
bote salvavidas (m) lifeboat
botella (f) bottle
botella de agua (f) water bottle
botón (m) button
botones (m) bellboy
boxeo (m) boxing
bragas (f) panties
bramante (m) twine
brazo (m) arm
brécol (m) broccoli
brillante shiny, glossy
brocha de afeitar (f) shaving brush
broche (m) brooch
bronquios (m) bronchial tubes
bronquitis (f) bronchitis
brújula (f) compass
brumoso hazy
bueno good

buenos días hello
bujía (f) spark plug
bulto (m) lump
buque mercante (m) freighter
burro/asno (m) donkey
buscar look for
buzón (m) mailbox

C
caballa (f) mackerel
caballete de pintor (m) easel
caballo (m) horse
caballo marino (m) seahorse
cabaret (m) cabaret
cabeza (f) head
cabina telefónica (f) telephone booth
cable (m) cable
cable de freno (m) brake cable
cable de red (m) network cable
cable para remolcar (m) towing cable
cables de empalme para la puesta en marcha (m) jumper cables
cabra (f) goat
cabrito (m) kid
cacahuate (m) peanut
cacao (m) cocoa
cada each
cada hora hourly
cadena (f) chain
cadenas antideslizantes (f) snow chains
cadera (f) hip
caerse fall
café (m) coffee
café helado (m) coffee with ice cream
cafetera (f) coffee machine
caja (f) cash register
caja de cambios (f) gearbox
caja fuerte (f) safe
cajero (m) cashier
cajero automático (m) automatic teller (ATM)
calabacines (m) zucchini
calabaza (f) pumpkin
calamar (m) squid
calambre (m) cramp
calcetines (m) socks
calcetines largos (m) stockings
calculadora de bolsillo (f) pocket calculator

caldo de pollo (m) chicken broth
caldo de ternera (m) beef broth
calefacción (f) heating
calefacción central (f) central heating
calefacción de carbón (f) coal heating
calefacción eléctrica (f) electric heating
calefactor (m) heater
calendario (m) calendar
calentador (m) hot water heater
calentador de inmersión (m) immersion heater
caliente hot, warm
calle (f) street
callejón (m) alley
calor (m) heat
calor moderado moderately warm
calzoncillos (m) underpants
cama (f) bed
cama de niño (f) child's bed
cama individual (f) single bed
cama matrimonial (f) double bed
cámara (f) camera
cámara de aire (f) inner tube
camarera (f) chambermaid
camarero (m) waiter
camarote (m) cabin
camarote doble (m) double cabin
camarote exterior (m) outside cabin
camarote individual (m) single cabin
camarote interno (m) inside cabin
cambiar alter
cambio (m) change, exchange
cambio de divisa (m) money exchange
cambio de marchas (m) gearshift
camisa (f) shirt
camiseta (f) undershirt, t-shirt
camisón (m) nightshirt
campamento (m) campsite
campana (f) bell
campanario (m) steeple
campanilla (f) call-button

campo (m) field
caña de pescar (f) fishing rod
canal (m) canal
cáncer (m) cancer
candado (m) padlock
candelero (m) candlestick
canela (f) cinnamon
cangrejo (m) crab
canoa (f) canoe
cañón (m) canyon
cansado tired
capilla (f) chapel
capitán (m) captain
capó (m) hood
capón (m) capon
capuchino (m) cappuccino
caqui (f) persimmon
cara (f) face
carambola (f) carambola
caravana (f) trailer
carbón (m) charcoal
carboncillo (m) charcoal pencil
carburador (m) carburettor
cargadero (m) porter
carne (f) meat
carne de ave (f) poultry
carnero (m) mutton
carnicero (m) butcher
caro expensive
carpa (f) carp
carpintero (m) carpenter
carrera de caballos (f) horse racing
carrera de coches (f) car racing
carretera nacional (f) national highway
carretera regional (f) country road
carro de compras (m) shopping cart
carro de las maletas (m) baggage carts
carta (f) letter
carta de vinos (f) wine list
carta urgente (f) express mail
cartelera (f) billboard
cartera (f) billfold, wallet
carterista (m) pickpocket
casa de empeño (f) pawnbroker
casa de vacaciones (f) vacation house
casado married
cascada (f) waterfall
casco (m) helmet
caseta para cambiarse (f) beach cabin

casino (m) casino
casita de campo (f) bungalow
caspa (f) dandruff
castaña (f) chestnut
castaño (m) chestnut
castillo (m) castle
catálogo (m) catalog
catarro (m) head cold
catedral (f) cathedral
católico (m) Catholic
cazo para la leche (m) milk jug
cebada (f) barley
cebo (m) bait
cebollas (f) onions
cebolleta (f) scallion
cebollino (m) chive
ceja (f) eyebrow
celular (m) cell phone
cementerio (m) cemetery
cena (f) dinner
cenicero (m) ashtray
ceñido tight
centímetro (m) centimeter
centolla (f) spider crab
centrifugadora (f) spin-dryer
centrifugar spin-dry
centro comercial (m) department store, shopping center
centro de la ciudad (m) downtown
centro histórico (m) old city
cepillo de dientes (m) toothbrush
cepillo para el cabello (m) hairbrush
cepillo para fregar (m) scrubbing brush
cepillo para ropa (m) clothesbrush
cepillo para zapatos (m) shoe brush
cera (f) wax
cerámica (f) ceramic, ceramics
cerdo (m) pig
cereal (m) grain
cerebro (m) brain
cereza (f) cherry
cerrado closed
cerradura (f) lock
cerrajero (m) locksmith
cerveza (f) beer
cesta de compras (f) shopping basket
cesta de la ropa (f) laundry basket

chal (m) scarf
chaleco (m) vest
chaleco salvavidas (m) life jacket
champanero (m) cooler
champú (m) shampoo
chanclas (f) bath slippers
chaparrón (m) showers
chaqueta (f) jacket
chaqueta de cuero (f) leather jacket
charco (m) puddle
cheque (m) check
cheque de viajero (m) traveler's check
chile (m) chili
chimenea (f) chimney
chinches (f) thumb tacks
chocolate (m) chocolate
chófer (m) driver
chucrut (m) sauerkraut
chuleta (f) cutlet
chuletas (f) spare ribs
chupete (m) pacifier
ciática (f) sciatica
ciclismo (m) bicycle racing, cycling
ciclón (m) tornado
científico (m) scientist
ciervo (m) stag, deer
cigarrillo (m) cigarette
cima (f) mountain peak
cine (m) cinema
cinta adhesiva (f) adhesive tape
cinta elástica para el cabello (f) elastic
cinta métrica (f) measuring tape
cinturón (m) belt
cinturón de plomo (m) weight belt
cinturón de seguridad (m) seat belt
circo (m) circus
ciruela (f) plum
ciruela amarilla (f) yellow plum
cirujano (m) surgeon
cistitis (f) inflammation of the bladder
cita (f) appointment
cita de negocios (f) business meeting
citología (f) swab
claustro (m) cloister
clavel (m) carnation, clove
clavícula (f) collarbone
clavo (m) nail
climatizador (m) air-conditioning

club nocturno (m) night-club

coalición (f) coalition

cobre (m) copper

coche (m) car

coche-cama (m) sleeping car

coche-litera (m) sleeper

cocido cooked

cocido en el horno baked

cocina (f) kitchen

cocina / hornillo de gas (m) gas stove

cocina pequeña (f) kitchenette

cocina/hornilla eléctrica (f) electric range

cocinero (m) cook

coco (m) coconut

código postal (m) zip code

codo (m) elbow

codorniz (f) quail

col (f) cabbage

col blanco (f) white cabbage

col rizada (f) savoy cabbage

colaborador (m) collaborator

colador (m) strainer

colchón (m) mattress

colchón neumático (m) air mattress

coles de Bruselas (f) brussel sprouts

coliflor (f) cauliflower

colina (f) hill

collar (m) necklace

collar de perlas (m) pearl necklace

color (m) color

color del cabello (m) hair color

colorete (m) rouge

columna vertebral (f) spinal column

comedia (f) comedy

comer eat

comerciante (m) businessman

cometa (f) kite

comisión (f) commission

como like, as

compañero de trabajo (m) colleague

compartimiento (m) compartment

comprar buy

con with

con dibujos patterned

con motas knobby

con mucho contraste high-contrast

con poco contraste low-contrast

concierto (m) concert

condado (m) county

condiciones de entrega (f) delivery terms

condiciones de pago (f) payment terms

condimento (m) spice

condominio (m) condominium

condón (m) condom

conejo (m) rabbit

conexión telefónica (f) telephone connection

conferencia (f) conference

conferencia de prensa (f) press conference

conferencia interurbana (f) long-distance call

conmoción cerebral (f) concussion

conocer meet

conocido (m) acquaintance

consejo de administración (m) board of trustees

conservas (f) canned food

consigna (f) checkroom

consigna automática (f) locker

constitución (f) constitution

consulado (m) consulate

contable (m) bookkeeper

contaminación (f) pollution

contar tell

contestador automático (m) answering machine

contra reembolso COD

contrato (m) contract

contrato de compraventa (m) purchase contract

control de seguridad (m) security check

contusión (f) bruise

convención (f) convention

convento (m) cloister

cooperación (f) cooperation

corazón (m) heart

corbata (f) tie

corbata de pajarita (f) bowtie

corcho (m) cork

cordero (m) lamb

cordón (m) string

cordón eléctrico (m) electrical cord

cordón prolongador (m) extension cord

cordones (m) shoelaces

coro (m) choir

correa de pulsera (f) wristband

correa en cuña (f) v-belt

corrector (m) concealer

corredor (m) broker

correo aéreo (m) airmail

correo certificado (m) registered mail

correos (m) post office

corriente (f) current, power

cortina (f) curtain

corto short

cortocircuito (m) short circuit

costa (f) coast

costa rocosa (f) rocky shoreline

costilla (f) rib

costo (m) cost

creencia (f) denomination

creer believe

crema batida (f) whipped cream

crema de afeitar (f) shaving cream

crema para bebés (f) baby cream

crema para las manos (f) hand cream

crema para zapatos (f) shoe polish

cremallera (f) zipper

crespón (m) crepe

cripta (f) crypt

cristal de la ventana (m) window pane

cristianismo (m) Christianity

cristiano (m) Christian

cronómetro (m) stopwatch

croquetas (f) croquettes

cruce (m) crossroad

crucero (m) cruise

crudo raw

cruz (f) cross

cuaderno (m) notebook

cuaderno de anillos (m) loose-leaf notebook

cuadro (m) painting

cuadro de conexión manual (m) switchboard

cuándo when

cuánto how much

cuánto tiempo how long

cuarto (m) quarter

cuarto de aseo (m) washroom

cubierta (f) deck, cover

cubiertos (m) silverware
cubito de hielo (m) ice cube
cubo (m) hub, bucket
cubo de basura (m) garbage can
cubo de playa (m) sand pail
cubrecadenas (m) chain-guard
cuchara (f) spoon
cucharilla (f) teaspoon
cucharón (m) stirring spoon
cuchillo (m) knife
cuchillo para carne (m) meat knife
cucurucho (m) ice cream cone
cuello (m) neck, collar
cuenta (f) bill
cuerda (f) rope
cuerda de trepar (f) climbing belt
cuerda para la ropa (f) clothesline
cuero (m) leather
cueva (f) cave
cuidado breve del niño (m) babysitting
cuidado del niño (m) child care
culata (f) cylinder head
cultura (f) culture
cuna de viaje (f) travelling crib
cuota de arriendo (f) rental fee
cúpula (f) dome
curso de cocina (m) cooking course
curso de idiomas (m) language course
curso de pintura (m) painting course

D ....
dar give
dardo (m) dart
dátiles (m) dates
de out (of)
de aplicación exterior external
de colores colored
de mucho cuerpo full-bodied
de nuevo again
deber must
débil weak
decir say
declaración (f) statement

declaración de aduana (f) customs declaration
decoración del cristal (f) glass painting
decorador (m) decorator
dedal (m) thimble
dedo (m) finger
dedo anular (m) ring finger
dedo del corazón (m) middle finger
dedo del pie (m) toe
dedo índice (m) forefinger
dedo meñique (m) pinkie
dedo pulgar (m) thumb
degustar taste
dejar let
delantal (m) apron
delito (m) crime
demasiado too much
democracia (f) democracy
dentadura postiza (f) denture
dentista (m) dentist
denuncia (f) complaint
departamento (m) department
departamento de extranjería (m) immigration authority
deporte (m) sport
depósito de equipaje (m) baggage room
deprimido (m) depressed
derecha right
derecho de recusación de declaración (m) right to remain silent
derrota (f) defeat
desayuno (m) breakfast
descenso (m) descent
descuento (m) discount, rebate
deshielo (m) thaw
deshollinador (m) chimney sweep
desierto (m) desert
desinfectante (m) disinfectant
desmayado unconscious
desodorante (m) deodorant
despejo (m) clearing
despertador (m) alarm clock
después afterward
destapador (m) bottle opener
destinatario (m) recipient
destornillador (m) screw-

driver
desvalijar rob
detergente (m) dishwashing liquid
detergente para lavadora (m) laundry detergent
devolución del equipaje (f) baggage claim
día (m) day
día de llegada (m) date of arrival
día de salida (m) date of departure
diabetes (f) diabetes
diamante (m) diamond
diariamente daily
diarrea (f) diarrhea
diccionario (m) dictionary
diciembre December
diente (m) tooth
diésel/dieseloil (m) diesel
difteria (f) diphteria
dínamo (m) dynamo
dinero (m) money
dinero suelto (m) change
diputado (m) representative
dirección (f) address, steering
director (m) manager
disco duro (m) hard disk
discoteca (f) discotheque, disco
disposiciones aduaneras (f) customs regulations
distensión (f) strain
distribuidor (m) distributor
DIU (m) intra-uterine device
divertido amusing
divisa (f) currency
docena (f) dozen
documento de identidad (m) ID
dolor (m) pain
dolor abdominal (m) stomachache
dolor de cabeza (m) headache
dolor de espalda (m) backache
dolor de estómago (m) stomachache
dolor de garganta (m) sore throat
dolor de muelas (m) toothache
dolores de costado (m) stitch in the side
domingo (m) Sunday

dónde where
dorada (f) golden bream
dormitorio (m) bedroom
double cubierta, doble piso (f, m) double-decker
drama (m) drama
drogas (f) drugs
ducha (f) shower
dulce sweet
dulces (m) candies, candy
dulcificante (m) sweetener
duna (f) dune
durante el día during the day

E

economía (f) economy
economista (m) economist
edad media (f) Middle Ages
edificio (m) building
editorial (f) publishing house
eje delantero (m) front axle
eje trasero (m) rear axle
ejercicios aeróbicos (m) aerobics
ejército (m) army
elástico (m) elastic
elecciones (f) elections
electricidad (f) electricity
electricista (m) electrician
embajada (f) embassy
embarazada pregnant
embarazo (m) pregnancy
embarcadero (m) jetty
embrague (m) clutch
embudo (m) funnel
embutido (m) sausage
emergencia (f) emergency
empanado breadcrumb-fried
empaste (m) filling
empleado (m) employee
empresario (m) entrepreneur
en in
en blanco y negro black-and-white
en lista de correos general delivery
en, sobre on
enagua (f) slip
enamorarse fall in love
encendedor (m) lighter
encendido (m) ignition
encendido defectuoso (m) backfire
enchufe (m) plug
encía (f) gum

encontrar find
encrucijada (f) crossroad
eneldo (m) dill
enero January
enfermedad viral (f) viral illness
enfermera (f) nurse
enfermero (m) male nurse
enfermo sick
engañar deceive, cheat
engranaje (m) gear
enjuagar rinse
enojado angry
ensalada (f) salad
ensalada de lechuga (f) green salad
ensalada mixta (f) mixed salad
entender understand
entonces then
entrada (f) entrance
entreacto (m) intermission
eperlano (m) smelt
equilibrio (m) balance
equipaje (m) luggage, baggage
equipaje de mano (m) hand baggage
equipo estéreo (m) stereo system
equitación (f) horseback riding
equivocado wrong
erizo de mar (m) sea urchin
escala (f) stopover
escalera de mano (f) ladder
escalera mecánica (f) escalator
escaleras (f) stairways
escalofrío (m) chill
escalope (m) deep-fried cutlet
escalope / escalopa (m,f) scallop
escáner (m) scanner
escoba (f) broom
escobilla limpiapipas (f) pipe cleaner
escorzonera (f) viper's grass
escribir write
escritorio (m) desk
escuchar listen
escuela pública (f) public school
escultura (f) sculpture
escurreplatos (m) dishrack
ese, esa that one

esmalte de uñas (m) nail polish
esmoquin (m) tuxedo
esnórquel (m) snorkel
espaguetis (m) spaghetti
espárrago (m) asparagus
espátula (f) putty knife
especialista (m) specialist
espejo (m) mirror
espejos exteriores (m) sideview mirrors
espiga (f) ear of grain
espinaca (f) spinach
espléndido gorgeous
esponja (f) sponge
esposa (f) wife
esquí (m) ski
esquí a campo traviesa (m) cross-country skiing
esquí acuático (m) water-skiing
esquí alpino (m) downhill skiing
esquiar skiing
estaca (f) tent peg
estación de ferrocarril (f) railway station
estación de policía (f) police station
estación final (f) last stop
estacionamiento (m) parking place
estadio (m) stadium
Estados Unidos United States
estafador (m) swindler
estambre (m) worsted
estampilla, sello (f, m) stamp
estanco (m) tobacco store
estanque (m) pond
estatua (f) statue
éste, ésta this one
estilo románico (m) romanesque
estofado braised
estómago (m) stomach
estragón (m) tarragon
estrecho narrow
estrella marina (f) starfish
estreñimiento (m) constipation
estribor (m) starboard
estropajo (m) kitchen rag
estuche para gafas (m) glasses case
estudiante (m) student
estupefacientes (m) dope
estupendo great
etiqueta (f) label
excavaciones (f) excava-

excelente super, outstanding, excellent
exceso de equipaje (m) excess baggage
excursión por la costa (f) shore excursion
excursionismo (m) hiking
excusado (m) restroom
exento de derechos de aduana duty-free
experto de informática (m) computer expert
exportación (f) export
exposición (f) exhibition
exposímetro (m) exposure meter
expositor (m) exhibitor
exprés (m) espresso
exprimidor (m) lemon squeezer
extranjero (m) foreigner

F
fábrica (f) factory
fabricante (m) manufacturer
factura (f) invoice
faisán (m) pheasant
falda (f) skirt
fantástico fantastic
farmacéutico (m) druggist
farmacia (f) drugstore, pharmacy
faro (m) lighthouse
faro del automóvil (m) headlight
fax (m) fax
febrero February
fecha (f) date
feo ugly
feria (f) fair
ferretería (f) hardware
ferrocarril (m) railroad
festival (m) festival
fianza (f) security, deposit
fibra sintética (f) synthetic fiber
fiebre (f) fever
fieltro (m) felt
fijador (m) fixative
fijador para el cabello (m) hair-setting lotion
filete de lomo (m) loin steak
filete de solomillo (m) fillet steak
filología inglesa (f) English language and literature
filosofía (f) philosophy
filtro de pipa (m) pipe filter

filtro del aceite (m) oil filter
fin de semana (m) weekend
finanza (f) finance
firma (f) signature
fiscal (m) district attorney
física (f) physics
flan de manzanas (m) apple flan
flash (m) flashbulb
flatulencia (f) flatulence
floristería (f) florist
flotador (m) swimming ring
folklore (m) folklore
folleto (m) brochure
formato (m) format
forro del freno (m) brake lining
fortaleza (f) fortress
fósforo (m) match
fotógrafo (m) photographer
fractura del hueso (f) fracture
frambuesas (f) raspberries
franela (f) flannel
franqueo (m) postage
frenar brake
freno (m) brake
freno de emergencia (m) emergency brake
freno de mano (m) hand brake
freno de tambor (m) drum brake
fresa (f) strawberry
fresco (m) mural
frijol (m) wax-bean
frío cold
friso (m) frieze
frito fried
frustrado frustrated
fruta (f) fruit
frutería (f) fruit stand
fuego (m) fire
fuera de temporada (f) off season
fuerte strong
fumar smoke
funcionario (m) civil servant
funda dental (f) crown
funicular (m) cable railway
furúnculo (m) boil
fusible (m) fuse
fútbol (m) soccer

G
gafas de buceo (f) diving goggles

gafas para el sol (f) sun glasses
gafas para nadar (f) swimming goggles
galería (f) gallery
galería de arte (f) art gallery
galería del coro (f) choir loft
galleta (f) cracker, cookie
galleta dulce (f) rusks, zwieback
gallina (f) chicken
gallina de Guinea (f) guinea fowl
gallineta (f) red perch
gallo (m) rooster
gambas (f) prawn
gamuza (f) suede
ganso (m) goose
garaje (m) garage
garaje de estacionamiento (m) parking garage
garantía (f) guarantee
garbanzo (m) chick-pea
garrapiñado glazed
gas butano (m) butane gas
gasolina (f) gas
gasolina normal (f) regular gas
gasolina súper (f) extra (gas)
gasolinera (f) gas station
gasto (m) expense
gastos adicionales (m) extra costs
gastos de transporte (m) freight charges, transportation costs
gato (m) cat, jack
gemelos (m) cufflinks
geología (f) geology
gerente (m) manager
gimnasia (f) gymnastics
ginecólogo (m) gynecologist
girasol (m) sunflower
giro (m) transfer
giro postal (m) remittance, money order
gis (m) crayon
gis de acuarela (m) watercolor crayon
globo (m) balloon
globo de aire caliente (m) hot-air balloon
gobierno (m) government
golf (m) golf
goma de borrar (f) eraser
gorra (f) cap with visor
gorro (m) cap

gorro de baño (m) bathing cap
gotas para los oídos (f) eardrops
gótico Gothic
grabación digital (f) digital recording
grabador de casete (m) cassette recorder
grabadora de CDs (f) CD-writer
gracias thank you
gramo (m) gram
granada (f) pomegranate
grande large
granizo (m) hail
granja (f) farm
grapas (f) paper clips
grifo (m) faucet
gripe (f) flu
gris gray
grosella silvestre (f) gooseberry
grosellas (f) currants
grupo sanguíneo (m) blood type
guante para la ducha (m) face mitt
guantera (f) glove compartment
guantes (m) gloves
guardabarros (m) mudguard, fender
guardarropa (m) cloakroom
guarniciones (f) side dishes
guía de viajes (f) guidebook
guía telefónica (f) telephone directory
guisante (m) pea
guisar stew
gulasch (m) goulash
gustar like

H
habichuelas (f) beans
habichuelas blancas (f) white beans
habitación (f) room
habitación doble (f) double room
habitación en casa de huéspedes (f) guesthouse room
hablar speak
hacer do
hacer transbordo transfer
hacha de hielo (m) ice ax
hamaca (f) hammock
hambre (m) hunger

haragán (m) loafer
harina (f) flour
haya (m) beech
helada (f) frost
helado (m) ice cream
hemorragia (f) hemorrhage
hemorragia nasal (f) nosebleed
heno (m) hay
herida (f) wound
herida por corte (f) gash
herir injure
hermana (f) sister
hermano (m) brother
hermoso beautiful
herramienta (f) tool
hibisco (m) hibiscus
hidropatín (m) pedal boat
hielo (m) ice
hielo resbaladizo (m) sheet ice
hígado (m) liver
higo (m) fig
higo chumbo (m) cactus fruit
hija (f) daughter
hijo (m) son
hilo (m) thread
hinchado swollen
hinchazón (f) swelling
hinojo (m) fennel
hipermétrope far-sighted
hipertensión (f) high blood pressure
hipogloso (m) halibut
historia (f) history
hockey sobre hielo (m) ice hockey
hoja de laurel (f) bay leaf
hojas de afeitar (f) razor blades
holgado loose
hombro (m) shoulder
hongo (m) mushroom
honorario (m) fee
hora (f) hour
hora de llegada (f) arrival time
hora de salida (f) departure time
horario (m) timetable, schedule
horario de consulta (m) office hours
horario de vuelo (m) flight schedule
horarios de apertura (m) open hours
horas de trabajo (f) working hours

horquilla de rueda delantera (f) front wheel fork
horquillas (f) hairpins
horrible dreadful
hospital (m) hospital
hotel (m) hotel
hoy today
hueso (m) bone
hueva de pescado (f) roe
huevo duro (m) hard-boiled egg
huevo escalfado (m) poached egg
huevo frito (m) fried egg
huevo pasado por agua (m) soft-boiled egg
huevo revuelto (m) scrambled egg
humedad (f) humidity
huracán (m) hurricane

I
ictericia (f) jaundice
iglesia (f) church
imán (m) magnet
imperdible (m) safety pin
impermeable waterproof, raincoat
importación (f) import
impresionante awesome, impressive
impreso (m) printed matter, printed
impresora láser (f) laser printer
impresora por chorro de tinta (f) inkjet printer
impuesto (m) tax
inarrugable wrinkle-free
inclinación (f) gradient
indicador de gasolina (m) fuel guage
industria (f) industry
infarto cardíaco (m) heart attack
infección (f) infection
inflamación (f) inflammation
información (m) information
ingeniero (m) engineer
iniciativa cívica (f) citizens' initiative
inmigración (f) immigration
inquietante uncanny
insecticida (m) insecticide
insignia (f) badge
insolación (f) sunstroke
inspección aduanera (f) customs check

inspector (m) ticket inspector
instructor de esquí (m) ski instructor
instrumentos para pipa (m) pipe implements
insulina (f) insulin
intermitente (m) turn signals
intermitentes de emergencia (f) emergency flashers
internet (m) internet
internista (m) internist
interno internal
intérprete (m) interpreter
interruptor de luz (m) light switch
intestino (m) intestine
intoxicación (f) poisoning
inundación (f) flood
inusual unusual
inversión (f) investment
invierno (m) winter
invitación (f) invitation
inyección (f) injection
inyector de combustible (m) fuel injector pump
ir go
izquierda left

J

jabalí (m) boar
jabón (m) soap
jamón (m) ham
jaqueca (f) migraine
jarabe (m) syrup
jarabe para la tos (m) cough syrup
jardín (m) garden
jardín botánico (m) botanical gardens
jardinero (m) gardener
jarra (f) mug
jarrita para crema (f) creamer
jazz (m) jazz
jefe de departamento (m) department head
jengibre (m) ginger
jeringa (f) syringe
jeringa desechable (f) disposable needle
jogging (m) jogging
joven young
joyero (m) jeweler
jubilado (m) retired person
judías (f) bush-beans, kidney beans
judías verdes (f) green beans, string beans

judío (m) Jew
jueves Thursday
juez (m) judge
jugador de defensa (m) quarterback
jugo de fruta (m) fruit juice
jugo de manzana (m) apple juice
jugo de naranja (m) orange juice
jugo de uva (m) grape juice
juguete (m) toy
juguetería (f) toy store
julio July
junio June
junta (f) gasket

K

kárate (m) karate
kayak (m) kayak
kilo (m) kilo
kilómetro (m) kilometer
kilómetro cuadrado (m) square kilometer
kiwi (m) kiwi fruit

L

labio (m) lip
laca (f) hairspray
ladrón (m) thief
lago (m) lake
lámpara (f) lamp
lámpara de querosén (f) kerosene lamp
lana (f) wool
lancha inflable (f) rubber dinghy
langosta (f) lobster
langostino (m) crawfish
lápiz (m) pencil
lápiz de cejas (m) eyebrow pencil
lápiz de color (m) colored pencil
lápiz de labios (m) lipstick
largo long
lata (f) can
lata de gasolina (f) gas can
laurel (m) laurel
lavabo (m) washbasin
lavado con agua caliente (m) hot-water wash
lavadora (f) washing machine
lavandería (f) laundromat
lavaplatos (m) dishwasher
laxante (m) laxative
leche (f) milk

lechón (m) suckling pig
lechuga (f) lettuce
lector de CD (m) CD player
lector DVD (m) DVD player
leer read
lejos far
lengua (f) tongue
lenguado (m) sole, flounder
lente (m) lens
lente de contacto (f) contact lens
lentejas (f) lentils
lento slow
lesión (f) injury
ley (f) law
libra (f) pound
librería (f) bookstore
librero (m) bookseller
libro de cocina (m) cookbook
libro de documentación (m) non-fiction
libro ilustrado (m) picture book
libro infantil (m) children's book
libro técnico (m) technical book
licencia de navegación de vela (f) sailing licence
licencia submarinista (f) diving license
licor (m) liqueur
licorería (m) liquor store
liebre (f) hare
lienzo (m) canvas
lila purple
lima (f) lime
lima para uñas (f) nail file
limón (m) lemon
limpiaparabrisas (m) windshield wiper
limpieza (f) cleaning
limpieza en seco (f) dry-cleaning
línea telefónica (f) telephone line
lino (m) linen
linterna (f) flashlight
líquido del freno (m) brake fluid
lisa (f) mullet
literatura (f) literature
litro (m) liter
llamada de cobro revertido (f) collect call
llamada local (f) local call
llamada telefónica (f) phone call
llanta (f) rim

llave (f) key, wrench
llave de tuercas (f) wrench
llegada (f) arrival
lleno full
llover rain
llovizna (f) drizzle
lluvia (f) rain
loción para el cuerpo (f) body lotion
locomotora (f) locomotive
lombarda (f) red cabbage
lomo (m) loin, saddle (of lamb)
lubina (f) sea bass
lucha (f) wrestling
lucio (m) pike
lugar (m) place
lugar natal (f) birthplace
lugar turístico (m) vacation spot
lumbago (m) lumbago
lunes (m) Monday
luneta trasera (f) rear windshield
lupa (f) magnifying glass
luxación (f) sprain
luz (f) light
luz de parada (f) brake light
luz delantera (f) headlight
luz intermitente (f) blinker, flasher
luz trasera (f) taillight

M

macarrones (m) macaroni
madre (f) mother
maestro (m) teacher, master
magnífico splendid
maíz (m) corn
maleta (f) suitcase
maletero (m) trunk
maletín (m) briefcase
malo bad
mañana tomorrow
manantial (m) mountain spring
mandarina (f) tangerine
mandíbula (f) jaw
mando a distancia (m) remote control
manecilla (f) hands
manga (f) sleeve
mango (m) mango
manguera (f) hose
manillar (m) handlebars
mano (f) hand
manta (f) blanket
manta eléctrica (f) electric blanket

mantel (m) tablecloth
mantequilla (f) butter
manzana (f) apple
mapa (m) map
mapa de la ciudad (m) map of the city
máquina de afeitar (f) razor
máquina tragamonedas (f) slot machine
mar (m) sea
maravilloso terrific
marca (f) brand
marca de fábrica (f) trademark
marco para diapositivas (m) slide frame
marea alta (f) high tide
marea baja (f) low tide
mareado seasick
marejada (f) swell
margarina (f) margarine
margarita (f) daisy
marido (m) husband
marinero (m) sailor
mariscos (m) shellfish
marketing (m) marketing
martes Tuesday
martillo (m) hammer
marzo March
más more
más tarde later
más temprano earlier
matamoscas (m) fly swatter
mate matte
material (m) material
mayo May
mayonesa (f) mayonnaise
mecánico (m) mechanic
mecánico de automóviles (m) motor vehicle mechanic
mechado larded
mechón (m) strand
media luna (f) croissant
media pensión (f) half board
medianoche (f) midnight
medias (f) tights
medicamento (f) medication
medicina (f) medicine
médico (m) doctor
medieval medieval
medio (m) medium
medio, mitad half
mediodía (f) noon
medusa (f) jellyfish
mejillón (m) mussel
mejorana (f) marjoram

melocotón (m) peach
melón (m) melon
membrete (m) letterhead
membrillo (m) quince
memoria principal (f) RAM
mendigo (m) panhandler
menta (f) mint
menú (m) menu
mercader (m) merchant
mercado (m) market
mercería (f) dry goods
merluza (f) sea pike
mermelada (f) jam
mes (m) month
mesa (f) table
mesa plegable (f) folding table
mesita de noche (f) night table
metro (m) meter, subway
metro cuadrado (m) square meter
metro plegable (m) measuring stick
mezclado mottled
microfibra (f) microfiber
microondas (m) microwave
miel (f) honey
miércoles Wednesday
mierda (f) shit
mil millones billion
milímetro (m) millimeter
minibar (m) minibar
minuto (m) minute
miope short-sighted
misa (f) church service
mismo same
misterio (m) mystery
moca (m) mocha
mochila (f) backpack
moda (f) fashion
módem (m) modem
molesto annoyed
molinillo de café (m) coffee grinder
mollejas (f) sweetbread
mondongo (m) tripe
moneda (f) coin
monedero (m) purse
mono cute
monoesquí (m) snowboard
montaña (f) mountain
monumento (m) monument
moras (f) mulberries
mordedura (f) bite
mosquitero (m) mosquito net
mostaza (f) mustard
motel (m) motel

motolancha (f) motorboat
motor (m) motor
motor de arranque (m) starter
móvil (m) cellular
mozo de estación (m) porter
mucho much
muchos many
muebles (m) furniture
muela del juicio (f) wisdom tooth
muelle (m) dock
muñeca (f) wrist
músculo (m) muscle
museo (m) museum
música (f) music
musical (m) musical
músico (m) musician
muslo (m) thigh
musulmán (m) Muslim
muy very

N

nabicol (f) rutabaga
nabos (m) turnips
nabos rojos (m) red beets
nada nothing
nadaderas (f) water wings
nadadores swimmers
naipes (m) playing cards
naranja (f) orange
narciso (m) narcissus
nariz (f) nose
nata (f) cream
nata ácida (f) sour cream
náusea (f) nausea
navaja (f) jacknife, pocket knife
nave (f) nave
nave central (f) center nave
nave lateral (f) side aisle
nave transversal (f) transept
navegación de vela (f) sailing
Navidad (f) Christmas
negociación (f) negotiation
negro black
nervio (m) nerve
neumático (m) tire
nevar snow
nevera (f) cooler, insulated bag
niebla (f) fog
nieto (m) grandson
nieve (f) snow
nieve granizada (f) sleet
nieve-polvo (f) powder (snow)

niños (m) children
níspero (m) medlar
nivel de dificultad (m) degree of difficulty
no no
no nadadores non-swimmers
no necesita plancha no ironing
Noche Vieja (f) New Year's eve
notario (m) notary
noticias (f) news
novela corta (f) short novel
novela policíaca (f) detective novel
novia (f) fiancée
noviembre (m) November
novio (m) fiancé
nube (f) cloud
nublado cloudy
nudo (m) knot
nueces del Brasil (f) Brazil nuts
nuera (f) daughter-in-law
nuevo new **nuez** (f)
nuez (f) nut, walnut
nuez moscada (f) nutmeg
número de casa (m) street number
número de la habitación (m) room number
número de teléfono (m) telephone number
número de vuelo (m) flight number
número del vagón (m) car number
número secreto (m) PIN

O

o or
objetos de valor (m) valuables
obrero (m) worker
obrero especializado (m) skilled worker
obtener get
océano (m) ocean
octubre (m) October
ocupado occupied
oferta (f) offer
oficial (m) official
oficina de cambio (f) exchange bureau
oficina de objetos perdidos (f) lost-and-found office
oír hear
ojo (m) eye

ola (f) wave
oleaje (m) surf
oler smell
olla (f) pot
olvidar forget
opaco dull
ópera (f) opera
operación (f) operation
opereta (f) operetta
opinión (f) opinion
óptica (f) eyewear store
orégano (m) oregano
oreja (f) ear
orinal de cama (m) bedpan
ornitología (f) ornithology
oro (m) gold
orquídea (f) orchid
ortodoncista (m) orthodontist
oscuro dark
ostra (f) oyster, mussel
otoño (m) autumn
otorrinolaringólogo (m) ear, nose and throat specialist
otros, otras other
oveja (f) sheep
ozono (m) ozone

P

pabellón (m) hall
pacana (f) pecan nut
padre (m) father
páginas amarillas (f) yellow pages
pago en efectivo (m) cash payment
paisaje (m) landscape
paja (f) straw
pala (f) shovel
pala de basura (f) dustpan
palanca del cambio (f) gearshift
paleta (f) palette
palo de la tienda (m) tent pole
paloma (f) pigeon
palos de golf (m) golf clubs
pan (m) bread
pan blanco (m) white bread
pan centeno (m) rye bread
pan con comino (m) caraway seed bread
pan integral (m) wholewheat bread
pan negro (m) black bread
pan tostado (m) toast
pana (f) corduroy

panadería (f) bakery
panadero (m) baker
pañal (m) diaper
panecillo (m) roll
panqueque (m) pancake
pantalla (f) screen
pantalón corto (m) shorts
pantalones (m) pants
pantano (m) swamp
pantorrilla (f) calf
pañuelo de papel (m) tissue
papa / patata (f) potato
papas fritas (f) fried potatoes, french fries
papaya (f) papaya
papel (m) paper
papel de aluminio (m) aluminum foil
papel de cartas (m) stationery
papel de regalo (m) gift wrap
papel higiénico (m) toilet paper
papel para acuarela (m) watercolor paper
papel para envolver (m) wrapping paper
papelera (f) wastepaper basket
papelería (f) office supplies
papeles del coche (m) car documents
paperas (f) mumps
papilla de avena (f) oatmeal, porridge
paquete (m) parcel
paquete pequeño (m) small parcel
par (m) pair
parabrisas (m) windshield
paracaidismo (m) sky diving
parachoques (m) bumper
parada (f) stopover, stop
paraguas (m) umbrella
parálisis (f) paralysis
paramédico (m) paramedic
parasol (m) lens shade
parca (f) windbreaker
parlamento (m) parliament
párpado (m) eyelid
parque (m) park
parque infantil (m) children's playground
parque natural (m) nature park

parque zoológico (m) zoo
párrafo (m) paragraph
parrilla (f) grill
parte trasera (f) rear
partera (f) midwife
pasa (f) raisin
pasado mañana day after tomorrow
pasador (m) barrette
pasaje (m) plane ticket
pasajero (m) passenger
pasaporte (m) passport
Pascua (f) Easter
pasear ride
pasillo (m) aisle
pasionaria (f) passion fruit
paso (m) pass
pasta (f) noodles
pasta dentífrica (f) toothpaste
pastel (m) cake, pastel
pastelería (f) pastry shop
pasteles (m) pastries
pastilla para dolor de cabeza (f) headache pill
pastillas para dormir (f) sleeping pills
pastillas para la garganta (f) cough drops
patatas dulces (f) sweet potatoes
patillas (f) sideburns
patín (m) skate
patinaje sobre hielo (m) ice-skating
patinar rollerblading
patines (m) rollerblades
patines de hielo (m) ice skates
patio (m) backyard
pato (m) duck
pavo (m) turkey
pedal (m) pedal
pediatra (f) pediatrician
pedir order
pegamento (m) glue
peine (m) comb
peletería (f) fur shop
película (f) movie, film
película transparente (f) plastic wrap
pelo (m) hair
pelota (f) ball
pelota de fútbol (f) soccer ball
pelota de golf (f) golf ball
pelota de ping-pong (f) ping-pong ball
pelota de tenis (f) tennis ball
peluca (f) wig

peluquero (m) hairdresser
pendiente (m) pendant
pendientes (m) earrings
pensar think
pensión completa (f) full board
Pentecostés (m) Whitsun
pepino (m) cucumber
pequeño small
pera (f) pear
perca (f) perch
percha (f) hanger
pérdida (f) loss
perdiz (f) partridge
perdón sorry
peregrino (m) pilgrim
perejil (m) parsley
perfume (m) perfume
perfumería (f) perfumery
perifollo (m) chervil
periódico (m) newspaper
periodista (m) journalist
perla (f) pearl
permanente (f) perm
permiso para pescar (m) fishing license
perro (m) dog
persiana (f) shutter
persona madura (f) senior citizen
pesa (f) weight
pesa/haltera (f) dumbbell
pesca (f) fishing
pescadería (f) fish store
pescado (m) fish
pez azul (m) bluefish
pez espada (m) swordfish
pezón (m) nipple
picadillo (m) meatloaf
picado ground, chopped
picadura de insecto (f) insect bite
picante tangy
pie (m) foot
piel (f) skin
piel sintética (f) artificial leather
pierna (f) lower leg, round steak, leg
piezas de recambio (f) spare parts
pijama (m) pajamas
pila bautismal (f) font
pimentón (m) pepper
pimienta (f) pepper
pimiento (m) green pepper
piña (f) pine cone, pineapple
pincel (m) paintbrush
ping-pong (m) ping-pong, table tennis

piñón (m) pine nut
pintor (m) painter
pintura (f) painting
pintura al óleo (f) oil
  paints
pinturas al pastel (f) pastels
pinza de ropa (f) clothespin
pinzas (f) tweezers
pipa (f) pipe
piragua (f) canoe
piragüismo (m) canoeing
piscina (f) swimming pool
piso (m) floor
pista de esquí (f) ski run
pistache (m) pistachio
pistón (m) piston
placa de identificación (f)
  name badge
plancha (f) iron
planetario (m) planetarium
plata (f) silver
plátano (m) banana
platija (f) flounder
platino (m) platinum
plato (m) dish, plate
plato hondo (m) bowl
platos de huevos (m) egg
  dishes
playa (f) beach
playa arenosa (f) sandy
  beach
playa de arena gruesa (f)
  pebble beach
playa privada (f) private
  beach
plaza (f) square
plazo (m) deadline
plazo de entrega (m) time
  of delivery
plomada (f) sinker
plomero (m) plumber
pluma fuente (f) fountain
  pen
poco little, few
poco asado browned
poder can, be able
policía (f) police, policeman
política (f) politics
pollo (m) chicken
pollo asado (m) grilled
  chicken
polluelo (m) chick
polo acuático (m) water
  polo
polvo de maquillaje (m)
  compact
pomada para las que-

maduras (f) ointment for
  burns
pomelo (m) pomelo
popa (f) stern
popelina (f) poplin
por through
por eso therefore
por favor please
por la mañana in the
  morning
por la noche at night
por la tarde in the
  evening, in the afternoon
por qué why
por, para for
porque because
portal (m) main entrance
postre (m) dessert
pozo (m) well
prado (m) meadow
precio (m) price
precio con descuento (m)
  discount price
precio de compra (m) purchase price
precipicio (m) cliff
preferentemente preferably
prefijo (m) area code
preguntar ask
prensa (f) press
presa (f) dam
presentar introduce
presidente (m) president,
  chairman
presión alta (f) high pressure
pretemporada (f) pre-season
primavera (f) spring
primero first
primo (m) cousin
principiante (m,f) beginner
prisión (f) prison
prismáticos (m) binoculars
proa (f) bow
probar try on
procesador (m) processor
procesión (f) procession
proceso (m) trial
producción (f) production
productos de limpieza (m)
  cleaning products
productos lácteos (m)
  dairy products
profesor (m) professor
profundo deep
**programa para lavado de
  ropa delicada** (m) gentle
  wash

programador (m) programmer
propano (m) propane
propina (f) tip
prostituta (f) prostitute
protección solar (f) sunblock
protestante (m) Protestant
proveedor (m) supplier
prueba del embarazo (f)
  pregnancy test
psicología (f) psychology
psicólogo (m) psychologist
psiquiatra (m) psychiatrist
puente (m) bridge
puente dental (m) dental
  bridge
puerro (m) leek
puerta (f) door
puerto (m) harbor
puesta del sol (f) sunset
pularda (f) young fattened
  hen
pulmón (m) lung
pulmonía (f) pneumonia
púlpito (m) pulpit
pulpo (m) octopus
pulsera (f) bracelet
puños (m) cuffs
punto de encuentro (m)
  meeting place
puré (m) mashed potatoes
puritos (m) cigarillos
puros (m) cigars

Q

qué what
quemadura (f) burn
quemadura por el sol (f)
  sunburn
querido darling
queso (m) cheese
queso de leche de cabra
  (m) goat's milk cheese
queso de leche de oveja
  (m) sheep's milk cheese
quién who
química (f) chemistry
químico (m) chemist
quingombó (m) okra
quinqué (m) hurricane
  lamp
quiosco (m) newsstand
quitaesmalte (m) nail polish remover
quitamanchas (m) stain
  remover

R

rábano (m) radish
rábano picante (m) horseradish

rabo (m) tail
radiador (m) radiator
radio (f) radio
radiografía (f) X-ray
raíz (f) root (of the tooth)
rape (m) anglerfish
rápido fast
raqueta de ping-pong (f)
  ping-pong racket
raqueta de tenis (f) tennis
  racket
raquetas de badminton
  (m) badminton rackets
raro strange
rascacielos (m) skyscraper
raso (m) satin
rastro (m) flea market
raya (f) part (hair), ray
raya mediana (f) center
  part
rayo (m) spoke (wheel)
readaptación profesional
  (f) retraining
recepción (f) reception
recibo (m) receipt
recomendar recommend
recorrido por el puerto
  (m) harbor tour
reducción (f) reduction
reflector (m) reflector
refresco (m) soft drink
refrigerador (m) refrigerator
refugiado político (m) political refugee
refugio (m) mountain hut
regadera (f) watering can
regalo (m) gift
regata (f) regatta
regional regional
registro (m) reception desk
regla (f) ruler
rehogado steamed
reino (m) kingdom
relámpago (m) lightning
relieve (m) relief
religión (f) religion
relleno stuffed
reloj (m) watch
reloj de buzo (m) diving
  watch
reloj de pared (m) wall
  clock
reloj de pulsera (m) watch
relojero (m) watchmaker
remar rowing
remitente (m) sender
remolcar tow
remos (m) oars
reparar repair
repetir repeat
reportaje (m) report

representante (m) representative
requesón (m) curd
reserva (f) reservation
reservar reserve
resfriado (m) cold
responsabilidad (f) liability
restaurante (m) restaurant
restos (m) remains
retardador de disparo (m)
  self-timer, automatic
  shutter release
retraso (m) delay
retrovisor (m) rearview
  mirror
reumatismo (m) rheumatism
revisor (m) conductor
revista (f) magazine
revuelto stirred
rímel (m) mascara
riñón (m) kidney
río (m) river
rizador (m) curler
rizo (m) curl
robar steal
roble (m) oak
robo (m) theft
rodaballo (m) turbot
rodilla (f) knee
rodillo (m) rolling pin
rojo red
romántico romantic
romero (m) rosemary
romper break
ropa de color (f) colored
  laundry
ropa interior (f) underwear
rosa (f) rose
rosado pink
rosbif (m) roast beef
rosetón (m) rosette
rotulador (m) felt tip pen
rubeola (f) German
  measles
rueda (f) wheel
rueda de recambio (f)
  spare wheel
rugby (m) rugby
ruibarbo (m) rhubarb
ruina (f) ruin

S..........................
sábado Saturday
sábana (f) bed sheet
saber know
sabor (m) flavor
sacacorchos (m) corkscrew
sacapuntas (m) pencil
  sharpener**s**

acerdote (m) priest, minister
saco de dormir (m) sleeping bag
sacristía (f) sacristy
sal (f) salt
sala (f) living room
sala de conciertos (f) concert hall
sala de espera (f) waiting
  room
salida (f) gate, takeoff,
  exit, departure
salida de emergencia (f)
  emergency exit
salida del sol (f) sunrise
salir de excursión hike
salmón (m) salmon
salmón ahumado (m)
  smoked salmon
salmonela (f) salmonella
salón de belleza (m)
  beauty salon
salpullido (m) rash
salsa de soja (f) soy sauce
saludo (m) greeting, salutation
salvavidas (m) life preserver, life guard
salvia (f) sage
sandalias (f) sandals
sandía (f) watermelon
sangramiento (m) bleeding
sangre (f) blood
santuario (m) sanctuary
sarampión (m) measles
sarcófago (m) sarcophagus
sardina (f) sardine
sartén (f) frying pan
sastre (m) tailor
saúcos (m) elderberries
sauna (f) sauna
secador (m) hairdryer
secadora (f) dryer, clothes
  dryer
secar con secador blow-
  dry
sección de fumadores
  smoking section
sección de no fumadores
  non-smoking section
seco dry
secuoya (f) sequoia
sed (f) thirst
seda (f) silk
seda dental (f) dental floss
sedal (m) fishing line
sedante (m) tranquilizer,
  sedative
segadora-trilladora (f)
  harvester

segundo second
seguro (m) insurance
selección directa (f) direct dialling
semáforo (m) traffic light
semillas de girasol (f) sunflower seeds
sémola (f) semolina
señal de línea libre (f) dial tone
señal de línea ocupada (f) busy signal
sendero (m) footpath
sendero de ascensión (m) climbing path
seno (m) breast
sentir feel
septiembre (m) September
servicio de atención al cliente (m) customer service
servicio de averías (m) breakdown assistance
servicio de grúa (m) towing service
servicio de habitaciones (m) room service
servicio de playa (m) beach patrol
servicio público (m) public service
servilleta (f) napkin
servilletas de papel (f) paper napkins
sesión judicial (f) legal proceedings
si if
sí yes
siempre recto straight ahead
sierra (f) saw
silla (f) chair
silla de cubierta (f) deck chair
silla de niños (f) highchair
silla de ruedas (f) wheelchair
silla plegable (f) folding chair
sillín (m) saddle
sillón (m) armchair
sin without
sin plomo unleaded
sinagoga (f) synagogue
sobre (m) envelope
sobrina (f) niece
sobrino (m) nephew
socio (m) business partner
soda (f) soda
sol (m) sun
sollo (m) sturgeon

sólo only
soltero single
sombra (f) shadow
sombra de ojos (f) eyeshadow
sombrero (m) hat
sombrilla (f) sun umbrella, parasol
sopa (f) soup
sopa de fideos (f) noodle soup
sopa de verdura (f) vegetable soup
sostén (m) brassiere
sotavento leeward
squash (m) squash
submarinismo (m) diving
suceso (m) event
suegra (f) mother-in-law
suegro (m) father-in-law
suela (f) sole
suela de cuero (f) leather sole
suela de goma (f) rubber sole
suéter (m) sweater
suficiente enough
suite (f) suite
sujetapapeles (m) paper clips
sujeto a derechos de aduana dutiable
suministro de agua (m) water supply
supermercado (m) supermarket
suplemento del billete (m) surcharge
surf (m) surfing
surtidor de gasolina (f) gas pump
sustituto del azúcar (m) sugar substitute

T ....
tabaco (m) tobacco
tabla de patín (f) skateboard
tabla de planchar (f) ironing board
tabla de surf (f) surfboard
tacómetro (m) rev counter
tacón (m) heel
taladradora (f) drill
tallarines (m) flat noodles
talón (m) heel
tamaño (m) size
tamarindo (m) tamarind
tampones (m) tampons
tanque (m) tank
tapón (m) plug, stopper

taquilla (f) ticket counter
tarde late
tarifa (f) charge
tarifa de estacionamiento (f) parking fee
tarjeta de crédito (f) credit card
tarjeta de embarque (f) boarding pass
tarjeta de esquí (f) ski pass
tarjeta de red (f) network card
tarjeta de sonido (f) sound card
tarjeta gráfica (f) graphics card
tarjeta postal (f) postcard
tarjeta profesional (f) business card
tarjeta telefónica (f) phone card
tarta (f) pie
tarta de fruta (f) fruit tart
tarta de manzanas (f) apple pie
tasa de licencia (f) licensing fee
taxista (m) taxi driver
taza (f) cup
té (m) tea
té de fruta (m) fruit tea
té negro (m) black tea
teatro (m) theater
techo corredizo (m) sunroof
teclado (m) keyboard
técnico dental (m) dental technician
tejador (m) roofer
tejido de rizo (m) terry cloth
teléfono (m) telephone
teléfono de tarjeta (m) card telephone
teléfono público (m) pay phone
teléfono público de monedas (m) coin-operated telephone
telegrama (m) telegram
telémetro (m) distance meter
teleobjetivo (m) telephoto lens
telesilla (m) chair lift
telesquí (m) ski lift
televisión (f) television
televisor (m) TV
télex (m) telex
templo (m) temple

temporada alta (f) high season
temporada baja (f) low season
temprano early
tenazas (f) pincers, pliers
tendedero (m) clothesrack
tendón (m) tendon
tenedor (m) fork
tener have
tenis (m) tennis
terciopelo (m) velvet
termo (m) thermos
termómetro (m) thermometer
terraza (f) terrace
tétano (m) tetanus
tía (f) aunt
tiburón (m) shark
tienda (f) tent
tienda al por menor (f) retail store
tienda de alimentos naturales (f) health food store
tienda de antigüedades (f) antique store
tienda de artículos baratos (f) dime store
tienda de artículos de deporte (f) sporting goods store
tienda de artículos usados (f) second hand store
tienda de bicicletas (f) bicycle shop
tienda de comestibles (f) grocery store
tienda de comestibles finos (f) delicatessen
tienda de fotografía (f) photo store
tienda de informática (f) computer store
tienda de objetos artísticos (f) arts and crafts store
tienda de regalos (f) souvenir shop
tienda de ropa (f) clothing store
tienda de telas (f) fabric store
tienda de vinos (f) wine store
tienda electrodomésticos (f) electrical appliances store
tienda musical (f) music store
tierra firme (f) mainland
tifón (m) typhoon

tijeras (f) scissors
tijeras para uñas (f) nail scissors
tilo (m) lime tree
tímalo (m) grayling
timón (m) rudder
tinta (f) ink
tinte para el cabello (m) hair dye
tinte temporal para el cabello (m) color rinse
tintorería (f) dry cleaning
tío (m) uncle
tipo de cambio (m) exchange rate, course
tirador de puerta (m) door handle
tirantes (m) suspenders
tirita (f) band-aid
tisana (f) herbal tea
tiza (f) chalk
toalla (f) towel
toalla de playa (f) beach towel
toalla pequeña (f) hand towel
toallita higiénica (f) sanitary napkin
tobillo (m) ankle
tocino (m) bacon
todavía still
todos all
toma de corriente (f) socket
tomar take
tomates (m) tomatoes
tomillo (m) thyme
tonelada (f) ton
tormenta (f) storm, thunderstorm
tornillo (m) screw
toronja (f) grapefruit
torre (f) tower
tortilla de huevos (f) omelet
tos (f) cough
tos ferina (f) whooping cough
tostador (m) toaster
trabajar work
tractor (m) tractor
tragedia (f) tragedy
traje (m) outfit, suit
traje de baño (m) swimming trunks
traje de buceo (m) wetsuit
tranquilo quiet
transbordador de automóviles (m) car ferry
transbordador/ferry (m) ferry

transfusión de sangre (f) blood transfusion
transmisión (f) transmission
tranvía (m) streetcar
trapo para limpiar (m) cleaning rag
trastorno cardíaco (m) heart problem
trastorno de la circulación (m) circulatory disorder
tratamiento de la raíz (m) root canal work
travesía (f) transit
tren de cercanías (m) commuter train
tren rápido (m) express train
trepadores (m) crampons
triángulo de emergencia (m) warning triangle
trigo (m) wheat
trineo (m) sled
trípode (m) tripod
tripulación (f) crew
trizar shatter
trompas de Falopio (f) fallopian tubes
trucha (f) trout
trueno (m) thunder
tubo de escape (m) exhaust
tuerca (f) nut
tumba (f) grave
tumbona (f) deck chair
tumefacción (f) swelling

U
úlcera (f) ulcer
un poco a little
un, uno, una a, an
unidad (f) unit
unidad de CD-ROM (f) CD-ROM drive
universidad (f) college, university
urólogo (m) urologist
útero (m) uterus
uva (f) grape

V
vaca (f) cow, beef
vacío empty
vagina (f) vagina
vaginitis (f) vaginitis
vagón-restaurante (m) dining car
vainilla (f) vanilla
vajilla (f) dishes
valle (m) valley
valores máximos (m) maximum (values)

valores mínimos (m) minimum values
válvula (f) valve
varicela (f) chickenpox
vaso (m) cup
vejiga (f) bladder
vela (f) candle, sail
veleta (f) float
velocímetro (m) speedometer
vena (f) vein
vendaje (m) bandage
vendedor (m) salesperson
vender sell
vendimia (f) vintage
venir come
ventana (f) window
ventanilla (f) counter
ventilador (m) ventilator, fan
ver see
verano (m) summer
verde green
verdulería (f) fresh produce stand
verduras (f) vegetables
vesícula biliar (f) gallbladder
vestido (m) dress
veterinario (m) veterinarian
viaje de ida y vuelta (m) round-trip

viaje por el río (m) river boat trip
victoria (f) win
videocasete (m) videocassette
videograbadora (f) VCR
vidriero (m) glazier
vidrio (f) glass
viejo (m) old
viento (m) wind
viernes Friday
Viernes Santo (m) Good Friday
viña (f) vineyard
vinagre (m) vinegar
vinagre balsámico (m) balsamic vinegar
vino (m) wine
vino blanco (m) white wine
vino tinto (m) red wine
violación (f) rape
violar rape
viruela (f) smallpox
visión, agudeza de la vista (f) vision
vista al mar (f) ocean view
vodka (m) vodka
volante (m) shuttlecock, steering wheel
volcán (m) volcano
voleibol (m) volleyball
voltaje (m) voltage
voto (m) vote

vuelo (m) flight
vuelo de enlace (m) connecting flight
vuelo de vuelta (m) return flight
windsurf (m) windsurfing

Y
y and
yate (m) yacht
yerno (m) son-in-law
yogur (m) yogurt
yudo (m) judo

Z
zanahoria (f) carrot
zapatería (f) shoe store
zapatero (m) shoemaker
zapatillas (m) sneakers, slippers
zapato (m) shoe
zapatos de deporte (m) track shoes
zapatos de excursión (m) hiking boots
zapatos para niños (m) children's shoes
zarzamoras (f) blackberries
zona peatonal (f) crosswalk
zoología (f) zoology
zumo de tomate (m) tomato juice

© Copyright 2001 by Koval Verlag GmbH, Weilerbachstrasse 44, D-74423 Unterfischach, Germany
First edition for the United States and Canada published in 2003 by Barron's Educational Series, Inc.

All inquiries should be addressed to:
Barron's Educational Series, Inc.
250 Wireless Boulevard
Hauppauge, New York 11788
http://www.barronseduc.com
ISBN-13: 978-0-7641-2280-4
ISBN-10: 0-7641-2280-0
Library of Congress Catalog Card Number 2002101235

Printed in China
9